Information, Systems and Information Systems
– making sense of the field

Information, Systems and Information Systems
– making sense of the field

Peter Checkland
and
Sue Holwell

Lancaster University, UK

JOHN WILEY & SONS

Chichester · New York · Weinheim · Brisbane · Singapore · Toronto

Copyright © 1998 by John Wiley & Sons Ltd,
Baffins Lane, Chichester,
West Sussex PO19 1UD, England

National   01243 779777
International (+44) 1243 779777
e-mail (for orders and customer service enquiries):
cs-books@wiley.co.uk
Visit our Home Page on http://www.wiley.co.uk
or http://www.wiley.com

Other Wiley Editorial Offices

John Wiley & Sons, Inc., 605 Third Avenue,
New York, NY 10158-0012, USA

VCH Verlagsgesellschaft mbH, Pappelallee 3,
D-69469 Weinheim, Germany

Jacaranda Wiley Ltd, 33 Park Road, Milton,
Queensland 4064, Australia

John Wiley & Sons (Asia) Pte Ltd, 2 Clementi Loop #02-01,
Jin Xing Distripark, Singapore 129809

John Wiley & Sons (Canada) Ltd, 22 Worcester Road,
Rexdale, Ontario M9W 1L1, Canada

Library of Congress Cataloging-in-Publication Data

Checkland, Peter.
    Information, systems and information systems : making sense of the
field / Peter Checkland and Sue Holwell.
        p. cm.
    Includes bibliographical references and indexes.
    ISBN 0-471-95820-4 (cloth)
    1. Management information systems.   2. Information technology.
I. Holwell, Sue.   II. Title
T58.6.C425 1998
303.48'33—dc21   97-34187
                                                                     CIP

British Library Cataloguing in Publication Data

A catalogue record for this book is available from the British Library

ISBN 0-471-95820-4

Typeset in 11/13 Bembo from the authors' disks by Dorwyn Ltd, Rowlands Castle, Hants
Printed and bound in Great Britain by Biddles Ltd, Guildford and King's Lynn
This book is printed on acid-free paper responsibly manufactured from sustainable forestation, for
which at least two trees are planted for each one used for paper production.

To
Jo, Ben, Tom and Jamie
PC

To
Jean, and the memory of Ken
SH

Contents

There were many types of extremes. The extremes of language, for example . . . the contrived and concocted language that McCarthy and I invented almost instinctively and spontaneously with intimate understanding. A strange and wonderful contrivance considering our very different backgrounds: an Irish working-class socialist from Belfast; an English ex-public schoolboy and international journalist . . . In this linguistic haven we established a refuge for ourselves and at the same time made a world richly meaningful for us.

> Brian Keenan, *An Evil Cradling*,
> describing the time when he and John
> McCarthy were held as hostages.

'Only words? *Only* words? Oh, dear. But you see words are what I do believe in. They're all we've got.'

> Penelope Lively, *Day of Judgement*

I checked my e-mail and found as usual I got two exciting messages from friends who now also have e-mail. They say things like 'I've got e-mail. E-mail me' . . . When I first had a fax machine we all faxed each other senseless, just because we could. We didn't actually say anything we couldn't say via much more old-fashioned technology but that's not the point is it? The point is to be modern and show off about it, to pretend you're at the cutting edge . . .

> Suzanne Moore in a *Guardian* column.

Preface

The world we now live in is one which is shaped physically by technology. This is obvious enough as we look around us at cities, at motorways linking cities, or at landscapes stitched with electricity pylons and wind farms. But the shaping is more than physical. Since technology expands the range of possibilities open to us, it also helps to shape our mental perceptions of the world. If we can send faxes to Australia in an instant, rather than consign letters to a boat which takes six weeks to arrive there, this changes our relation to Australia, and our mental image of it.

It is in fact *science-based* technology in particular which has revealed itself to be so powerful a force, shaping both our physical and our mental worlds. Much technology, such as pottery or paper making, was developed long before the scientific revolution of the 17th century, but it is the expansion of technology based on scientific knowledge rather than slowly-acquired craft skill which can now so rapidly transform both us and our world.

In recent times the biggest impact on our daily lives from technology which has its base in science has come from the development of tiny pieces of semiconductor called 'microchips' which carry many electrical circuits. Thanks to these we can now 'check our e-mail', 'visit a Web site', 'surf the Net' or shave with a battery shaver whose chip indicates on a liquid crystal display the percentage of battery power remaining.

At the core of these recent technological changes is the development of the digital computer, together with allied telecommunications; and with that comes the emergence of 'information technology' (IT) as a new field of study. Our concern in this book is in one sense with IT, but we do not focus on the technology itself, on such things as hardware configurations or, say, the specification of software engineering needed to support collaborative work, on which there is no lack of literature.

Our aim is more fundamental. Our concern is with the *context* of IT, with its place in human affairs in general and in organizations in particular. This is what many would regard as the associate field of study, that of 'information systems' (IS). And our motivation for writing this book is the feeling that thinking about IS is not yet out of its Stone Age. Yes, there is a rapidly growing IS literature; but it exhibits two characteristics which are disquieting. Firstly it reveals much confusion, even about such basic concepts as 'data', 'information', 'knowledge' and the relation between them. Secondly, conventional wisdom, as embodied in college textbooks for young students, is well out of touch with reality, being rooted in ideas about organizations from the 1960s. In the texts in question students are presented with a model of managing as decision-making in pursuit of declared goals; information systems are then presented as supporting that decision making, a model which anyone with real experience of organizational life knows to be absurdly, often farcically inadequate. There must be serious problems for an IS field which is both full of conceptual confusions and tied to out-of-date thinking about the nature of management and organizations. Our aim is to initiate conceptual cleansing in the IS field, to try to create a 'clearing in the forest', something which Peter Keen (1991), in thoughtful reflections on IS research, sees as a useful role for books in this area in its present state of development.

In this book we are concerned with both IT and IS, but especially with IS and its relation to IT. In principle you could think out the fundamentals of information systems without reference to the technology used in actual systems, which might consist largely of telephones, written messages and maps, as in the spectacular system described in Chapter Five. But, given the ubiquity of computer and telecommunication technology, it is nowadays necessary to think of IS in relation to IT, not least because the rapidly changing technology offers possibilities for new kinds of information system well beyond the capabilities of earlier technology. This then makes possible new activities, new ways of doing things and new thinking, none of which would have been possible without the new technology.

Equally, the IT experts ought to be richly conscious of the nature of information systems and their context as a background to their expert role in making them possible. Unfortunately, the fascinations of IT are strong enough to make it a rather closed world, with many IT professionals not really interested in IS and its influence in organizations. Some even assume that IS and IT are synonyms, as they strive to stay within their cosy world! The authors remember an experience in the Management Services Department of what was then ICI Plastics Division. Its leader felt that his biggest problem was to persuade his two groups of people, business analysts and IT professionals, to work together on the problems the group tackled. The business analysts were keen on joint working; the IT experts were not. One of them said: 'Look, all we need is a precise specification of what is required of the system. We will then provide an efficient and elegant technical solution. That's our role'. We think the IT expert was wrong. Just as IS cannot ignore IT, so work on IT needs to be done in relation to the human and social context which provides its ultimate justification and truly defines its role. This is why what we aim at here is a clear fundamental account of the IS field which meets several requirements:

- it needs to make sense both to those who work in IS and to those whose concern is IT;
- it needs to encompass changes in practice which are made possible by technical developments;
- finally, it must be robust enough to remain valid as the technology itself and ways of using it continue to develop.

The aim is to give an account of the field which meets these criteria, is fed by experience, but is more than simply an account of 'what works in practice', this being all that much of what currently passes for 'IS theory' amounts to.

Going beyond 'what works in practice', however, does not mean that we are attempting to lay down a philosophy for the field in a technical sense, a would-be permanent theory of IS. The research was driven by a belief in the need to link ideas to experience and experience to ideas. Given that belief, we are trying to develop a coherent and defensible concept of IS which matches experience; it could perhaps open the way for professional philosophers to contribute their kind of scrupulous intellectual agonizing to this subject.

The motivation for writing this book comes from personal experiences. Peter Checkland, after 15 years in industry, as a manager in ICI, moved to Lancaster University and started a programme of action research in real-world problem situations. Out of that programme has come the holistic approach to dealing with such situations known as Soft Systems Methodology. In the research which led to it, and to its refinement over the years, the situations tackled never failed to reveal problems related to information and its provision. In this context it seemed remarkable that an area called 'information *systems*' made very little use of systems ideas or the process of thinking systemically. The experiences in more than 25 years of this research underpin the thinking in this book, which can in one sense be seen as a third book in the sequence which began with *Systems Thinking, Systems Practice* in 1981 and continued with *Soft Systems Methodology in Action* in 1990.

Sue Holwell worked in both IS and IT in the Australian Government Service for 20 years, concerned at different times with systems design and implementation, information strategy, introduction of communication networks and provision of professional computing for architects and engineers. Latterly she headed an IS function which covered both IS and IT. In the course of this experience of many aspects of computing she felt frustration at the irrelevance of both academic and trade literatures, which never seemed to be quite in touch with issues in the front line as she was experiencing them. She moved to study and research at Lancaster University in an attempt to understand the sources of her frustration as a professional in the field, and to find ways of moving beyond it.

These motivations explain the nature of the book: it seeks to make a substantive contribution. It is not another book *about* IS, its possible boundaries, its feasible research methods, its debatable curriculum. There is a role for such books, and never a shortage of them in any field within the groves of academe. In this field the collection edited by Mingers and Stowell (1997) provides a good current example. But such books always remind us of Roy Campbell's well-known lines on some South African novelists: 'They use the snaffle and the curb all right, But where's the bloody horse?' We are here interested in the horse rather than the snaffle and the curb.

Thus, although written within a university management school, the book is not, at least for us, its authors, a piece of academic writing of a kind that would appeal to an ivory-tower purist. Academics are very good at creating images and ideas, and building them into structures about which arguments can rage. ('Why are academic disputes so heated?', someone once asked. Came the reply: 'It's because the stakes are so small.') Many academics, even including some in management schools, never move beyond the disputes over ideas and theory construction, being interested in the arguments for their own sake. But the ideas matter ultimately only in proportion to their relevance to lived experiences. Given our backgrounds in both the real world and academe, we are committed to the development of ideas out of, and in, practice. We are interested both in how ideas shape what people do and in the way in which what people do shapes the ideas: in ideas and action mutually creating each other. So we have tried to make the work described here a product of that constant interaction. Ideas not grounded in action are arid; equally, unreflective action amounts to little more than 'whistling in the wind.'

The relevant audiences for this book are necessarily wide, given its aspirations. It is relevant to management consultants, managers and similar professionals because it is based in management and consultancy experience; and it is relevant to those who work as professionals in IS and IT because it tries to make sense of that world. It is also relevant to students studying IS and/or IT who wish to gain a greater understanding than that provided by the flawed conventional wisdom of their textbooks, since it seeks to replace that simplistic model, subsuming it within a richer account more relevant to the real world of life in organizations.

In struggling to make sense of the research experiences, and to forge the argument of this book, we have been helped by a number of people to whom we are very grateful. Action research by definition requires active collaborators and we are grateful to all those willing people in industry and in the National Health Service who have taken part in our researches over the last five years. Special thanks go to Chris Atkinson, Steve Clarke, Kek Goh, John Hardy, Vic Peel, John Poulter, Caroline Rea, Bob Steele and Peter Wood, all of whom were close associates.

More broadly, our thanks for their stimulating influence over the years go to our colleagues in the Department of Management Science in Lancaster University's Management School: Dave Brown, Paul Dunning-Lewis, Geoff Walsham, Brian Wilson, Mark Winter; and to consultants Sheila Challender and Mike Haynes, reflective practitioners both. Everyone who has taken part in the Lancaster programme of action research over more than 25 years owes a considerable debt to the post-graduate students of what is now the MSc in Information Management. Our thanks go to the many who have worked with us on projects.

Finally, since we can write properly only by using pen and paper, many thanks go to the ever-cheerful, ever-willing Jenny Seddon, who, with calm professionalism, turned a much-worked-over manuscript into clean copy.

Part One

The Field of Information Systems and its Problems

Chapter One

The Field of Information Systems: Crucial but Confused

INTRODUCTION: A SECOND INDUSTRIAL REVOLUTION?

We all live very different lives from those lived by our ancestors, even by our parents and grandparents, and we now accept without giving the matter much thought that change is a constant feature of our world.

We are probably readier than any previous generation to accept that fact, since the pace of change in this century has been so great. Life was slower and steadier for the medieval peasant. It was also shorter and more brutish, and if we can expect our own lives – at least in the developed world – to be both longer and more interesting, this is in major part due to the fact that we have at our disposal something which is also one of the main sources of the constant change we experience: namely, *science-based technology*. Technology which is based not only on handed-down craft skill but also on scientific knowledge is a source of both material well-being and much of the continual change we experience in our lives.

Technology is older than the scientific method, and much technology (pottery making and metal extraction, for example) existed long before the Greeks created the scientific outlook and initiated the process which culminated in the Scientific Revolution of the 17th century. Thereafter the combination of science and technology has been a uniquely powerful source of the kind of changes which can profoundly alter the lives of very large numbers of people in many countries.

In 1782, James Watt used steam to drive a piston in both directions, and in inventing a steam engine capable of rotary motion created the basis of changes so profound that nobody now questions the aptness of the phrase 'the Industrial Revolution' to describe them. That revolution, starting with changes in science-based technology, also became, with urbanization, a social, political and economic revolution, one which continues today. Describing the industrialism and urbanism which started in late 18th century Britain and then spread across Europe, the historian Thomson (1966)points out that

> A European born in 1815 who lived to the age of eighty-five lived through greater changes than had any of his ancestors – though perhaps not through greater changes than his descendants would experience. Not the least important fact about the acceleration of historical development that began around 1800 is that it still continues. (page 115)

Every reader of this book will be experiencing that acceleration, and hence will be living through the consequent continuing changes. Indeed, they are currently so obvious and so profound that they are continually referred to as constituting no less than a *second* industrial revolution, one based upon information rather than energy and linked to the development of the computer. We are told repeatedly, so much so that it has become a cliché, that we are now in the 'Information Age' and can tread an 'information superhighway', or 'surf the Internet'.

The concept of a second industrial revolution emerged in the 1960s. The Princeton economist Fritz Machlup drew attention to the increasing proportion of knowledge workers in the workforce (Machlup 1962) and talk began of the 'knowledge society'. Daniel Bell of Harvard published in 1973 an extensive analysis of what he called 'the coming of *post-industrial* society', in which the crucial resource is no longer capital but knowledge. Much of the writing in this vein, and especially that which gives such ideas wide currency, is inevitably journalistic in nature. Examples are John Naisbitt's *Megatrends* (1982) and Alvin Toffler's *The Third Wave* (1980) and *Powershift* (1990): suitable for the airport departure lounge, perhaps, but not scholarly. (A scholarly analyst of the 'information society' (Webster 1995, page 218) describes Toffler as a 'techno booster', and includes James Martin, of *The Wired Society* (1978) in the same category.) A sprightly critic, Theodore Roszak (1986), himself no stranger to the demotic, describes such writing as 'an ungainly hybrid of potted social science, Sunday supplement journalism and soothsaying' (page 34).

Nevertheless, we should not dismiss such journalism too peremptorily. Books of this kind become bestsellers because they chime in with vaguely-recognised notions; and there is impact in such nuggets as Naisbitt's three-word history of the American people: farmer, labourer, clerk!

Naisbitt acknowledges his debt to Bell, suggests that post-industrial society has been misunderstood as an economy based on *services* and asserts that 'it is now clear that the post-industrial society is the information society' (Naisbitt 1982, Chapter 1). The Japanese, grasping the concept in national terms, announced at the start of the 1970s their intention to build just such a society.

Back in the world of scholarship, Hirschheim (1985), in a broad social and organizational review of office automation, quotes a number of studies which indicate the steady decline in the fraction of the workforce employed in agriculture and industry, and the rise in the number of those employed in work which is largely information based. And many of us have in recent years been experiencing the change in the quality of our professional lives (not necessarily for the better) which is a result of the development and spread of such inventions as the fax machine and the computer network: the avalanche of messages increases, as does the need to extract, code, store, process and retrieve some of them from the mass of dross.

If we are to see the changes associated with the rise of the computer as a new industrial revolution, one based on information, then it is interesting to note that this second revolution was implicit in the first. In developing the steam engine, Watt, an instrument maker of genius, developed the centrifugal governor which controlled the speed of the machine, keeping it approximately constant and hence making it a powerful and reliable industrial device. Now, it is almost impossible to describe this device without using the language of data processing. Although it is a purely mechanical device, restricted to one set of movements, when thought of as the embodiment of a *process* it is seen as a processor of data. It senses (automatically) the speed of the machine and acts, or not, (automatically) to increase or decrease the supply of steam to the cylinders depending upon the data captured. It is, in this sense, a data processing device, one upon which the usefulness of the machine depends.

Roszak (1986) makes the distinction between *strong* machines and *smart* machines. The former (steam engines, dynamos, ships) characterize the first industrial revolution, while the second is characterized by 'smart' machines such as computers and all kinds of machines containing microprocessors which process data – such as, nowadays, even battery-driven shavers which display the shaving time left in minutes. Using this distinction, the steam engine with governor, introduced in 1788, is a 'strong' machine controlled by a 'smart' device: thus the first revolution presages the second, and it is an academic point as to whether the present changes constitute a new revolution or simply signal the inevitable progress of the first.

What is certain, though, is that 'smart' machines are widely recognized as having changed, and continuing to change, the nature of working life for millions of people.

It is argued, notably in the oft-cited work of Zuboff (1988), that the introduction of information technology (IT) can have very profound effects on both individuals and organizations, effects which go beyond the quantitative. The automation of existing clerical procedures is always likely to lead to a reduced need for clerks to record data, update files and analyze patterns in the data. But Zuboff's argument is that the most significant effects of IT are qualitative ones. In the early 1980s she was reading the history of the first industrial revolution, trying to grasp how the material changes in production altered people's everyday lives; meanwhile she was working as a consultant for a Wall Street bank and a daily newspaper, assessing the application of IT to clerical work in the bank, and the transition to computerized typesetting at the newspaper plant. During interviews, many workers voiced uncertainty and distress in the face of the change engulfing them. Zuboff realized that she was witnessing a change no less profound than that which overcame the spinners and weavers who in the 19th century had to cease their home production and move into the new factories. The bank clerks and linotype operators, similarly, were not simply using new tools, they were experiencing a deep-rooted change in their lives. Zuboff (ibid) writes:

> The material alterations in their means of production were manifested in transformations at an intimate level of experience – assumptions about knowledge and power, their beliefs about work and the meaning they derived from it, the content and rhythm of their social exchanges, and the ordinary mental and physical disciplines to which they accommodated in their daily lives. I saw that a world of sensibilities and expectations was being irretrievably displaced by a new world . . . (Preface)

Based on participant observation, interviews and small group discussions, Zuboff (ibid) presents rich accounts of studies of the effects of IT at seven sites. In making sense of this experience she was led to make up the word 'informate' to describe what IT does beyond the automation of procedures. IT, she argues, 'is not mute': as a result of the kind of thinking necessarily involved in its introduction,

> IT not only produces action but also . . . symbolically renders events, objects and processes so that they become visible, knowable and shareable in a new way. (page 9)

This *rendering visible* of events, objects and processes, so that the use of IT itself produces new information, will inevitably set in motion dynamics that

> will ultimately reconfigure the nature of work and the social relationships that organize productive activity. (page 11)

This has important consequences for organizations and for the process of managing them. Zuboff believes that the 'informating process' due to IT has the potential to set knowledge and authority on a collision course. The domains of managerial activity need to be rethought as the development of four things: intellectual skills (involving 'abstraction, explicit inference and procedural reasoning'); the technology itself; strategy; and the social system of the organization. The managing process, accepting 'post-hierarchical' relationships, ought to concern itself with organizational learning, with the way in which people in organizations continually construct the meanings which for them make sense of themselves and their world.

Of course, in real situations, such changes will be perceived by some as threatening traditional management authority. In the organizations she studied, Zuboff did observe attempts to suppress the 'informating' process and to direct potential innovation towards conventional automation: such situations will show all the rich messiness of human affairs. What is important for our purposes is to note that the use of IT *poses these new dilemmas*. Because of the kind of thinking it entails, IT is not simply a new tool with which to do traditional tasks. It stirs things up, introduces uncertainties, gets people perceiving their world in a new way.

An important consequence of this is that the introduction of IT will always have implications and consequences beyond the merely technical. There will always be political consequences of introducing IT. This is to use the word 'politics' to cover the set of processes which relate to the continual achievement and re-achievement of accommodations with respect to the disposition of power among people and/or groups of people. In this sense politics in human affairs is endemic, and is enacted at all levels, from the societal through the institutional and organizational, to the level of small parts of organizations, right down to the level of the relationship between two individuals. IT will affect the power balance at all levels because of the kind of thinking it entails, and also because 'information' is so relevant to power. Gaining access to information or denying others that access is one of the oldest moves in the power game! The first true printed book in Europe, the Gutenberg Bible, appeared in 1455, and by 1501 an astute Pope, head of one of the most powerful institutions in society at that time – the Church – was suggesting to bishops that control of printing technology might be the key to preserving the purity of the faith (Roberts 1980). Thus the importance of information dissemination linked to printing was quickly recognized in western culture. And we can feel sure that if Niccolo Machiavelli, writing *The Prince* in 1513 to tell his master what had to be done in order to gain and retain power, had been writing today, he would have urged that if you stage a coup then be sure to capture the TV and radio station at the same time as capturing the palace!

We have then, in the current industrial revolution with information at its core, a source of great technical and social change with which we need to come to terms. But to do so entails exploring and clarifying a set of concepts and activities which are currently both confused and confusing.

'INFORMATION SYSTEMS' AND 'INFORMATION TECHNOLOGY'

There are probably several reasons why the very broad field of 'information systems' (IS) and 'information technology' (IT) is in a confused state. Firstly, this is a relatively new field, emerging only in the late 1940s with the introduction of the first computers based on vacuum tubes (or 'valves'). And the really rapid development stems from the introduction of integrated circuits (transistors made on the flat surface of a semiconductor) in the mid-1960s. So these are early days for the development of the field, even though the rate of technical development has been astonishingly high, with the basic cost of computing power dropping 40 per cent a year, every year, during the 1970s (Large, 1980), and the time needed for one electronic operation falling, between 1958 and 1980 by a factor of 80 million (Porter and Millar, 1985).

Secondly, the rate at which thinking about the field has developed has not matched that at which the technology has changed. This is not surprising since the on-going development of ideas requires both real-world experience and much dialogue between interested people. This has its own rolling pace which cannot always be hurried.

Thirdly, as has been argued in the previous section, the nature of the changes brought about by IS and IT is that they extend beyond the mere use of new tools to cover deeper cultural change. The field is bound to be a hybrid one, with many candidates for inclusion: not only technology but also management and organization theory, sociology, systems thinking, political science, social psychology, etc.

On the face of it, the phrase IT refers to a technology, one which here might be taken to refer mainly to the hardware of computers and telecommunication equipment. But 'technology' is often interpreted in a broader sense; for example queuing theory is often taken to be part of the 'technology' of management science. This is the case here. IT, without being sharply defined, is usually regarded as a collection of both practices, techniques *and* devices concerned with collecting, storing, processing and distributing data or information (though those two terms are frequently confused, as we shall see). A recent handbook of management (Kempner 1987) described the phrase IT as being

> coined to mark the convergence of two technologies that had traditionally been separate: computing and communications. (page 25)

Zuboff (1988) suggests that it reflects the convergence of several streams of development including

> microelectronics, computer science, telecommunications, software engineering, and system analysis. (page 415)

The inclusion of the latter items here overlaps IT with the broader, also ambiguously-defined field of IS. This may be thought of as marking the *organizational* need to manage the use of IT in relation to an organization's activities and intentions. In the Series Introduction to a sequence of books on aspects of IS, Boland and Hirschheim (1985) describe this field as a combination of two primary fields: computer science and management, with a host of supporting disciplines eg psychology, sociology, statistics, political science, economics, philosophy and mathematics. IS is concerned not only with the development of new information technologies but also with questions such as: how they can best be applied, how they should be managed, and what their wider implications are. (page vii)

A current student text (Ahituv and Neumann 1990) lists no fewer than 19 'foundations' of IS, seeing it as the intersection of three main disciplines: exact sciences (including control theory, general systems theory, statistics), technology (including computer science, electrical engineering) and social and behavioural sciences (including management theory, sociology, psycholinguistics, economics, etc).

Given the overlaps and links between computer science, computer technology, and management and organization studies, it is not surprising that this is a confused field. The confusion is usefully illustrated within universities, which sometimes set up departments of computing, or computer science, while interests in information systems are pursued in management schools. And it is also not unknown for individuals whose interest is in IS development (in Boland and Hirschheim's (1985) sense above), to find themselves in departments of computer science where they feel somewhat beleaguered, since many of those taken up with the delights of a fast-moving technology are notoriously uninterested in the application of computer systems and their richly ambiguous organizational consequences.

Our aim in this book is to try and dispel some of the confusion which characterizes this field. This is a work of would-be conceptual cleansing. Its focus will be on information systems and their creation, mainly in an organizational context. Although we accept that technological developments may well create new possibilities which may lead to a re-thinking of organizational forms and processes, the focus on IS rather than IT is a conscious decision based on a particular view: information systems exist to serve, help or support people taking action in the real world (Checkland and Scholes 1990, Chapter 2), and it is a fundamental proposition that in order to conceptualize, and so create, a system which *serves,* it is first necessary to conceptualize that which is *served,* since the way the latter is thought of will dictate what would be necessary to serve or support it (Checkland 1981, page 234). For example, an industrial research and development operation could not sensibly be designed and built up without first thinking out the nature of the industrial activity served by that research and development,

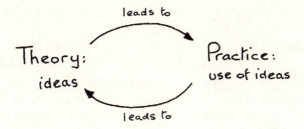

Figure 1.1. *The learning cycle in which theory and practice create each other*

since it is *that* conceptualization which dictates what will count as 'support' and 'service' in the industry in question.

The starting point of this work, then, is a re-thinking of what is entailed in providing informational support to purposeful action in the real world of organizations. From that a clearer view emerges of the nature of 'information systems' and IS as a field of study. It is not, however, primarily a theoretical work. Neither is it simply an account of real-world experiences in the world of IS, though such experiences do form an important part of it. Rather, it is based on the belief that thinking about the world and having experiences in it cannot properly be separated. The experiences are interpreted by, but also serve to create, ideas and concepts which in turn make sense of (new) experience. Neither the ideas nor the experiences are prime, since each creates and modifies the other. Hence the research work presented here is the product of the cycle shown in Figure 1.1. It is the *learning cycle* shown in that figure which is prime, and this work is the outcome of traversing that cycle many times. Of course the account of the work we give here is inevitably rather more coherent than we felt the work itself to be while we were doing it! Not all the false trails will be followed, not all the cul de sacs explored.

Like everything else in human affairs, this work is the product of a particular history – of particular people in a particular context of time, place, and ideas – and it is probably helpful to explain briefly both its context and the mode in which it was carried out.

THE CONTEXT OF THIS WORK: DEVELOPMENT OF SOFT SYSTEMS METHODOLOGY

The present work was carried out in association with what is now a more-than-25-year programme of action research. The programme, though based in a post-graduate university department, has always been conducted outside the university – in the messy real–world problem situations in which managers of all kinds and at all levels try to cope with the complexity of 'life's rich pageant'. The research has aimed at finding ways of dealing holistically with such situations using systems thinking. Several hundred systems studies have been carried out by Lancaster University teams as part of the research programme, and its main outcome is the methodological approach to tackling real–world problems which is known as 'soft systems methodology' (SSM). This development has been described in many papers (some of which are referenced here, where appropriate) and three books from the original Lancaster group. There is also a growing secondary literature. *Systems Thinking, Systems Practice* (Checkland 1981) describes the first decade of the research, placing it within a framework of the development of systems thinking, which itself had to be rethought during the course of the research. *Soft Systems Methodology in Action* (Checkland and Scholes 1990a), written for would-be practitioners, describes the second decade of the research, seeking to show the flexible-but-rigorous use of the methodology in the hands of experienced users; Wilson's *Systems, Concepts, Methodologies and Applications* (1984) describes his involvement in the research programme, starting from the intellectual stance of a control engineer and embracing 'softer' elements experientially.

We will describe current SSM more fully in Chapter Six; at this stage, we will briefly outline its core characteristics and the context of its development.

At the start of the programme the approach adopted was deliberately to attempt a naive transfer of what would now be called 'hard' systems engineering from its use in such tasks as optimizing the output of a petrochemical complex to the more ambiguous area of the problems of managing, broadly defined. The 'hard' systems engineer chooses to see the world as a set of systems, and hence assumes that it is easy to answer the question: what is the system in question? He or she then carefully defines the named system's objectives; and numerous techniques are available to enable the system to be engineered to meet those objectives. Alternatives are modelled, and carefully defined criteria are used to choose between them. It was discovered that in the kind of problematical situations within and between organizations with which managers have to cope, the inability to decide 'the system' and name 'its objectives' was often what caused the situation to be regarded as problematical in the first place. (For example: was the Anglo-French Concorde project to be regarded simply as a system to create the world's first supersonic aircraft? Or as a political system to persuade the French the British could be good European partners? Or as a system to help maintain a UK precision engineering industry? Or as a system to ensure that the Europeans – not the Americans – were world leaders in at least one advanced technology? In the real Concorde project all these considerations and many others were relevant.)

Gradually a different approach emerged (Checkland 1972). It was based on the fact that all real-world 'management' problem situations have at least one thing in common: they contain people interested in trying to take *purposeful action*. The idea of a set of activities linked together so that the whole set, as an entity, could pursue a purpose was taken to be a new kind of system concept, called 'a human activity system'. Ways of naming and building models of such systems were developed (Smyth and Checkland 1976; Checkland 1979; Checkland, Forbes and Martin 1990; Checkland and Scholes 1990b). It was accepted from very early on in the research that in building such models it was necessary to declare the set of values, the outlook, the worldview *(Weltanschauung)* which makes a particular model meaningful, since the purposeful action which one observer perceives as 'freedom fighting' will be perceived as 'terrorism' by another observer with a different taken-as-given image of the world. The models are clearly not would-be *descriptions* of reality; they are very much less complex than they would need to be to fill that role! They are, rather, concepts relevant to exploring what we perceive as 'reality'. They are best described as 'holons', using the word which Koestler (1967 and 1978) made up for the abstract notion of an entity which is simultaneously both an autonomous whole and in principle a part of larger wholes (Checkland 1988a).

Given a handful of models of this kind, that is to say models of concepts of purposeful activity built from a declared point of view, they could be used, in the so-called 'comparison stage' of SSM, to give a coherent structure to debate about the problem situation and what might improve it. This 'comparison' was normally carried out by using the models as a coherent source of cogent linked questions to ask of the real situation as the participants perceived it. This created a debate among people with an interest in or concern for the problem situation, the purpose of the debate being collectively to learn a way to possible changes in the problem situation, changes which were regarded as being both desirable and feasible. This normally entailed the finding of *accommodations* between conflicting interests, situations which did not satisfy

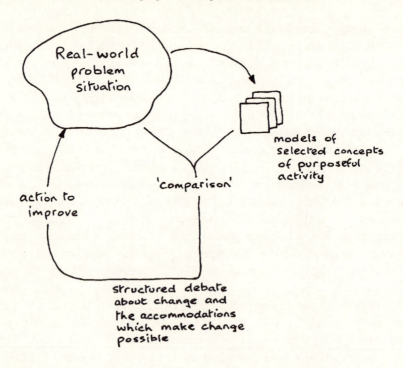

Figure 1.2. *The learning cycle of soft systems methodology*

everyone (or maybe anyone!) but could be lived with, enabling action to be taken. *Occasionally* an overall consensus could be achieved, a consensus being a special case of the more general (and common) notion of reaching accommodations.

Thus SSM emerged as a learning system having the form shown in Figure 1.2. In principle the learning may go on and on, and to end a systems study is to take an arbitrary step, since problematical situations (and all human situations fit into this category!) will continue to evolve and will never be free from differences of interest, opinion and values. The nature of the methodology is well captured by von Bülow (1989):

> SSM is a methodology that aims to bring about improvements in areas of social concern by activating in the people involved in the situation a learning cycle which is ideally never-ending. (page 35)

The 'activation' of the learning cycle is through the use of models, as outlined above, but in recent years the model-based stream of analysis has been supplemented and complemented by a second stream which

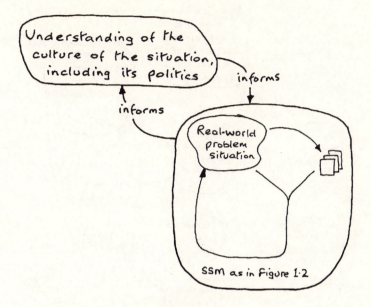

Figure 1.3. *SSM including the cultural exploration*

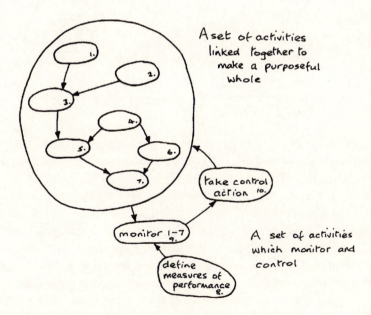

Figure 1.4. *The form of activity models in SSM*

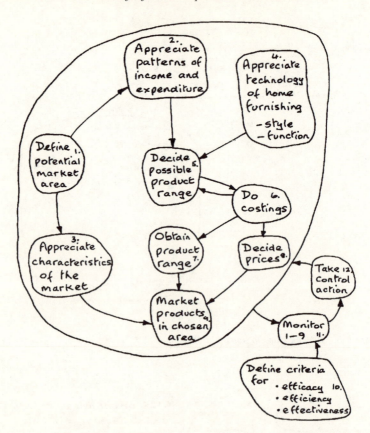

Figure 1.5. *An SSM-style activity model from the modified IKEA mission statement, concerned with marketing home furnishing items of good design and function at prices low enough to enable a majority of people to be able to affort them*

explores the problem situation as a culture. This gives a process for SSM which is illustrated in Figure 1.3 (and discussed in detail in Checkland and Scholes 1990a).

Now, the models of human activity systems used in SSM consist of a structured set of activities constituting an operational sub-system within a boundary, together with a monitoring and control sub-system which could in principle modify the operations or their structure if they were thought of as 'failing'. The basic structure is shown in Figure 1.4, and there are a number of examples of such models later in this book.

Figure 1.5 shows a model we built from a modified version of the mission statement of IKEA, the Scandinavian home furnishing company. (We used the word 'marketing' since the only verb in the original statement is 'offer' – and the company intends more than that.) Figure 1.5 is a picture of a holon which represents the 'logical machine' required to pursue the purpose expressed in the mission statement. Clearly any such holon could in some circumstances be thought of as a potential set of operations which human agents might in principle try to make happen in a real situation. If that occurred then people undertaking the activities of that holon in a real situation would need information support.

This is the thought which links SSM to work on IS. Each activity in the holon has a place in a structure of activities. It may be contingent upon some of the other activities (as, say, 'convert raw material to product' would be contingent upon the prior 'obtain raw material') and some of those activities may be contingent upon it. Given this context, it would in principle be possible to carry out an analysis of the information required to help people carrying out the activities in the model. For example, any agent carrying out the activity 'obtain raw material' would in logic need information concerning the nature of the raw material, suppliers of it, their reliability, quality, price, etc. And carrying out the activity would yield further information about raw material supply. In this way models of purposeful holons can be used to initiate and structure sensible discussion about information support for the people undertaking real-world pur- poseful activity. It is along this route that SSM has moved in the direction of work on the creation of information systems (Checkland 1988b).

The basic idea that 'human activity system' models can be used as a vehicle for what is often thought of as 'information requirements anal- ysis' will be considerably amplified, and also partially modified, in the course of this book. Nevertheless, it remains the core idea behind the work described here, and information provision has remained an im- portant theme throughout the whole SSM research programme. Iron- ically, the first-ever conceptual model built during the development of SSM (Checkland and Griffin 1970), not yet expressed in the form shown in Figure 1.4, happened to be an ideal-type model concerned with the information necessary to enable decisions to be made in processing customer orders in a medium-sized textile company. It was a few years, however, before the implications of that model were followed up.

There is more about current thinking on SSM in Chapter Six. Meanwhile it is useful to make some preliminary remarks about the context in which SSM was developed. It was created in a research programme concerned not with classical-style hypothesis testing but with learning from intervention in real-world problem situations, with 'action research'.

THE MODE OF THIS WORK: ACTION RESEARCH

Hypothesis testing?

In 1600, William Gilbert, personal physician to Queen Elizabeth 1, carried out an experiment which tested a current theory that a magnet derived its strange properties from feeding on iron. He magnetized a piece of iron, stored it with iron filings, and carried out weighings periodically to show that the magnet was not in fact consuming the filings. Gilbert, writing *de Magnete* six years before Galileo's first publication, was an experimentalist ahead of his time, and what he did with the magnet would now be regarded as the very epitome of positivistic scientific research, the shape of which is shown in Figure 1.6. He made disciplined observations of a selected part of an external reality outside himself; and the observations, which tested a hypothesis to destruction, could be repeated to yield the same results by anyone who cared to repeat his experiment.

This method of conducting investigations in natural science, based on the three principles of reductionism, repeatability and the refutation of hypotheses (Checkland 1981, Chapter 2), has been so widely successful that it has become the dominating model of research activity. Many

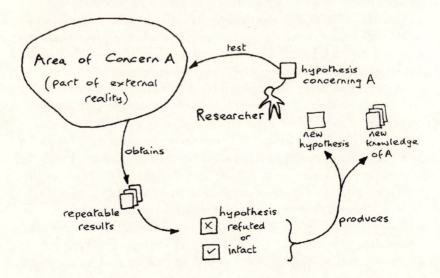

Figure 1.6. *The cycle of positivist hypothesis-testing research in natural science (after Checkland 1991a)*

people in many different fields make the unquestioned assumption that 'research' means the testing of hypotheses.

However, the hypotheses which natural scientists test concern the natural regularities of the universe, and all the evidence is that these are invariant: the inverse square law of magnetism is always that, every time it is tested no matter who (competently) does the testing. When we turn to human affairs, however, and to social phenomena, it is far from obvious that the same experimental hypothesis-testing approach applies.

Geoffrey Vickers, in developing the theory of 'appreciative systems' through which he sought to make sense of his 40 years of experience in the world of human affairs (Vickers 1965), was always cogently critical of those who blithely try to apply the method of natural science to social phenomena. In conversation he used to point out that while Copernicus and Ptolemy offer very different hypotheses about the basic structure of our solar system, we know that, irrespective of whether the sun or the earth is at the centre of the system, the actual structure is *entirely unaffected by our having theories about it*. Whereas when Marx propounds a theory of history this changes history! The methods of natural science, extremely productive in enabling external observers to discover the regularities of the natural universe, are exceptionally difficult to apply to human affairs.

This being so, we can be sure that the difficulty applies to work on information systems in organizations. The setting up of an information system is itself a social act, requiring some kind of concerted action by many different people; and the operation of an information system entails such human phenomena as attributing meaning to manipulated data and making judgements about what constitutes a relevant category. And of course meanings and judgements will differ from one person to another. Thus IS and IT are hardly part of the physical regularities of the universe, to be unambiguously explored using the hypothesis-testing approach. Nevertheless, the seductive attraction of the apparent certainty of the approach, as well as the prestige attached to being 'scientific' in one's work, leads to many valiant attempts to carry out this kind of research in information systems. This is especially so in the USA where positivism is very much the dominant research paradigm. To illustrate the difficulties in the IS field, it is probably useful briefly to examine an example.

Dennis et al (1990) describe a very carefully designed experiment based on the hypothesis that electronic meeting systems (EMS) have the capability to support and improve the strategic management of organizations. The researchers' form of EMS is one in which participants took part in meetings, face to face, in the same room at the same time 'with electronic communications used to support or replace verbal communications' (page 37). The meetings took place in an elaborately-prepared special room created at the researchers' university.

> Each participant has a separate networked, hard disk-based, color graphics micro-computer workstation that is recessed into the work area. Another one or two workstations serve as the facilitator's consoles which are used to control the EMS software. At least one large screen video display is located at the front of the room as an electronic blackboard, with other audio-visual support also available . . . (ibid, page 41)

Seventeen groups from different organizations held meetings in the EMS room while 'performing some aspect of strategic management' (ibid, page 41) and evaluation of the results was attempted.

Now the difficulties begin to pile up. Firstly, the concept of strategic management has no agreed sharp definition; hence, secondly, ascertaining whether or not EMS improve it, via improvement of meetings which supposedly relate to it, is not going to be easy! The researchers adopted and adapted 12 measures of system capability claimed to be relevant to supporting strategic management by previous researchers. These system capabilities included such items as enhancing idea generation, enhancing innovation, fostering managerial motivation, anticipating crises etc -- all items which are themselves far from being sharply defined.

After the meetings had taken place, much data concerning them was collected and evaluation included the use of questionnaires. Using a five-point scale, participants subjectively rated whether or not the EMS-supported meeting in the special room was 'much worse', 'worse', 'no different', 'better', or 'much better' than their usual meetings held without electronic support. Some time after the meeting the member of the group 'most responsible for the organization's strategic management activities' (ibid, pages 41 and 42) was interviewed. The 12 system capabilities were rated by the interviewers on the 1–5 scale, and a subjective overall rating was also made. Grades were averaged (to two decimal places!) and statistical analysis was carried out to ascertain if gradings were significantly different from non-EMS-supported groups studied by earlier researchers. The averaged interview-derived gradings ranged from 3.40 to 4.47, where 3 means the EMS-supported meeting was rated 'no different' from a manual process, and 4 means the computer-supported meeting was 'better' than a manual process. The final claim is made that the research shows that this form of EMS support for strategic management has been found to enhance six capabilities claimed by others to lead to more successful strategic management outcomes: idea generation, identification of key problems, communication of line managers' concerns, organizational learning, integration of diverse functions and anticipation of crises.

It would take a very benign critic, however, to accept without question the results of such an experiment, even though we may readily acknowledge the near-heroic effort made by the researchers in carrying it out. The ambiguity of the hypothesis; the ambiguities of the definition of the capabilities said to affect strategic management; the long and dubiously-causal link between 'better' meetings and 'improved' strategic management outcomes; the lack of any attempt at including an internal 'control' situation within the experiment itself: all these factors give pause for thought. And is not the sheer psychology of the situation likely to influence or even determine the results? The managers were invited along to hold their meeting in the elaborate university facility which the researchers had obviously taken great trouble to set up. Asked to judge if the subsequent meeting was 'better' or 'worse' than usual, it would be a churlish manager who was not prepared to say – *since saying it costs the manager nothing* – that the meeting was somewhat 'better' than usual. Would not the well-replicated 'Hawthorne effect' (Mayo 1933) that people respond well when interest is shown in their work and it is taken to be important, be enough to explain the results, independently of any effects which might be due to EMS technology?

These issues are raised not to put this particular research in the dock, but rather to indicate the profound difficulties of importing the methods of natural science into the study of 'social systems'. In the IS and IT field we need to think carefully about the research mode to be adopted and to declare it, being aware of its limitations.

The work described in this book, as mentioned in the previous section, was carried out in association with a research programme into the development of soft systems methodology. That programme as a whole was not based on hypothesis testing but on interpretive action research in real-world situations. This is the kind of research described here, and it is important to be clear about the nature of this approach to inquiry, its limitations, and the outlook upon which it is based (Checkland 1991a).

Action research

The implicit belief behind hypothesis-testing research in information systems is that social phenomena and social reality are at core not fundamentally different from the physical reality which biologists, chemists and physicists investigate. An alternative view is that social reality – what counts as 'fact' about the social world – is continually being constructed and re-constructed in dialogue and discourse among human beings, and in action which they take. Researching social reality then becomes an organized discovery of how human agents *make sense of* their perceived worlds, and how those perceptions change over time and differ from one person or group to another. That kind of researcher does not expect to discover unchanging 'social laws' to set alongside the laws of physics. The nature of this kind of *interpretive* research has been usefully summarized by Walsham (1993):

> Interpretive methods of research start from the position that our knowledge of reality, including the domain of human action, is a social construction by human actors and that this applies equally to researchers. Thus there is no objective reality which can be discovered by researchers and replicated by others, in contrast to the assumptions of positivist science. Our theories concerning reality are ways of making sense of the world and shared meanings are a form of intersubjectivity rather than objectivity. (page 5)

The development of this approach to researching human situations is usually taken to stem from Kurt Lewin's view of 'the limitations of studying complex real social events in a laboratory, the artificiality of splitting out single behavioural elements from an integrated system' (Foster 1972). The approach involves the researcher immersing himself or herself in a human problem situation and following it along whatever path it takes as it unfolds through time. Probably most interpretive action researchers would accept the notion of Argyris et al (1982) that the crucial elements in the approach are: a collaborative process between researchers and people in the situation; a process of critical inquiry; a focus on social practice; and a deliberate process of reflective learning. This falls short of being a prescription, however, and has one serious deficiency, as we shall now argue: namely, it omits the need for a declared-in-advance intellectual framework of ideas, a framework in terms of which what constitutes 'knowledge' about the situation researched will be defined and expressed. This is essential, since what constitutes 'knowledge' in human situations should not be taken as a given. The research might lead to the framework being modified, or, in an extreme case, abandoned; but without a declared-in-advance epistemological framework it is sometimes difficult to distinguish researching from novel writing. Such a declared framework also allows those interested in the research and its outcomes to recover the process by which the results were obtained. Hence they can see how these arose and decide how believable they are.

It is unfortunate that the absence of an emphasis on this crucial requirement – crucial, that is, if the findings are to be openly arrived at, not based on hidden hunches and intuition – is rather too characteristic of the modest stream of literature on action research since the 1950s, a stream which may be sampled via Blum 1955, Foster 1972, Clark 1972, Susman and Evered 1978, Hult and Lennung 1980, Warmington 1980, Argyris et al 1982, Susman 1983, Gilmore et al 1985, Stowell and West 1994.

At a basic level, any piece of research in any mode may be thought of as entailing the elements shown in Figure 1.7 (Checkland 1985). A particular set of linked ideas F are used in a methodology M to investigate some area of interest A. From doing the research, the alert

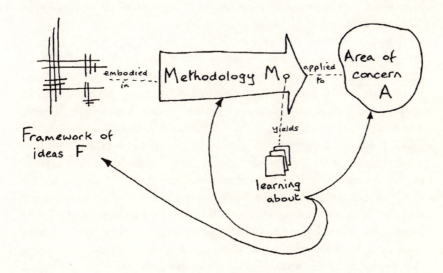

Figure 1.7. *Elements relevant to any piece of research (after Checkland 1985, 1991a)*

researcher may learn things about all three elements. Plate tectonics are an example of a contemporary F, when A consists of earthquakes and vulcanicity. The phlogiston theory of heat is a failed F from the 18th century. In natural science M is the process of Figure 1.6: the testing to destruction of hypotheses.

Even so simple a model is useful in understanding programmes of research. In the 25-year development of SSM at Lancaster University, in a programme of action research, the definitions of F, M and A shifted as learning was achieved. Initially, A was how to tackle hard-to-define, ill-structured, 'wicked' problem situations with which managers have to cope. The chosen M, at first, was systems engineering, the idea being to see if its use could be extended to 'softer' problems than those for which it was developed. F was the set of ideas underlying systems engineering, namely ideas from systematic systems thinking and control engineering. Gradually, as the research programme evolved, F M and A all changed. A was still 'how to tackle management problems' but came to place special emphasis on the organized provision of information in so-called 'information systems', this being an area especially susceptible to the new M, since that had also changed. The new M was SSM, which came out of the failed attempts to use 'hard' systems engineering in messy real-world situations. F became *systemic* rather than *systematic* systems think-ing, and more specifically included the notion of modelling concepts of purposeful activity in holons constructed from declared points of view or *Weltanschauungen*.

This change to, or extension of F, M and A is typical of action research, and must be expected when researching in that mode. How-ever, it is clear that the recognition that the changes have occurred and lessons have been learnt will be much helped if we have declared in advance the intellectual framework within which 'lessons' are defined. The framework in this case is that in Figure 1.7. But the principle is a general one. If we are going to plunge into the flux of events and ideas in a real situation, which is always both exciting and daunting, and hope to be able to extract lessons from the experience (in other words, do the 'research' part of action research) then we must declare in advance the framework in terms of which research lessons will be expressed. (Tech-nically, we must define the epistemology which will be the source of what counts as 'knowledge' in this experience.) In general, neglecting this crucial principle leaves the action research literature vulnerable to positivist critics – even though they, in turn, have a difficult time de-fending hypothesis testing in the domain of human action.

We must emphasize very emphatically the importance of this principle of declaring the intellectual framework which will define the lessons learned. For example, the work by Zuboff (1988), referred to earlier, is generally regarded as important and has been described by Keen (1991) as

> by far the most scholarly contribution to date to the discussion of the link between information technology and changes in work, working and the future of workers. (page 43)

But that research would be stronger if the principle had been followed more rigorously. In her section on research methodology, Zuboff says that she wished to understand the interchange between 'human responsiveness' and the experienced 'life world' (ibid, page 423), believing that each shapes the other (as in our Figure 1.1). Her main methodological devices were the small-group discussion and the open-ended interview. She says that she began her project with 'a range of themes I wanted to explore and an extensive interview protocol designed to translate those themes into appropriate questions' (ibid, page 427). Unfortunately she does not tell us what the 'interview protocol' was which ensured that the questions were 'appropriate'. Had she done so this would have improved the research, making it less anecdotal, enabling the reader to reconstruct its course more convincingly.

From the argument so far we can construct Figure 1.8 as a version of Figure 1.6, modified to cover action research. The researcher here deals not in hypotheses but in research themes within which lessons can be sought. The researcher joins a real-world problem situation (A), taking part in the deliberations which lead to practical outcomes – usually taking the form of action to bring about perceived improvement. The researcher also declares a framework and methodology, so that critical reflection can yield findings of various kinds, such as learning about F, M, A, or about the research themes; or new themes may be defined as a result of the experience.

We can now build upon Figure 1.8 to develop a more prescriptive (though still 'ideal') account of what action research entails.

Initially the researcher will find a real-world situation which seems relevant to research themes which he or she regards as significant. Then it is important, and certainly prudent, to negotiate carefully the respective roles of researcher(s) and people in the problem situation. This is important because there is always some ambiguity in the complex dual

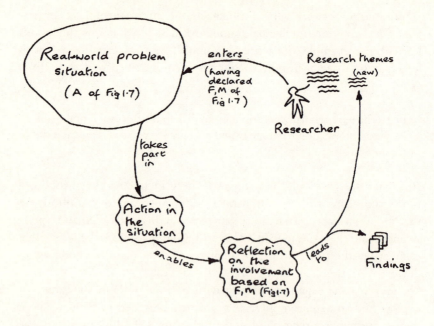

Figure 1.8. *The cycle of action research in human situations (after Checkland 1991a)*

role of the researcher: both involved in the action as participant and consciously reflecting upon it to extract useful lessons. Next, on the grounds argued above, it is essential to declare both the framework of ideas and the methodology in which they are embodied. Substantive work can now begin. This will consist of the researcher becoming involved in the action in the situation (though not always, obviously, with the same degree of involvement as those who would be tackling the problem even if no researcher were present), the aim being to help bring about changes felt to be 'improvements'. While doing this the researcher tries to make sense of the accumulating experience, doing so using the declared F and M. This may well cause a re-thinking of earlier stages – and again it is the explicit declaration of the intellectual framework which makes this poss-ible. Finally, the researcher negotiates an exit from the situation (which may be an arbitrary act since the situation itself will continue to evolve through time) and reflects on the experience in order to extract the various lessons learnt. This process is shown in Figure 1.9.

It is our experience that SSM provides one way of implementing the process modelled as an ideal type in Figures 1.8 and 1.9. Since the field of information provision is part of the domain of human affairs, action

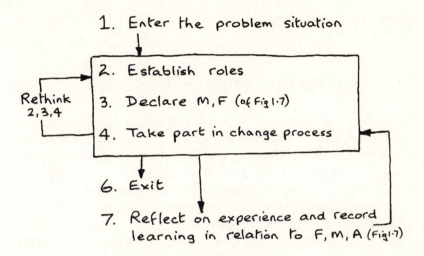

1. Enter the problem situation

2. Establish roles

3. Declare M, F (of Fig 1·7)

4. Take part in change process

Rethink 2,3,4

6. Exit

7. Reflect on experience and record learning in relation to F, m, A (Fig 1·7)

Figure 1.9. *The process of action research (after Checkland 1991a)*

research is a relevant way of investigating it and the issues surrounding it. And since the models of purposeful activity built as part of the process of SSM can be examined with a view to defining required information support, as discussed in the previous section on the context of this work, SSM is a particularly relevant approach for structuring action research concerned with information systems. It was used that way in the field studies described in Chapter Seven.

Obviously we cannot extract law-like statements from the detailed involvement in particular situations which characterizes action research. In any case, action research is underpinned by a belief that in human situations such laws, except at a vacuous level, are not lying there waiting to be 'discovered', not in the same way that the inverse square law of magnetism can be thought of as 'waiting to be discovered' in that phenomenon. It is not surprising, in fact, that the generalizations arising out of the 25 years of action research at Lancaster University are mainly at the level of methodology, together with principles of 'good practice' derived from the experiences (Checkland 1981, Wilson 1984, Checkland and Scholes 1990a). In the work described here we use the lessons from a number of action-research experiences to try to establish a coherent account of the IS field which makes sense of its many strands and hence ought to be able to help with the planning and carrying out of work within the field. Action research based on SSM is the mechanism we have used to traverse the cycle of learning shown in Figure 1.1, carrying out the action research based on the process of Figure 1.8.

THE STRUCTURE OF THIS BOOK

Although each part of this book will, it is hoped, make sense if read on its own, the book is conceived as a whole. It is the result of executing many times the cycle between experience and reflection, which is always a complex process, never free from confusion. The book does not try to express all the confusion on the journey; but it does try to express with as much clarity as we can muster, the outcome of that journey, and to do so via a structure which will be outlined here.

So far, in introducing the work, we have set the scene with an argument which may be summarized as follows. The first industrial revolution made available sources of power which led to the factory system and the growth of an industrial society. It was founded on science-based technology and, as that has continued to change at an ever-increasing tempo, the further changes have come to be seen as a second industrial revolution, this time based on information or knowledge rather than energy. These developments have led to the emergence of a new field of concern and study, namely the broad field of information systems and information technology. This now has such big effects on our lives that we need to come to terms with it if we wish to avoid simply being carried along on the tide of technological development. So this is an important field. But it is also a confused one with unclear boundaries, overlaps and multiple interpretations of commonly used phrases (IS, IT, etc).

Hence there is a need for conceptual cleansing, and that is what is attempted here. It is done by relating ideas concerning the field with real-world experiences, executing the process of Figure 1.1.

The context in which the work has been done is that of the development of SSM and, in keeping with the 25-year tradition of that development, an action research approach has been taken. This has involved participation in real-world situations in which the issues of concern relate to information, the overall theme being informational support for purposeful action.

Out of these experiences and the reflections upon them comes the research finding: an account of the IS field which makes sense of it and hence ought to help in planning and carrying out coherent work within it.

Table 1.1. *The shape of the book*

Section	Focus	Content
PART ONE Chapter One	Scene setting: the problem area	The main themes are established: an important but confused field; context: SSM-based action research in IS-related problem situations; aim: conceptual cleansing of the field.
Chapter Two	Scene setting completed: the strands within it	The main strands in IS are reviewed, establishing the lack of any clear accepted structure for it.
PART TWO Chapter Three	Organization	The context of much would-be concerted action, namely the organization, is clarified as an important concept relevant to IS.
Chapter Four	Information in support of intentional action	A basic account of forming intentions and taking purposeful action is established.
PART THREE Chapter Five Chapter Six Chapter Seven	Field work in six settings, military, industrial and in the UK National Health Service (Including an account of SSM (Chapter Six))	These accounts derive from action research in problem situations in which information provision was an important factor.
PART FOUR Chapter Eight	The field of information systems	In the light of Chapters Three and Four and the experiences in the action research (Chapters Five to Seven) a sense-making overall conceptualization of the field is presented.

In this chapter we have identified the problem area and described the context in which we have approached it as a research problem. In Chapter Two, we complete the scene setting by anatomizing the confusion in the field. In Part Two, comprising Chapters Three and Four, we take a fundamental look at some of the basic concepts relevant to the theme of providing information in support of purposeful action. Since the context of work on information systems is normally that provided by organizations (and this is true also of inter-organizational and global systems), in Chapter Three we examine the concept of 'the organization'. This is a surprisingly slippery idea, considering what a rich intuitive sense of 'organization' we all have from our everyday knowledge and experience. In Chapter Four we then argue for a basic model in which real-world experience and discussion of it lead to intentions being formed and action taken, this entailing the generation and transfer of information.

The conceptualization developed in Part Two represents the 'theory' part of the cycle in Figure 1.1. This both helped to shape, and was itself shaped by, the experiences described in Part Three, Chapters Five to Seven. This includes, in Chapter Six, a more extensive account of SSM than that given in this first chapter. The experiences themselves derive from military (Chapter Five) industrial and health-care settings (Chapter Seven). Those experiences led (though not linearly!) to the view of the IS field and its implications for future work which is described in Part Four, consisting of the reflections in Chapter Eight.

For ease of reference the shape of the book is summarized in Table 1.1.

Chapter Two

Information Systems: The Anatomy of a Confusion

INTRODUCTION

Our aim in this book is to try to make sense of a broad field, and to do so by working from both practice-based theory and theory-based practice. The field is that which focuses on the organized provision of information in support of people taking purposeful, or intentional, action, this action being usually — but not exclusively — initiated within organizations. We have tried to do this by linking experience of the IS world with the development of ideas relevant to that experience, those ideas informing the experience just as the experience leads to the ideas, as shown in Figure 1.1. Traversing such a cycle in an organized way can, we believe, make sense of the field of IS. And this is worth doing because it will enable work within it to be more coherently organized, carried out and discussed.

In order to realize that aim it is useful (as well as prudent!) to understand the nature of the confusion it is hoped to reduce or dispel. That is the object of this chapter: to show the anatomy of some of the confusion, to indicate the interacting strands in the field — if, indeed, it is sufficiently coherent to be regarded as one. For there is no agreement even on that central point, as we shall see.

INTELLECTUAL FIELDS

The concept of an intellectual field or, more sharply defined, 'a discipline', implies a shared concern to accumulate knowledge in a particular

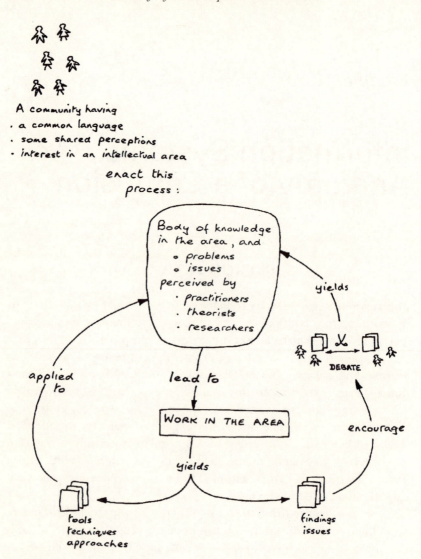

Figure 2.1. *An intellectual field*

area, to resolve issues within it, to solve puzzles or problems, and to influence action taken. There is an implication that the body of knowledge will grow, and that the field or discipline will spawn institutional activity: conferences, courses, journals, probably professional bodies. As problems are tackled and investigations made, the field will create and/ or import tools, techniques and approaches which will themselves develop in use. As findings accumulate, debate among members of the relevant community will lead to the enrichment of the body of knowledge and to the definition of new issues and problems. The process envisaged is that shown in Figure 2.1.

Such clusterings of activity and thinking in relation to shared concerns are not usually invented or designed. Rather they *emerge* as the sharing of perceptions grows (Banville and Landry 1989).

The process illustrated in Figure 2.1 has two aspects – cognitive and social, thinking and doing – and will not be tidy. The cognitive aspect concerns the development of what counts as knowledge in the field: what constitutes accepted findings, issues, topics, tools, etc. But the investigations and debate which create this knowledge constitute a social process taking place within a particular community of interested people, and they will have to share language and perceptions to a significant degree if investigation and debate are to be possible. In an established mature field, such as chemistry, for example, this sharing of language and concepts is likely to be so well established as to be virtually invisible. In that field, to take an example at random, the making of organic compounds with seven-membered rings of carbon atoms is a problem, since nature favours six-membered rings. The community of chemists in universities, research institutes and industry agree on both the relative importance of the topic and the nature of the problem. The preparative and analytical techniques to be applied are well understood, and they are known to produce reliable results in other areas of chemistry. Also, the present body of knowledge about seven-membered ring compounds is accessible in published papers and books. The problem for the chemist is actually achieving results, either using the known methods or developing new ones, and that is what the literature of chemistry describes. There is now little concern about the general structure and content of the field of chemistry and its processes as such. They are 'transparent'; they are taken as given by workers in the field, who simply assume the existence of structures and processes like those in Figure 2.1 and get on with the substantive work.

In the case of information systems, even the most cursory examination of the literature (for example in eclectic volumes such as Langefors et al (1986), Boland and Hirschheim (1987) Nissen et al (1991), Cotterman and Senn (1992) and Galliers (1992a)) suggests that no such 'transparency' exists. In the 1990s a field may now be piecing itself together, but it is very far indeed from being a taken-as-given structure-with-content within which the energy and attention can be concentrated on substantive work.

Practically everything about it is problematical: its focus, methods, norms, language and standards.

This may, of course, simply reflect the fact that it is a relatively recent development. There is no reason in principle why it should not have emerged early on as a concern within the broader field of management. But in fact the pioneering writers who helped to create management as a field of inquiry – Frederick Taylor, Henri Fayol, Mary Parker Follett, Chester Barnard, for example – simply ignore information. Tricker (1982, page 21), in a happy phrase, says that to them information was 'like sunlight to the Victorian botanists', namely crucially important to the process in question but either available or not; it was not a matter for scrutiny. The attention to information as being worthy of study emerged only with the arrival of the digital computer, and the birth pangs of the field of IS (if that's what they are) have been accompanied by, and have often stemmed from, the rapid development of computing.

IS: HISTORY AND TOPICS OF CONCERN

It might be expected that the emergence of the field of IS could be approached by examining the emerging history of a cycle like that in Figure 2.1 over the last 40-odd years – the period of computerization. This is indeed possible; but it is immediately interesting, when we try to do it, to find that there is no clear agreement on the shape of that history.

Anyone who has lived through the period of computerization in an organization will have a strong intuitive sense of phases of development. Such a person will have seen their organization both purchase its first mainframe computer, which was housed in an air-conditioned room, and recruit a new kind of professional to run it. They will have witnessed the changes as computing moved beyond transaction processing, and seen networks of now-powerful microcomputers replace mainframes. They will have observed the increasing power of users to develop their own systems, as well as the rise of systems which support the forming of judgements rather than automate some well-defined task. During this time they will have been dismayed or amused by the ever-changing jargon and will have felt excited or threatened by the torrent of technical developments.

It might be expected from common experience that there is agreement on the phases in computing development and that the history of that development is hardly controversial. But this is not the case. Phases

Table 2.1. *Phases in the history of computing*

	Earl (1989)		Somogyi & Galliers (1987)			Smith & Medley (1987)					Rockart (1988)			
No. of Periods	2		3			5					4			
Period Description	Data processing	Information technology	Data processing	Management services	Information processing	Data processing	Information system	Management information system	End user	Information resources management	Accounting	Operational	Information	Wired society
'Distinctor' Technology Characteristics	computing	multiple	cumbersome ltd. reliability ltd.I/O	large mainframes screen I/O minis databases	converging packages PCs workstations							PCs		communications cost effective hardware & software
Characteristics of Systems			stand alone batch	on-line real-time	user friendly networked	batch processing	applications	database applications integration	4th generation languages	5th generation systems	batch processing	on-line direct access real-time	4th generation languages relational databases	
Systems Development Role of User			empirical	structured project management	EUC participative prototyping CASE IS planning	I/O processor	project involvement	project management	builds small systems	full partnership	'subject'	line management involvement	line partnership	line leadership
Applications Orientation	tactical cost saving	strategic investment	scientific administrative economies of scale	management support & control corporate databases efficiency	DSS expert systems routine business advantage	limited financial	financial & operational	management information systems	DSS integrated systems	expert systems	financial transactions	operational transactions	use of information DSS	links functions & organizations
Manager Type and Posture	delegate abrogate	leadership involvement				uninitiated supervisor	computer trained	managerially trained	broad-base company	executive level	information systems staff abrogation			full participation

are recognised but there are a number of versions of what those phases are. Table 2.1 brings together some aspects from four accounts of the history (Earl 1989, Somogyi and Galliers 1987, Smith and Medly 1987, Rockart 1988). Although they have a broad-brush picture in common, from simple data processing to more sophisticated technology and operations, the differences between them are striking. They suggest, respectively, two, three, five and four historical phases or periods and use different phrases to describe the periods and what marks them as distinct.

The broad theme in all these accounts, namely technological development, is a significant factor in another, lengthier history of computer systems development, that of Friedman (with Cornford, 1989). Their account is persuasive. Its argument is that computer systems development can be seen in terms of the interaction of changes in the core technology with changes in applications, the two being linked by activities which 'mediate' between them (ibid, page 48). Such mediating activities include systems analysis, programming and computer operations. Acting upon these three elements: core technology, applications and mediating activities, are 'agents of change', factors 'which may be thought of as driving the history, of stimulating long-run changes' (ibid, page 53).

These change agents may be internal to the computer world, such as technical improvements to hardware, or external, such as changes in employment contracts and conditions which, for example, might push managers to replace clerks with automated processes.

Given this framework of analysis, Friedman and Cornford see the history of the development of computer systems as resulting from attempts to overcome factors which constrain further computerization at a given time. This leads to their belief in three different phases of computerization.

> These phases are each defined by a 'critical factor' or problem that has limited the development of computerization during that period. (ibid, page 58)

The phases they identify as having occurred so far are characterized by constraints on further computerization dominated by: firstly, hardware costs and capacity and reliability limitations (until the mid-1960s); then software constraints in the shape of productivity limits and difficulties of delivering reliable systems on time and within budget (from the mid-1960s until the early 1980s); and now user-relation constraints arising from inadequate perception of user demands and inadequate servicing of their needs (the current phase). They speculate that a fourth phase of computing history may be characterised by a focus on tackling problems associated with large-scale inter-organizational systems or with strategic support systems within organizations; they label this potential fourth phase 'the phase of organization environment constraints' (ibid, page 337).

The history of computerization as analysed by Friedman and Cornford is less tidy than this drastic summary may suggest. They point out that problems are alleviated rather than solved and that 'old' problems continue to get attention, so that the history reflects past as well as current issues. They point out, for example, that as the computing field has passed through each phase sub-communities have emerged dedicated to overcoming the perceived constraints. (Verrijn–Stuart (1986) describes this happening in his history of the IFIP Technical Committee 8, 'Information Systems'.) In later phases such groups persist, so that overall

the direction of technological progress in the field reflects the chief issues of the past as well as current fashionable issues. (ibid, page 354)

In other words this history is as complex as that of any human situation! Nevertheless, the coherence and detail of Friedman and Cornford's account (more than 400 pages of it) does suggest that it is not unreasonable for observers to see this history as that of a field piecing itself together, drawing on established disciplines. But it is certainly not yet a field with well-defined content and clear boundaries.

The different views on the disciplines contributing to IS as a field were alluded to in the previous chapter, and it is useful to note this variety as further evidence that IS is at best only an emerging field. It has been defined as the *integration* of six fields (Davis 1980), as the *intersection* of three domains (Cooper 1988), as a *combination* of two fields with seven supporting disciplines (Hirschheim and Boland 1989); or as having six *necessary* disciplines Teng and Galetta 1990), three *contributing* fields (Thuan et al, 1988) or three *necessary foundations* (Culnan and Swanson 1986).

Within the field itself reviewers have in recent years ranked topics significant for practitioners (Dickson et al 1984, Brancheau and Wetherbe 1987, Brancheau et al 1996, Niederman et al 1991), significant for researchers (Teng and Galetta 1990) or prominent in the literature (Farhoomand 1987), as summarized in part in Table 2.2. In Utopia we

Table 2.2. *Rankings of IS topics in terms of significance by various audiences*

a) Practitioners (**Wetherbe and associates**)

Rank	1987	1996
1	Strategic planning	Responsive IT infrastructure
2	Competitive advantage	Business process redesign
3	Organizational learning	Distributed systems
4	IS role and contribution	Information architecture
5	IS alignment in organization	Communication networks
6	End user computing	Software development
7	Data as corporate resource	Data as resource
8	Information architecture	IS human resources
9	Measuring effectiveness	IS alignment in organization
10	Integrating DP, OA, automation	Strategic planning
11	Telecommunications	Collaborative support systems
12	Human resources	Measuring effectiveness
13	Software development	IS role and contribution
14	Multi-vendor integration	Organizational learning
15	AI	Managing legacy portfolio
16	Application portfolio	End user computing
17	Factory automation	Competitive advantage
18	Security and control	Multi-vendor integration
19	Packaged software	Electronic data interchange
20	IS funding	Outsourcing

b) Literature and researchers

Rank	Literature (Farhoomand 1987)	Researchers (Teng and Galetta 1990)
1	Cost benefit analysis	Decision support systems
2	Database and software design	AI
3	IS resource management	Database management systems
4	DSS, decision theory	System development
5	End user computing	End user computing
6	Expert systems, AI	Human factors
7	Human-computer interaction	Telecommunications
8	Impact of IS	MIS evaluation
9	Implementation	Organizational impact of MIS
10	Information requirements analysis	MIS education
11	Inter-organizational systems	MIS management
12	Management and planning of IS	Software engineering
13	Organizational design	
14	Strategic use of IS	
15	Technology transfer	

might expect good correlations between these rankings, but in view of what we have said of the IS field so far, it is perhaps not surprising to find no great correlation between these rankings of particular topics, such as you might expect to find in a mature field. And there is considerable volatility of rank order revealed in the three reviews by Wetherbe and his associates over a period of twelve years, as topics go in and out of fashion. Table 2.2 contains two ranked lists of topics considered important by IS executives (from Wetherbe and his associates) as well as topics important to researchers and in the literature in the late 1980s. Volatility is the impression conveyed.

Given the features of the IS field which we have illustrated so far – its problematical history, the different views on its structure and reference disciplines, the volatility of the topics of interest within it – it is not surprising to find that there are fundamentally different schools of thought within it. These are based upon very different perceptions of its core concerns, and different approaches to investigation within the field. This will be illustrated in the next sections.

IS: THE CORE CONCERN

Figure 2.1 shows a cycle of activities which you would expect to observe taking place in a well-established field. In the previous section we found no agreed account of the history of such a cycle, as it might apply to IS, no agreement on relevant reference disciplines outside the field itself, and no common perception of the topics of interest and their relative importance. This suggests that it is worth examining the most basic core concern of the field, the concern without which it would not make sense even to discuss the idea of IS as an emerging field.

Nowadays, we take the *core* concern of the field to be the orderly provision of data and information within an organization using IT, that information being relevant to the ever-changing activity of the organization and/or its members. Work in this field will thus affect and influence real-world action. This concept is the most basic one in the field, but can be extended without distortion to consider information/data transfers between organizations or, most generally, between groups of people, this particular case becoming increasingly important today as a result of developments in computer and telecommunication technology.

Such a concern carries certain implications. Anyone taking it seriously would have to take some view on several elements within the concept.

They would have to think about the notion of 'information' and 'information system'; they would have to work with some coherent idea of what we mean by 'an organization'; and if the idea of providing information by the use of IT, a changing technology, is accepted, then the provision of information in an organization has to be regarded as something which will develop and change. Hence the interested person would have to take a stance on how to make investigations and do research within the field, that research aiming ultimately to influence action.

These apparently straightforward concepts might not be thought controversial. However, within the IS field we find people making very different assumptions about them, either consciously or implicitly, and this leads to the very different schools of thought in IS work. (See, for example, Boland (1979), Ehn (1988), Iivari (1991), Floyd et al (1992), Hirschheim et al (1995)). No doubt the existence of these schools, often unacknowledged or disregarded by mainstream thinking, provides at least a partial explanation for some of the confusion characteristic of the field.

Dominating IS work is a set of assumptions which sees organizations as goal seeking. The prime organizational activity is then decision-making in pursuit of goals, objectives or some longer-term mission. Information required by the organization is then that which supports and services decision making. This essentially 'scientific' view of organizations and information is usually associated with would-be scientific methods of investigation and research, based on systematic data collection aimed at hypothesis testing. These ideas constitute an intellectual stance which Walsham (1993) neatly sums up as reflecting

> a rational-economic interpretation of organizational processes, and a positivist methodology which is based on the view that the world exhibits objective cause-effect relationships which can be discovered, at least partially, by structured observation. (page 4)

It is not difficult to criticize this view of the world, at least where information systems are concerned, and there is currently some growing recognition in IS that an alternative strand of thinking is also relevant. This is the strand which appeals to those who feel that being a member of an organization is more like being part of a tribe than being the servant of a rational machine. For such people social reality is constantly being constructed and reconstructed in a social process in which meanings are negotiated. For them an 'organization' does not exist as an independent entity but is part of sense making by a group of people engaged in dialogue. This makes the idea of 'information' and 'information system' much more problematical – though not peripheral, since 'information' is obviously related in some profound way to meaning attribution and sense making. Equally, this view will not automatically embrace would-be-scientific hypothesis testing as an appropriate mode of research. It will seek alternative processes of inquiry in such areas as semiotics, hermeneutics or interpretative action research based on soft systems thinking (Andersen 1991, Boland 1986, Checkland 1988b, Galliers 1992, Rathswohl 1991, Stamper 1987 and 1991).

The difference between these schools of thought in IS work is similar to that in the field of management science and systems thinking, where the difference is captured in the words 'hard' (for the objective positivistic scientific view) and 'soft' (for the subjective/interpretative view). There the sharp definition of 'hard' and 'soft' (Checkland 1983) hinges upon the assumption made about the nature and location of what are thought of as 'systems'. Hard systems thinking assumes that the world contains systems which can be 'engineered' to achieve their objectives. Soft systems thinking regards the world as problematical but assumes that *the process of inquiry* into it can be knowingly organized as a system. It thus shifts systemicity from the world to the process of inquiry into the world. In the IS context the hard approach assumes that organizations are 'systems' with 'information needs' which IT can supply; the soft approach, as we have articulated it here, takes a process view of organizations and explores, using soft systems ideas to structure action research, the way in which people in organizations inter-subjectively attribute meaning to their world and hence form a view on what information is relevant.

The concept of these two strands of thinking is useful in providing understanding of some of the confusion in the IS field, and we shall examine them briefly in the next section – though it must be remembered that all such polarized concepts are never to be regarded as accurate *descriptions*; they are 'ideal types' by use of which we can better understand some of the real-world complexity.

IS: SCHOOLS OF THOUGHT, HARD AND SOFT

The 'hard', functionalist approach

A good way to find out the conventional wisdom in any field is to see what the introductory university-level student textbooks have to say on the subject. The task of such books is not to draw too much attention to the ambiguities and problems of the field – students will encounter those later – but to provide an account of the field in a straightforward way. Authors of such texts naturally give the account which embodies the most common conceptualisation of the field, the currently conventional view of it.

In IS there is remarkable agreement on what this is. The typical view expounded is that organizations, assumed to be social entities, seek to achieve goals. Management activity then contains much decision making in pursuit of goals and information systems provide support for this decision making. That is why information is now regarded as a vital corporate resource. As examples to illustrate this, we may take an influential textbook from the 1970s (Davis 1974), its mid-1980s updated version (Davis and Olson 1985) and a contemporary textbook (Zwass 1992).

The two versions of Davis' textbook are built upon the same core concepts, though the second edition (1985) usefully separates IS from IT in the early remark that

> management information systems as an academic discipline is more an extension of organizational behaviour and management than computer science. (page 22)

A management information system is 'an integrated user-machine system' (ibid, second edition, page 22), or, in the earlier edition, 'an integrated man/machine system' (page 5). Its purpose, and here the crucial features of its stance begin to be revealed, lies in

> providing information to support the operations, management, and decision-making functions of an organization. (second edition, page 22)

Organizations are seen as open systems containing a set of functional sub-systems

> with goals and objectives which cannot be achieved without management of the material and human resources. (ibid, second edition, page 116)

Each sub-system (manufacturing, marketing, accounting, etc) then requires its own tailored information systems. Managing is seen as consisting of planning, organizing, staffing, co-ordinating, directing and controlling, while decision making (in both editions of the book) is seen as analysing alternatives in relation to a decision and making a choice among the alternatives. All this conveys very clearly the concepts which emerged in the management science and 'hard' systems paradigm of the 1960s, as embodied in classical operational research, systems engineering, system dynamics and RAND Corporation systems analysis (Checkland 1981, Chapter 5). (Miles (1985) discusses what he calls 'the constraint of the "hard" systems paradigm' on conventional computer systems analysis, another version of 'hard' systems thinking.)

These same ideas are presented over and over again in basic student texts, of which Zwass' *Management Information Systems* is a current example. Organizations are 'formal social units devoted to the attainment of certain goals' (Zwass 1992, page 16). As a member of such a 'social unit' a manager is

> a problem solver, and the fundamental activity in problem solving is decision making. Decision making is the process of identifying a problem, identifying alternative solutions, and choosing and implementing one of them. (ibid, page 491)

Information systems have an important role in this. They are there 'to support individual decision making' (ibid, page 485). And here also 'an organization is an open system' (ibid, page 388).

These authors are drawing on a ubiquitous element in the conventional wisdom on IS, namely the Gorry and Scott Morton framework of 1971 which provides a simple classification of information systems in terms of the level and type of decisions which managers take. (IS literature is full of such frameworks for making sense of the field or some part of it – Mok (1993) collects and discusses no fewer than 30 of them; but Gorry and Scott Morton's has been the most influential with writers of student texts.)

They construct their framework by combining the work of Anthony (1965) and Simon (1960). Anthony distinguishes three levels of activity concerned with planning and control: operational control, management control and strategic planning. Simon postulates a range of decision types from programmed to unprogrammed which Gorry and Scott Morton render as 'structured', 'semi-structured' and 'unstructured'. Combining these gives the matrix of Table 2.3, which Lucas (1994) describes as 'very appealing' (page 48) and 'a unifying paradigm for the IS field for three decades' (page 57).

Table 2.3. *The Gorry-Scott Morton framework*

Classification of Decisions	Operational Control	Management Control	Strategic Planning
Structured	Order processing Accounts payable	Budgets Personnel reports	Warehouse location; Transportation mode mix
Semi-structured	Inventory control Production planning	Analysis of variance	Introduction of new product
Unstructured	Cash management	Management of personnel	Planning for R and D

This influential framework is one example, in fact, of the most pervasive underlying influence on textbook accounts of the IS field, namely the work of Herbert Simon (Boland 1987). Simon is responsible for what is undoubtedly the most influential body of work in the management sciences in the period since the mid-1950s, and Simon's analysis has been widely adopted within IS. It is Simon who has persuaded so many people to assume the nature of 'managing' to be problem solving through decision making. This is freely acknowledged in the textbooks quoted above, and Lewis (1991) writes more generally of the dominance of these ideas in introductory texts. Of 39 such texts he analysed, three-quarters defined the role of information systems as being to serve decision making. Of these, 84 per cent described Simon's model of decision making, with more than half giving this as the sole conceptual framework through which to understand decision making.

In a paper summarizing Simon's influential contribution, given to a conference 'round table' on Simon's work, Zannetos (1984) describes Simon's legacy as

> a theory of problem solving, programs and processes for developing intelligent machines and approaches to the design of organization structure for managing complex systems. (page 75)

This neatly summarizes the fields in which Simon's contribution has been made. The central theme of the work of Simon and his collaborators has been to try to establish a true science of administrative behaviour and executive decision making, something he refers to in the title of a short but influential book published in 1960: *The New Science of Management Decision* (Simon 1960). The core idea underlying this attempt to establish such a science is that human behaviour, both individual and corporate, can be taken to be *goal-seeking*. On this view both individuals and organizations try to achieve a succession of goals; that is their fundamental concern.

In pursuit of goals, managers (and, for that matter, organizations as a whole, which are not treated as being fundamentally problematical) *take decisions* and so *solve problems*. Simon has made important contributions to both these areas. In his theory of decision making, Simon shrewdly abandons the classical model of a perfectly rational decision maker whose aim is optimizing, the model formulated in classical economic theory. Instead – and this better matches most peoples' experiences in organizations – the decision maker exhibits a limited or 'bounded rationality', searching for decisions which are 'good enough' in the circumstances rather than optimal, in that they move the manager towards his or her goal, which may be adjusted as a result of incremental decisions. The aim is what Simon calls 'satisficing' rather than optimizing (Simon 1960).

The 'satisficing' is itself part of problem solving, of which Simon and his collaborators have provided an influential model. Simon and March, in developing a behavioural theory of the firm, see 'problems' as 'indicated by gaps between performance and goals' (March and Simon 1958, page 73) and 'problem solving' is then a matter of closing the gap by finding a suitable means to achieve the goal, which is taken as already known. In Simon's words (1960)

> Problem solving proceeds by erecting goals, detecting differences between present situation and goal, finding in memory or by search tools or processes that are relevant to reducing differences of these particular kinds, and applying these tools or processes. Each problem generates subproblems until we find a sub-problem we can solve . . . We proceed until, by successive solution of such sub-problems, we eventually achieve our overall goal – or give up. (page 27)

He envisages a three-stage process of problem solving/decision making, namely: problem identification and data collection; outlining alternative solutions and their outcomes; selecting a solution and monitoring its application.

These are the general principles which underlie the conventional wisdom expressed in the college textbooks concerning information systems. For example, in another contemporary text (Ahituv and Neumann 1990),it is no surprise to find that Simon's three stages of problem solving/decision making are used to illustrate the different forms which information systems may take:

> It is obvious that each stage in the decision-making process requires a different type of information and is therefore supported by information systems with different characteristics. (ibid, page 38)

But the model which sees human and organizational behaviour as decision making/problem solving in pursuit of goals is not the only way to conceptualise organizations and hence the information needs of them and their members. It has been the dominant model in IS so far, but there is increasing interest in an alternative perspective, which matches the 'soft' systems thinking of the 1970s and 1980s, just as the goal-seeking perspective was a foundation of the 'hard' systems approach of the 1960s.

The 'soft', interpretive approach

There is no single body of work which underlies the 'soft', or interpretive approach to information systems in the same way that Simon's work is taken as given, and so shapes the 'hard', or functional approach. But we may introduce the 'soft' orientation by referring to the work of Sir Geoffrey Vickers, not least because Vickers himself sees his work as not only indebted to, but also in rather profound conflict with that of Simon, since it takes a fundamentally different view of human action (Vickers 1965 and 1974).

Sir Geoffrey accumulated 40 years experience in the world of affairs and then in his retirement boldly set about trying to make sense of it in a general theory of the social process! The outcome of this final career was a series of books and papers unique in the field of social thinking in general and management thinking in particular. (A collection of his papers edited at the Open University contains a memoir of his life (Vickers 1984), while Blunden (1985) provides a useful short introduction to his ideas. A recent issue of *American Behavioural Scientist* edited by Blunden and Dando (1994) is devoted to Vickers' ideas and their current relevance to policy making. Adams et al (1987) edit a collection of Vickers' essays.)

In seeking an understanding of human affairs in general, and organizational life in particular, Vickers (1974) started by rejecting the goal-seeking model of human behaviour as being too poverty-stricken to match the richness of life as we experience it. He turned to systems ideas, but rejected the cybernetic model since there the course which the 'helmsman' (or controller or manager) tries to follow is a single course given from outside the system controlled,

> whilst the human regulator, personal or collective, controls a system which generates multiple and mutually inconsistent courses. The function of the regulator is to choose one of several possible *mixes*, none fully attainable. (present authors' italics)

Another major consideration is that the *standards* or criteria by which the 'mix' of courses to be followed will be judged are not given from outside. They are themselves internally generated by *the previous history of the system itself* and its interactions with its environment. Finally, the actions taken in the mix of courses to be followed are perceived as *relationship maintaining* (or eluding) rather than as a striving to achieve goals. It is the replacement of goal seeking by *relationship managing* which most clearly marks Vickers' theory of what he calls 'appreciative systems' as different from Simon's model. Seeking a goal is, for Vickers, the occasional special case of managing a relationship. (See Checkland and Casar 1986, and also Checkland 1991b and 1994a for a systems model of an appreciative system.)

In Simon's model, goal *definition* does not get much attention, but in Vickers' 'appreciative system', the core of the activity concerns debate about possible courses which might be followed and the relationships they will affect. For Vickers, in contrast to Simon, managers set standards or norms rather than goals, and the focus on goals is replaced by one on managing relationships according to standards generated by previous history. Furthermore, the discussion and debate which leads to action is one in which those taking part make judgements about both 'what is the case' (Vickers' 'reality judgements') and about its evaluation as 'good' or 'bad', 'satisfactory' or 'unsatisfactory' – what Vickers calls 'appreciative judgements'. This places Vickers work firmly in the interpretive tradition which sees social action as based upon personal and collective *sense making*. It takes a process view of organizations, is philosophically part of the tradition of phenomenology and hermeneutics, and is sociologically linked to the interpretive approach of Max Weber rather than the positivist sociology deriving from Durkheim which underpins Simon's work and the 'hard' systems tradition. Table 2.4 defines some characteristics of the two broad traditions.

Table 2.4. *Two broad traditions, versions of which underpin much IS work*

	The 'Hard' Tradition (Simon)	The 'Soft' Tradition (Vickers)
Concept of organization	Social entities which set up and seek to achieve goals	Social entities which seek to manage relationships
Concept of information system	An aid to decision making in pursuit of goals	A part of interpreting the world, sense making with respect to it, in relation to managing relationships
Underlying systems thinking	'Hard' systems thinking: the world assumed to be systemic	'Soft' systems thinking: the process of inquiry into the world assumed to be capable of being organized as a system
Process of research and inquiry	Predicated upon hypothesis testing; quantitative if possible	Predicated upon gaining insight and understanding; qualitative
Social theory	Functionalism (stemming from Durkheim)	Interpretive (stemming from Weber)
Philosophy	Positivism	Phenomenology

As we have indicated above, Vickers' work has not yet been as influential as Simon's, and its relevance to IS work is only now beginning to be discussed (Boland 1979, Lewis 1991 and 1994, West 1990 and 1992, Stowell and West 1994, Crowe, Beeby and Gammack 1996). Nevertheless, the strand of 'interpretive' thinking we have exemplified by the work of Vickers is itself coming to be reasonably well-represented in IS literature, even though it is not usually mentioned in the conventional wisdom of the college textbooks. (Hirschheim (1992) usefully reviews the history of the epistemology of IS.) It is present, however, in a strand of IS literature which includes such authors as Boland, Hirschheim, Klein, Land, Lee, Lyytinen, Mumford and Walsham, who write from a humanistic stance outside the conventional positivist hypothesis–testing norm. It is also at the core of the writing of Winograd and Flores (1986) whose much-noticed *Understanding Computers and Cognition* is written from the point of view that language as a medium does not simply reflect the world 'out there' but constitutes it in the social process of interaction. This leads them to the view that organizations are constituted as networks of conversations in which commitments are generated. Computer systems can support such conversations: 'Computers are a tool for conducting the network of conversation' (page 172). Arguing in this vein, they write explicitly that they 'want to break with the rationalistic tradition' (page 77). Similar thinking is found even in a recent book on software engineering (Floyd et al 1992) in which one of the editors speaks of 'our active role in constituting what we hold for real' (page 16), while a contributor (Goguen) argues that

> In proposing methodologies to guarantee the absence of error, we deny the incredible richness of our own experience, in which confusion and error are often the seeds of creation. (page 193)

This may well frighten many who produce software, but it must be said that the book says very little about the practicalities of 'interpretive' software development amid all the statements that software engineering should somehow be informed by the hermeneutic tradition.

Another author within this humanistic strand of thinking which offers an alternative to the conventional wisdom is Ciborra. He argues (1987) that organizations should be seen as networks of communicative exchanges, and that computer-based information systems should be thought of as making such exchanges easier. They are 'exchange support systems' (page 262). He contrasts this with the more conventional view within IS work, and makes the same distinction which is being argued here when he writes:

> Present-day (information system) designers . . . either tend to a 'data view' of organizations, or, in the case of those most influenced by business needs, to a decision-making view. These two ways of looking at the problems of computerization are so widely accepted and have been so much taken for granted that they can be said to form the conventional wisdom of today. The origins of the former can be traced directly back to the EDP field, while the latter stem from the influential work of Herbert A. Simon. (page 253)

THE FIELD OF IS: GENERAL

Since they are based upon such very different assumptions, it is clear that the 'hard' and 'soft' strands of thinking within IS work will lead to very different approaches to doing research; and very different bodies of knowledge will emerge from that research. In the previous chapter we outlined the research in which Dennis et al (1990) sought to test the hypothesis that sophisticated computer support would lead to 'better' management meetings and hence 'better' strategic management. There could hardly be a greater contrast between this and the work which Boland (1986) refers to in his paper 'Phenomenology: a preferred approach to research on IS', in the section headed 'Some attempts at doing phenomenology' – a modest sub-heading which usefully indicates that ways of doing 'soft' IS research are by no means yet well-established. One study began as a conventional examination of two different ways in which systems analysts could conduct interviews in order to design information systems to support hospital nurses. Potential designs were produced, and these were judged and scored by panels of experts. However, the experiment moved into an analysis 'below the surface' (page 345) of how the very way in which the experiment had been set up had determined the results obtained. The two interview methods

> mediated different images of the nature of control in the hospital and these . . . guided the analyst's interpretation of the nurses' situation. (page 346)

What happened was this. The researcher, Boland himself, assumed at the start that 'the nurses' real needs' (page 345) existed in some objective sense and would be matched to different degrees by the two different approaches to interviewing, this being revealed by the experts' scores. He came to see that the 'trappings of objectivity' (embodied in the ways in which the scores were normalized according to education and background of participants, etc) were actually irrelevant, as were the scores from the expert panel. What he found himself researching was the way in which the two interview approaches embodied different worldviews and would in fact 'create different kinds of worlds for the nurses' (page 345), thus conditioning their response to questions from the systems analysts.

> The early, positive science view of the experiment took the outcome at its surface value and had the judges 'objectively' score it. The later phenomenological view of the experiment tried to look beneath the surface of the outcome to the structures of meaning that gave rise to these particular interpretations by these analysts. (page 345)

Boland found himself researching how the use of language in the analyst–nurse conversations was not simply *reflecting* the participants' world but was helping to *constitute* it. The 'nurses needs' could not be taken as something pre-existing in the situation, waiting to be uncovered.

The researcher's stance here is so different from that of positivist hypothesis testing that very different images of the nature of the IS field will inevitably emerge from the two approaches.

Of course, it might be argued that the existence of different schools of thought within a field is the normal state of affairs even when that field approaches maturity. For example, a recent book on marketing theory (Sheth et al 1988) devotes itself to discussing no less than 12 schools of thought within that area – the systems view, the buyer-behaviour view, the social-exchange view, etc. However, our point is that, whereas everyone interested in marketing would both acknowledge the existence of debate between different schools of thought and take the existence of marketing as a field as given, within IS even recognition of the different schools of thought is not common; and in addition there is far from being a ready agreement that 'the field of IS' is itself a meaningful phrase. In our model here of what we mean by a field (Figure 2.1), the element of debate is crucial. It is in a sense the engine which drives the process, since it both discusses findings, topics, issues, etc and contributes to the body of knowledge which leads to further practice, yielding new findings etc. Such debate is not at the moment a strong feature of an embryo IS field. There is of course much practical activity, and this is carried out by practitioners who, on the whole, are unimpressed by the contribution which academic activity has made to IS so far. And there is also much reporting of hypothesis–testing research carried out in the 'hard' strand of thinking. Finally, there are not a few assertions that the 'soft' interpretive/ hermeneutic/phenomenological strand of thinking is a more relevant approach than the would-be scientific one, but these assertions are not yet matched by many actual accounts of practical work based on 'soft' thinking. Meanwhile, the debate which should be defining IS as a field, if it is to become one, has so far been largely a dialogue of the deaf.

A dramatic illustration of this is provided by the remarkable statement made by the senior editor of a well-known and respected IS journal, indicating what would-be authors should aim for. The statement is from *MIS Quarterly* (September 1989), and both Trauth and O'Connor (1991) and Keen (1991) have drawn attention to its significance:

A paper in the Research and Theory category should satisfy the traditional criteria for high quality scholarly research. It should be based on a set of well-defined hypotheses, unbiased and reproducible procedures for collecting evidence that supports or refutes the hypothesis, and sound analytical procedures for drawing appropriate conclusions from the evidence. This research often involves the collection of considerable quantitative data through such means as laboratory experiments or survey instruments. The data are then subjected to statistical analysis to draw the appropriate inferences from the research. (page xi)

This is an austere statement indeed! The senior editor's only concession is that 'a well-constructed case study can also meet the tests of rigorous research.'

This statement is remarkably one-dimensional, not least when we consider that scholarly journals are a main vehicle for carrying the debate about how to conceptualize a field, its topics, its issues and its research approaches. It illustrates unwittingly the stranglehold positivism has had on those who work in the North American groves of academe.

More recently there has been some shading of this stark position. In the 'Editors' Comments' section of the March 1993 issue of *MIS Quarterly*, the new senior editor for theory and research amends the position with the statement

> . . . we welcome research based on positivist, interpretive, or integrated approaches. Traditionally, *MIS Quarterly* has emphasized positivist research methods. Though we remain strong in our commitment to hypothesis testing and quantitative data analysis, we would like to stress our interest in research that applies interpretive techniques, such as case studies, textual analysis, enthnography, and participant/observation.

This is a very welcome broadening, but it follows a paragraph which speaks of 'identifying variables for scientists to study', and 'insight into cause/effect relationships'. It also assumes the existence in the social world of 'underlying phenomena' having 'properties and behaviours' which, once understood, would 'facilitate understanding *and prediction* of events in the world' (present authors' emphasis). This is the language of natural science, and is hardly compatible with the interpretive/phenomenological stance, which assumes that 'social reality' is continually constructed and re-constructed socially; it implies unquestioned editorial assumptions of a deeply positivist kind, namely assumptions that the social world is characterized by core regularities of the same kind as those studied by the natural sciences.

The statements from *MIS Quarterly's* editors would be unexceptional if they came from a mature field of natural science but are surprisingly axiomatic in an area of social science whose status is problematical: certainly not 'a discipline'; dubiously 'a field'; at best a primitive one.

IS in Whitley's typology

The structure of scientific fields has been extensively studied by Whitley. He sees an intellectual field in scientific work as a social context in which competencies and research skills are developed and employed, the aim being the production of new knowledge, and, for the researcher, the establishment of reputation in the field. For a practically-oriented potential field like IS, we would accept Keen's (1991) arguments that research in it is not simply aimed at finding out new knowledge, but

> is intended to *influence action* in some domain, such as public policy, systems design and implementation methods, education, management decision making or information systems planning. (page 27, present author's italics)

Nevertheless, it is interesting to look at the credentials of IS as a field against Whitley's typology. (Keen's argument simply means that, in a practical field, questions of the relevance of the research have to be settled prior to discussion of its rigour, since 'Until relevance is established, rigor is irrelevant' (ibid, page 47)).

Whitley (1984a) argued that recognized fields showed institutionalization at both the cognitive and the social level, the two not being independent. In his model, the way members of a field interactively produce knowledge and interpret each other's research results can be expressed in three main variables. These are:

1. the degree to which members of a field have to use established results, ideas and procedures in order to achieve knowledge claims regarded as useful ('functional dependence');
2. the degree to which problem formulations are agreed, in terms of their importance and significance ('strategic task uncertainty');
3. the degree to which members of a field have to persuade colleagues of the importance of their work to gain a high reputation (ie a measure of the degree of political co-ordination and control) ('strategic dependence').

Each of these three variables could have a 'high' or 'low' value, giving eight possible combinations which provide a framework in terms of which the nature and evolution of a particular field could be discussed.

It is interesting to examine the first editorial quotation from *MIS Quarterly*, discussed above, in terms of Whitley's variables. It reads like an attempt to establish *a particular procedure* for IS research, tackling a *particular class of problem* (those susceptible to quantitative data collection and statistical analysis) and implying the *sanction* of non-publication for would-be authors who fail to conform. This, in Whitley's language, represents high functional dependence, low task uncertainty and high strategic dependence: the combination, which he calls a 'conceptually integrated bureaucracy', and which represents Kuhn's 'normal science' (1962). Whitley exemplifies this combination by claiming that modern physics is a field which exhibits these characteristics. Well, we may reasonably doubt that IS is quite ready to take its place alongside physics as an intellectual field!

Whitley (1984b) also suggests that management studies (or the administrative sciences) can be described in terms of low functional dependence, low strategic dependence and high task uncertainty. This field, he suggests, is

seen as a largely academic enterprise with few connections to managerial actions and one which is highly internally differentiated . . . into separate ideas and approaches. (page 775)

To many this will sound like a good description of the present state of IS, and indeed Banville and Landry's detailed examination of IS in relation to Whitley's schema (1989) concludes from the evidence they assemble that the strong fragmentation of research themes and methods in IS supports classification as what Whitley calls a 'fragmented adhocracy'. This is a combination (low functional dependence; low strategic dependence; high task uncertainty) which has characteristics such as:

* weak barriers to entry in the field
* standards which can be affected by 'amateurs'
* 'common-sense' language (rather than well-defined terms)
* fluid reputations, often based on narrowly specific work
* personal, weakly-co-ordinated research agendas.

Most people working in IS will accept that this is a reasonable description of what they observe and experience! Banville and Landry (1989) provide a convincing demonstration that IS can be described as a 'fragmented adhocracy', and this fits in with the intuitive perceptions of those in this pluralistic and weakly coherent field. However, these are not necessarily debilitating criticisms of IS. The characteristics of a fragmented adhocracy listed above are not necessarily 'bad' features of IS which we should strive to change. In a field which seeks practical knowledge and aims to affect the behaviour of people in organizations, it is not necessarily a bad thing that entry to the field is easy, that 'amateurs' can contribute and that reputations are often both fluid and local. It is the other two characteristics in the list above which perhaps point to needs in the IS field. The work would probably be more effective in establishing knowledge and changing behaviour in organizations if the language of the field were more precise, enabling ideas to be expressed with greater clarity and hence helping to stimulate better debate. For example, the confusion over even the core words 'data' and 'information' cannot be helpful to the field. And if the language could be used with something approaching scholarly precision, this would help to improve the coherency of the field by enabling personal research programmes to be better related to each other.

This short excursion into the notion of an intellectual and practical field is, we believe, helpful in getting a grasp of the nature of IS as a field and its currently primitive state. It also points to the need to examine its language and core concepts at a fundamental level if sense is to be made of it. And finally it leads us to ask why the IS field is in the state it is.

Reasons for confusion in the IS field

There is no doubt a complex of reasons why this is so. For a start, it is a recent development. Physics may now be what Whitley terms 'a conceptually integrated bureaucracy', but in the 17th century, when Descartes' physics competed with Newton's, that field was probably more like a 'fragmented adhocracy'. In the case of IS, its development is closely linked to the development of a technology which is very recent, the first computers being built in the 1940s and the first business applications following as recently as the 1950s. What is more, the glamour of that technology has been seductive, so that many people fascinated by IT are simply not interested in lifting their eyes to such wider questions as what information systems people working in an organization need, how they should be developed, how they should be managed, and what the wider implications of computer technology are, both within and between organizations – all questions which the IS field must address if it is to be seen as a serious intellectual enterprise. Finally, the pace of development in the technology of computers, cogently chronicled by Friedman and Cornford (1989), has been very rapid indeed. The development of new technical possibilities has always been much quicker

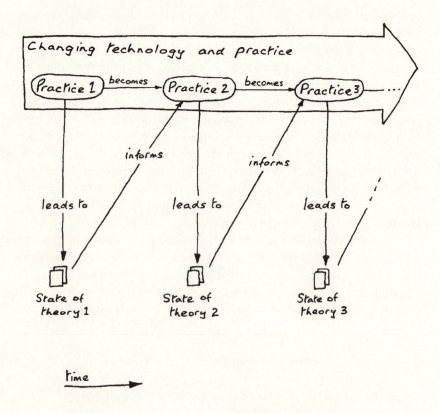

Figure 2.2. *In a technology-dominated field where technology changes rapidly, theory will always lag behind practice*

than the development of the thinking about IS. In any field this will lead to imbalance and confusion, as shown in Figure 2.2.

In any developing field allied to a changing technology, there will be a relationship between the discovery and exploitation of technical possibilities ('practice') and the development of the thinking which makes sense of the happenings ('theory'). Each will inform the other in some kind of symbiosis. But, where the technology is developing very rapidly, new practical possibilities will be found and developed by users whenever and wherever the new possibilities are found to be useful; they will not wait for relevant theory! Hence practice will tend to outrun the development of the thinking in any field in which the technological changes come very quickly indeed, as has been the case with computing hardware and software.

Thus in recent years the expressions 'groupware' and 'computer supported co-operative work' (CSCW) have come into use. They are not tightly defined, with different authors defining their scope differently, (an aspect discussed by Grudin (1991), but they refer broadly to computer and telecommunication support for groups of people engaged in such things as collaborative writing, meeting scheduling, communicating, conferencing and work management. This ill-defined sub-field within IS (called 'unruly' by Grudin, page 3) has come to be recognized, after the event, as something users were finding their way to doing for themselves. The conceptualizing of this potential field as some kind of whole has come later, as is illustrated by conference discussions in this area. (See, for example, the Proceedings of the ACM Conference on Computer Supported Co-operative Work, Los Angeles, 1990, and Hendriks 1991). This is an example in the real world of how, in a practice-driven field like IS, there will tend to develop the mismatch between practice and theory illustrated in Figure 2.2, with yesterday's theory always trying to catch up with and make sense of practice which has meanwhile moved on. This will not do much for the clarity of such a field!

This discussion suggests that, as an intellectual field, IS is in a fragmented state, with much of the work done within it seeming to be ad hoc rather than part of larger structures of thinking and debate such as one finds in mature fields like physics, chemistry or geography. Given the fact that this is a field with a practical aim – improving action taken in and by organizations and their members – and one whose associated technology (computing and telecommunications) is now ubiquitous, it seems worthwhile to attempt the project proposed in Chapter One: the conceptual cleansing of the field in the hope of contributing to its greater effectiveness.

THE FIELD OF IS: A PRAGMATIC MODEL

The idea of 'an intellectual field' is an abstract concept, and much of the discussion in the previous section has necessarily been at a rather abstract level. Practical people, feet firmly on the ground, may feel impatient with this, regarding it as academic in the worst sense. They will feel that they know, in a practical sense, the scope and content of the field.

There is force in this argument, and it is probably useful to declare the pragmatic model of the IS field which underlies the research described in

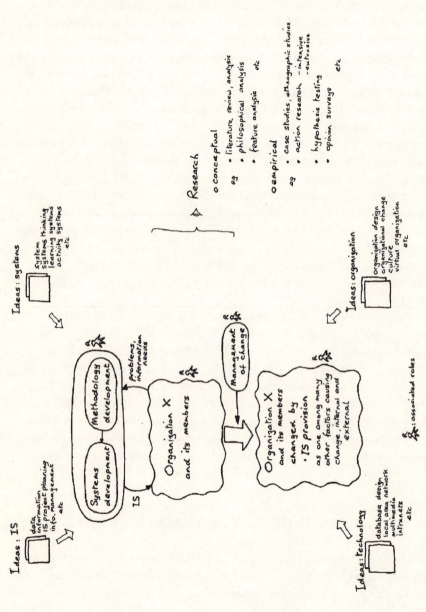

Figure 2.3. *The IS field: a pragmatic model of aspects relevant to describing it and research in it (after Checkland and Holwell 1995)*

this book. This is put on the table not as a self-evident description of the field but as an account of the context of IS work as we have assumed it to be during the studies described later. It is presented in the spirit of action research as described in the previous chapter; there it was argued that such research requires that the intellectual frameworks, in terms of which what counts as 'knowledge' will be defined, must be declared if the work is to be research, rather than simply unreflecting action. Figure 2.3, then, represents one of our frameworks: our pragmatic account of the core topics in the IS field and the bodies of knowledge which feed them (Checkland and Holwell 1992). It has been tested via our experiences, and we imagine that it will be 'recognizable' both to managers in organizations and to IS (including IT) professionals, but its status is only that of a model to which we can relate all the practical experiences which have gone into the making of this book; it is not prescriptive.

At the centre of the model is the core concern: the orderly provision of information in organizations as one important aspect of organizational change. Accepting this is to assume that organizations can never be static but are always changing in response to changing circumstances, both internal and external. Wise people in organizations will try to ensure that problems are perceived, framed and tackled consciously; and a ubiquitous feature of such organizational problem-solving activity will be work to create orderly systems of information provision. In any case, the provision of information systems, even if done only in response to technological imperatives (doing things because it's now technically possible to do them) will itself bring about organizational change. Again, if good sense prevails, the process of organizational change will itself be managed rather than simply left to happen. These are the elements at the centre of the model, and each may be associated with particular roles, such as: organization manager, information manager, system designer, consultant, etc. Note that these are roles, not individuals. One person may occupy, wholly or partially, a role or several roles. Thus a manager in an organization might also be in the role 'system designer' in a situation where users create their own systems.

It is assumed that this organizational change activity will in principle be capable of being fed by four particular bodies of relevant knowledge, represented by four streams of thinking and activity. The 'information systems stream' is that concerned with fundamental ideas of data, information and knowledge, also with methodology for IS planning and development and the managing of the information resource in organizations. The 'systems stream' consists of the body of systems thinking which emerged with general systems theory in the 1950s and is relevant to anything which may be thought of as a complex whole. The relevance of this thinking to work in IS is normally noted in the IS literature in a ceremonial way, but there is as yet not much in the way of determined persistent effort to forge the link between systems thinking and the organized provision of information in organizations (Checkland 1984). The 'technology stream' refers to the body of knowledge and work which focuses on IT itself and its development. It is important because, although IT provides a possible means (a 'how') to achieving the end of a working system to provide information (a 'what'), this is a technology in which new ways of doing things technically, new 'hows', can change ideas about possible 'whats'. The fourth stream is concerned with understanding organizations, organizational behaviour, and behaviour in organizations. This is the context of IS work, work which can hardly be undertaken without taking as given (preferably consciously) some concept of what an organization is. It has already been argued that the current conventional wisdom of IS is based upon a rather poverty-stricken view of what an organization is; there remains much work to be done in this area.

These elements give us a pragmatic picture of IS work as entailing a basic process of continual organizational transformation fed by the four areas of thinking and activity: information systems, systems thinking, IT and organization theory. Any particular piece of work in IS may draw upon any or all of these areas.

Also included in Figure 2.3 is a set of concepts which enable research into IS to be described. The main division is into conceptual/empirical, based respectively, as the words suggest, on thinking about aspects of the field as opposed to gathering evidence about such aspects. Conceptual work could include constructing an argument, making a review of the field as part of it, or providing a description/interpretation, essentially from the researcher's perspective (Galliers 1992b). Work based on collecting evidence concerning IS could include: conducting a survey in order to capture the outlook and opinions of users; carrying out hypothesis-testing experiments (whether conducted in an artificially-created laboratory situation or in the field itself); or carrying out collaborative action research, whether within one organization ('intensive') or with a group of organizations ('extensive').

Of course it is probable that in order to describe any actual piece of research work a number of these categories will have to be called on. Most actual research will not slot neatly into a category as if it were a pigeon hole. We have already indicated that our own preference is for empirical action research in which there is a fundamental contribution of a conceptual kind, namely the explicitly-declared intellectual framework in terms of which findings will be expressed.

Finally, we cannot over-emphasize that all such models or pictures like Figure 2.3 are never descriptive accounts of 'what is the case'; rather they provide categories and language enabling us to describe what is perceived to be the case. We have to remember all the time, and regularly remind ourselves of it, that the rich pageant of 'reality' is always more complex than any of the notations by means of which we try to make sense of it. What we are saying here is that, at a pragmatic level, Figure 2.3 provides a notation in whose terms we can provide accounts of the research studies upon which this book is based. Its main message at this stage is that there are a multiplicity of elements which impinge upon the process with which IS work is associated, namely organizational transformation. This implies that the view, not uncommon among technology enthusiasts, that the field of IT is synonymous with the field of IS, rather than being a part of it, is a view very difficult to sustain.

SUMMARY AND CONCLUSION

It is easier to describe a cup and saucer than a briar patch, and this has not been an easy chapter to write because we find the IS field not unlike the confused tangle of intertwined strands which characterize a briar patch: both boundary and content are unclear. Because of this, it is probably useful to summarize briefly the argument which this chapter has developed.

1. Intuitively there is enough meaning in the phrase 'the IS field' to make it worth investigating its form and content, taking an intellectual field to be a recognized learning system which addresses a particular topic area, as in Figure 2.1, in order to acquire knowledge and influence action.
2. In a well-established field it would be possible to describe the field in terms of the history of such a learning cycle. But as soon as this is attempted for IS, by going to its literature, confusion reigns, with many contradictory positions and approaches adopted, often without acknowledgement of the existence of alternatives.

3. Given this confusion, the IS field can be examined only on the basis of a declared perspective or worldview. Here its core concern is taken to be the orderly provision of information in (and between) organizations using IT, this being a part of on-going organizational change, the purpose of which is to influence action.

4. From that perspective the IS field exhibits two major strands of thinking, 'hard' and 'soft', which will yield very different bodies of knowledge and research approaches. The 'hard' approach assumes that organizations are goal-seeking entities and that the role of information is to aid decision making; research can take the form of hypothesis-testing experiments in the manner of the natural sciences. The 'soft' or interpretive approach takes a more 'tribal' view of organizations and sees them as relationship-managing entities (of which goal seeking is a special case). Information is relevant to sense making (with decision taking a special case) and research approaches – not yet well established – will derive from interpretive social science and hermeneutics; they will explore how sense making occurs in particular circumstances. At present the dialogue between 'hard' and 'soft' stances is rather threadbare.

5. Light can be shed on this via Whitley's work on the nature of intellectual fields in the sciences. The disparate pattern of unrelated work in IS makes it close to what Whitley calls a 'fragmented adhocracy' (a category also useful for describing management studies). The account of such a field which Whitley gives suggests the need to examine its language and core concepts at a fundamental level if greater coherence is to be achieved in the interests of the greater effectiveness of a practice-oriented subject area.

6. The reasons for the present state of the IS field are no doubt complex; they will include its newness, the seductive glamour of computer technology and the fast rate of technological change. The pace of change technically has been so great that practice will inevitably outstrip the thinking which makes sense of it (Figure 2.2); this will not help the coherency of the field.

7. In spite of the many intellectual ambiguities in IS, most people with an interest in it will have a practical sense of its shape and content. Figure 2.3 shows our 'pragmatic model' of IS, a model to which all the research described in this book can be related. In

this model IS work is one very significant feature of organizational change, something to which four streams of thinking and activity are relevant. These encompass information systems, systems thinking at a more general level, information and communication technology and organization theory. The figure also includes an indication of the categories of research approaches likely to be relevant in IS, from hypothesis testing to interpretive action research, from argumentative critique to surveys which capture actors' points of view.

In chapters One and Two we have suggested the need to examine some of the core concepts of IS at a fundamental level. We will do this in Part Two, before describing a number of research experiences in organizations in Part Three.

Part Two

Basic Thinking: Information in Support of Purposeful Action

Chapter Three

'Organizations': The Main Context of Work on Information Systems

INTRODUCTION

We argued in Part One that if IS is at all a definable intellectual field, it is at best only an emerging one. At the moment its structures and processes are rather confused, being far from those which characterize well-established areas of inquiry and action; IS is at best a 'fragmented adhocracy'. We also argued that in order to understand the field better, to make some progress in its conceptual cleansing, it is necessary to examine some of its fundamental concepts at a fundamental level. This we shall do here, starting with the context of most IS work: organizations. In this chapter we examine the concept of organization in order to understand better the idea of an information system which is established with the intention of serving or supporting members of an organization and the organization itself in the everyday world. Such clarification will be relevant not only to situations in which an organization establishes an information system internally, but also in situations – which are becoming more common – in which the concern is the electronic transfer of often large quantities of data or information between organizations (Konsynski 1992). Setting up either kind of information system will be an intervention which will change the organization(s) concerned, since it has the potential to change any or all of such features of an organization as the members' knowledge, their working and managerial practices and the disposition of power. This has been recognized throughout the development of IS. As long ago as 1958 (virtually pre-history in this

field) an influential paper in *Harvard Business Review* by Leavitt and
Whisler concluded that what they proposed to call 'information technology' would have important far-reaching effects on managerial
organization.

So the concept of organization must be relevant to the organized
provision of information; it had also better be clear. It is surprising what
a slippery concept it turns out to be!

'ORGANIZATION' IN IS LITERATURE

The 'hard', functional strand

IS conferences and IS literature do not pay much serious attention to the
question of what an organization is. Ovsenik's (1989) historical study of
the concept – from the Trojan Wars to the present day – is a rare find at
an IS meeting. Normally 'organization' is not taken to be a problematical concept; notions of organization are usually accepted without being

Table 3.1. *Some typical textbook references to the concept 'organization' (after Aiba 1993)*

Ahituv and Neumann (3rd edition 1990)	1. The users belong to a system called 'organization'. (page 2) 2. A social system, which is an organized and coordinated group of people who operate together to achieve common purposes – ie organizations (page 96)
Alter (1992)	Both organizations and information systems are systems in their own right. A system is a set of interacting components that operate together to accomplish a purpose (page 45)
Lucas (5th edition, 1994)	An organization is a rational coordination of activities of a group of people for the purpose of achieving some goal (page 78)
O'Brien (7th edition, 1994)	One way to understand the organizational impact of information technology is to view an organization as a sociotechnical system (page 414)
Schultheis and Sumner (3rd edition, 1995)	1. The organization is also a system (page 42) 2. The five parts of an organization are the operating core, the strategic apex, the middle line, the technostructure, and the support staff (page 42) 3. The five parts of the organization are joined together by flows – of authority, work material, information, and decision processes (page 43)
Zwass (1992)	Organizations are formal social units devoted to the attainment of specific goals. Organizations use certain resources to produce outputs and thus meet their goals (page 16)

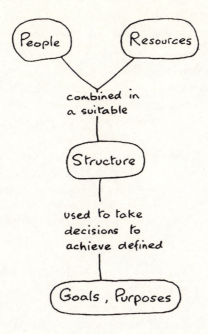

Figure 3.1. *The simple model of 'an organization' presented, or implicit, in much of the IS literature (after Aiba 1993)*

questioned. Robey and Zmud (1992) for example, suggest that research studies in IS 'often appear to be grounded in a theoretical void' (page 11). When the matter does get attention, the taken-as-given idea, as indicated in the previous chapter, is that organizations are goal-seeking entities, with managerial activity being seen as decision-making in pursuit of the declared goals (Jackson 1987). Table 3.1 collects some typical examples of how IS literature refers to 'organization', taken from a study by Aiba (1993).

The threads which run through accounts of organization in this field are that an organization consists of a group of people who together can seek to achieve objectives which would be beyond the reach of an individual, and that the entity, the organization, can be thought of as a system, usually 'a socio-technical system'. This latter abstract thought usually conveys the view that an organization's members will be working in several different functional parts connected together; changing any one of these will have some affect on all the others. Aiba examined the elements in definitions of organization in IS literature and concluded that the general image presented is no more sophisticated than that shown in Figure 3.1; it can be mapped onto Leavitt's well-known framework (1964) which consists of the four interconnected elements: people, structure, task and technology.

This simple model embodies what was described in the previous chapter as the conventional wisdom deriving from the influential work of Herbert Simon, a neat summary of his great contribution being provided in a current student textbook of IS by Zwass (1992):

> Decision making as the fundamental managerial activity. Use of quantitative models to support decision making. Recognition that, in general, an individual makes decisions with bounded (limited) rationality; organizations should compensate for these individual limitations. Organizations should be structured to facilitate the decision-making process. (page 413)

Acceptance of this model, together with the well-known analysis of levels of managerial activity (strategic planning, management control, operational control) derived from Anthony (1965) (extended to include the organization's operations themselves by authors such as Ein-Dor and Segev (1978) and Davis and Olson (1985)) leads to classification of types of IS which serve different managerial levels, as in the Gorry and Scott Morton framework (1971) presented in Table 2.3. Transaction processing systems support the operations; structured decision systems support operational and management control; decision support systems support the management control and strategic planning levels. In another schema of this type, Ahituv and Neumann (1990, page 124), for example, describe a well-thought-out 'comprehensive model' by Blumenthal (1969) which brings together the management ideas of Anthony and Simon with Forrester's 'industrial dynamics' model of an organization's physical network of stocks and flows (1961). This creates a rational model of an organization as a goal-seeking machine. It promotes coherent discussion of the information requirements at different organization levels which different types of IS could provide.

Such clear models are obviously helpful to inexperienced students, though they may make more experienced managers uneasy, since managers know how much of their time and energy is taken up, not with the substantive facts and the generic logic of their situations, but with the idiosyncrasies of interpretation of specific situations, and with the motivating myths and meanings which are as characteristic of organizations as the facts and the logic.

The 'soft', interpretive strand

It might be expected that the alternative strand of thinking in the IS world, the 'soft' (interpretive) strand identified in the previous chapter, would offer an alternative model or models of organization to set alongside the 'hard' goal-seeking-machine model just discussed. But those who advocate taking a more tribal view of organizations, and adopting a more interpretive approach to inquiry in the IS field, have not yet offered clear-cut sharply-defined models of organization which might underpin their approach. Like the mainstream of IS writers, the interpretivists have also focused mainly on the nature of IS, to the relative neglect of the concept of organization. Their writings do of course imply particular views of organization which are different from the goal-seeking model and which resemble each other. They imply that an organization is to be seen at core as a social process, essentially a conversational process, in which the world is interpreted in a particular way which legitimates shared actions and establishes shared norms and standards. But they do not at present offer well-defined models of organization which could be used in any detailed sense to shape and guide the provision of IS within an organization.

Illustrations of this may be found, for example, in the work of Ciborra, Kling, Goldkuhl and Lyytinen, and Walsham. Ciborra (1984 and 1987) argued for a contractual view of organizations:

> Organizations are stable networks of transactions regulated over a period of relative stability by a set of contracts to govern transactions between their members. (1984, page 138)

Information systems are then thought of as the data-based networks needed to create, establish, maintain and control the organization's set of contracts. No detailed model of 'organization' is offered, although the approach is suggested as a counter to the normal concept of organization in IS work based on 'individual decision making' (ibid, page 135).

Kling is concerned that system designers generally draw very narrow boundaries round what they are designing (Kling and Scacchi 1982, Kling 1987 and 1992). On the basis of 20 years of empirical work on how computer systems are adopted, developed and used in organizations, Kling argues for 'web models' of IS which place them in their social context. Such models take into account the social relations between participants, the infrastructure available to support the IS, and the history of commitments made in developing and operating computer-based technologies (1992, page 368). Again, no model of organization is provided but Kling's less than lucid advice is:

> Use a naturalistic open-systems organizational model, such as a negotiated order or institutional model of social activities, to best describe the social relations among key participants. (ibid, page 372)

Goldkuhl and Lyytinen, describing collaborative work by university-based groups in Sweden and Finland, urge a 'language action' approach to IS. This approach sees IS as formal communication systems which are socially constructed (Goldkuhl and Lyytinen 1982 and 1984, Goldkuhl 1987). The purpose of such a system is to 'influence certain people and their actions' (Goldkuhl 1987, page 336) and hence the approach to creating such systems should involve the system designer, acting in the role of 'catalyst/emancipator' rather than 'observer', studying how meanings are created by particular kinds of language use in the (social) situation of concern. Again, no model of 'organization' is suggested, but a 'negotiated order' model (Strauss 1978) is implied.

More recently Lyytinen (1992) has examined the possibility that work in IS might be based on the critical social theory of the Frankfurt School, especially the work of Habermas. He finds a growing interest but little in the way of substantive work, concluding that 'critical IS research', combining a broad view of the design, delivery and use of IS with a specific focus, is yet to emerge.

Finally, to round off these examples, we may briefly examine the approach of Walsham (1993), who develops an interpretive approach to understanding 'the process of organizational change associated with a computer-based information system' (page 52). Although he does not propose a particular model of 'organization', Walsham develops an analytical framework through which to examine IS case studies which leans heavily on the process view of organizations. The first element in his framework is an examination of change *content*, in terms of organization products or processes; he then draws on several other bodies of work. Following Morgan (1986), he draws on the 'culture' and 'political system' models of organization in order to examine the *social process* of organizational change, on Kling's 'web models' to explore *social context*, and on Giddens' 'structuration theory' (1979 and 1984) to conceptualize the link between social context and social process. (In Giddens theory, interactions between human beings draw on social structure, seen as rules and resources in human minds, and in so doing produce, reproduce and change that structure. This duality is similar to that in Vickers' notion of 'appreciative systems', briefly discussed in Chapter Two, where it was presented as a counter notion to Simon's goal-seeking model of human behaviour. For Vickers, we always see the world through a 'filter' created by previous judgements about it. New judgements both reproduce the previous 'settings' and create new ones, changing the filter in so doing: the appreciative system is always a product of the previous history of the system itself and its interactions with its environment.)

In Walsham's (1993) approach, then, we see another example of current work in the interpretive tradition which clearly places itself outside the dominating conventional wisdom. He robustly declares

> the concept of a 'complete and correct set of requirements ' (Davis and Olson 1985, page 474) for an information systems development sweeps away the multiple perspectives and ambiguities of organizational life and hides them under the carpet of the mechanistic metaphor. (page 29)

However, as in the other work considered here, the emphasis is on features of IS and organizational change rather than organization as such, and though the research is explicitly predicated on an interpretive view of an organization, no sharply-defined model of organization is developed, the implicit model being good enough for the purpose in hand.

This absence of an alternative model of organization from the interpretive school of thought is no doubt one reason why the model based on rational-decision-making-in-pursuit-of-goals dominates in IS literature. But there are also other reasons. There is no doubt that the goal-seeking framework, leading to clear-cut analysis of levels of managerial creativity, and hence well-defined types of information system, is exceptionally clear; it is also intuitively convincing, as long as it is not questioned closely, and eminently teachable. No wonder it gets taught! Finally, the most cogent reason for the dominance of the bureaucratic model of organizations may well be that it is the model which fits best of all with the fundamental nature of the computer: after all what is a computer but an electronic version of a bureaucracy? The point is well made by Dahlbom and Mathiassen (1993) in their thoughtful discursive book about software development, *Computers in Context*:

> In a bureaucracy, management is kept separate from actual production. Workers are not supposed to make decisions. They produce goods or

services according to instructions, only informing their managers about deviations and problems. Managers make decisions. They develop new plans and formulate instructions based on previous plans and status information.

A bureaucracy is like a computer, it is a powerful expression of mechanistic ideals. A bureaucratic organization is programmed, its work tasks are explicitly defined and formalized. It is a machine in which computing machines have their natural place, providing efficient processing and communication of information about products, activities, and resources. The computer is a perfect bureaucrat . . . (page 16)

Viewed overall, IS literature offers only the rather mechanistic model of organization which derives from Simon and is based on rational decision making in pursuit of organizational goals. The alternative interpretive strand of thinking is currently the source of much lively work, but its writers do not yet offer a detailed carefully-worked-out model of organization upon which a re-think of the IS field could be built.

'ORGANIZATION' IN THE ORGANIZATION THEORY LITERATURE

It might be expected that a more sophisticated model of 'organization' than the bureaucratic one might be plucked ready-made from organization theory (OT) literature for use in better understanding IS. This section briefly explores that possibility.

The literature of OT reflects a field which gives every impression of being more mature than that of IS. It is more mature in the sense that while its literature does not home in on generally agreed and accepted ways of thinking about and modelling its object of concern (as happens in a *very* mature field, such as chemistry), nevertheless the different strands of thinking are recognized and acknowledged; and there is debate between them of a kind which the IS field does not yet produce.

As an intellectual field, OT predates IS by about 20–25 years, one of its founding texts being Chester Barnard's *The Functions of the Executive*, published in 1938. OT's existence as a field of intellectual study stems from our general readiness to treat as a meaningful entity the abstract notion 'organization'. Of course, in everyday language we do this all the time, without worry. We say 'Shell has decided to build a refinery in Singapore', and everyone accepts without question that this is a meaningful statement, even though what it is which has done the 'deciding' is very problematical. The sentence speaks of the organization Shell as if it had a unitary brain and a consciousness and was capable, like a person, of deciding on certain courses of action. But 'Shell' is an abstract idea; it is something which somehow transcends the people who at any given time make up the membership of the company. How can this abstraction 'decide' anything? Yet we all intuitively accept the everyday statement as meaningful.

> The OT field exists, and can only exist, because we are ready to assume that once firmly established, an organization tends to assume an identity of its own which makes it independent of the people who founded it or those who constitute its membership. (Blau 1968, page 54)

OT exists to wrestle with, and understand this abstract notion of the 'organization' which somehow is beyond and independent of its members. OT's task is to develop useful knowledge about this abstract idea which could influence the design and operation of real-life organizations.

Since our concern here is only with the fact that organizations – whatever they are – are the context in which most IS work is done, we can afford to summarize drastically for brevity. This account of OT draws on Reed's historically oriented and very well-read account of the OT field (1985 and 1992), to which the reader is referred for more detail. Summarizing really savagely: an orthodoxy was established in the field, which dominated from the 1930s until the 1970s. Challenges to that orthodoxy eventually produced many different ways of analyzing organizations.

This produced a much more complicated picture of the field, though a common thread among the alternative approaches was a desire to reinstate the importance of the ability of organization members to interpret their social situation in their own ways.

In fact, the 'hard' and 'soft' strands in thinking in the IS field, identified in Chapter Two, are themselves reflections of thinking in OT. The orthodoxy which held sway for so long in OT is that of the scientific, functional, decision-making-in-pursuit-of-goals model derived from Simon, the model which still holds sway in IS. (Reed (1985) regards Barnard and Simon as 'the key figures' (page 13) and 'the true "founding fathers" of modern organization theory' (page 6).) The challenges to the orthodoxy, similarly, encompass the interpretive approaches which we find in the 'soft' strand of thinking in IS.

Within OT the orthodoxy was established as the field saw itself as

an applied science of organizational structure and functioning, directed to
the manipulative needs of an enlightened managerial elite . . .

This view

. . . became the dominant ethos of the 1950s and underwent subsequent
refinement and extension during the 'heyday' of modern systems theory
in the 1960s. (Reed 1985, page 5)

It also led to an approach to research based upon hypothesis testing,
most noticeably in the big programmes of work seeking, broadly, to
relate organizational structures to organizational tasks in order to
develop an empirically-based general theory of organization. See, for
example, Pugh et al (1963), Pugh and Hickson (1976), Woodward
(1965). This view is often referred to as the 'systems view', the 'contingency view', or the 'contingency-systems paradigm' (Donaldson
1985). Two of its protagonists, Kast and Rosenzweig (1973) describe it
thus in the foreword to a book of readings on the approach:

The contingency view of organizations and their management suggests
that an organization is a system composed of subsystems and delineated by
identifiable boundaries from its environmental supra system. The contingency view seeks to understand the interrelationships within and
among subsystems as well as between the organization and its environment . . . (page ix)

The nature of the system itself is that it is set up 'for accomplishing
specific purposes'. (page vii).

An important occurrence in OT was the publication in 1970 of
Silverman's *The Theory of Organizations*, a book continually referred to
by writers in the field. Silverman presented an alternative to the systems
model of organization which he calls 'the action frame of reference'.
This focuses not on the organization perceived as an abstract system in an
environment, but on the meaningful nature of social interactions for
individuals. It takes the view that social reality is not a 'given' but is
continually constructed and reconstructed by the actors in organizational
situations. Silverman regards the action approach not as a theory of
organizations but as 'a method of analysing social relations within organizations' (page 147). He provides a path along which such an analysis
might proceed; this consists of looking at six areas in sequence which can
be summarized as:

1. the historical development of the organization's role structure and pattern of interaction;
2. the nature of the involvement of ideal-type actors and the ends they pursue, that involvement deriving from experience both within and outside the organization;
3. the definition of their situations which these ideal-type actors offer, and their expectations of the likely behaviour of others, especially with regard to disposition of organizational resources;
4. the typical actions of different actors and the meaning they attach to the action;
5. the nature and source of the intended and unintended consequences of these actions, and the effects on the institutionalized role expectations;
6. changes in actors' involvements and ends, and changes in the role system, brought about by both internal and external transformations.

An analysis of this kind would clearly create a very different agenda from that derived from seeing an organization as a goal-seeking machine – and its implications for organizational information systems would also be very different.

This critique of the then conventional wisdom was widely influential in OT in the 1970s and helped to open up the field to the kind of critique and rejoinder which follows dethronement of an orthodoxy. (Donaldson, for example, offered an energetic defence of the traditional approach to organizational analysis in 1985.) There are now many strands of 'interpretivist' thinking, broadly defined, in OT, and Reed (1985) describes the mid-1980s state of the field as: 'a condition of upheaval over fundamentals and their implications for the practice of analysis' (page 213).

In a later book, Reed (1992) surveys the strands in this upheaval, doing so by an approach which includes outlining the most influential analytical frameworks since the mid-1960s. These perceive organizations as: social systems directed to achieving collective goals; negotiated orders created by members; structures of power and domination, advancing dominant economic, political and social interests; symbolic constructions (cultural artefacts); and social practices, that is to say administrative mechanisms 'through which collective action can be co-ordinated and mobilized in support of productive activity' (page 114).

It is clear that all of these different perspectives, none of which constitutes a new orthodoxy commanding general acceptance, would entail very different perceptions of the kinds of information systems an organization needs! This richness of analysis makes the current conventional wisdom of the IS field seem very naive indeed.

In summary, there is considerable similarity between the literatures of OT and IS. The two fields, with OT the more mature, map each other to the extent that each reveals an orthodoxy, a conventional wisdom, which has then been challenged – significantly in the case of OT, more tentatively so far in IS – by alternative ways of conceptualizing the nature of an organization. The orthodoxy is the same in both fields: it is the model of an organization which sees it as a social unit functionally organized to achieve corporate goals, and an approach to inquiry based upon the kind of positivistic hypothesis testing which is so well established in the natural sciences. In both fields 'hard' systems thinking (which assumes that the world is, or can be taken to be a set of systems) is used to express the model in more detailed form. The challenges to the conventional wisdom are also similar in the two fields, being broadly based on re-establishing the human agent as an actual creator of social reality through the attribution of meaning to observations and experience. These challenges draw upon phenomenology, hermeneutics and interpretive sociology rather than positivism, and lead to a variety of modes of inquiry other than hypothesis testing. In neither OT nor IS, and this is our main concern here, do the challenges to orthodoxy provide a model of organization as sharply defined as that expressed in the conventional wisdom.

These are considerable similarities; indeed at this level there is only one major difference between OT and IS. This is that in the latter field some of the work on the new approaches, building on earlier work within the management sciences, is also expressed in the language of systems thinking, though this time 'soft' systems thinking rather than 'hard', the 'soft' variety assuming not that the world is systemic but that the process of inquiry can be organized as a learning system (Checkland 1981, Checkland and Scholes 1990a). There is as yet no evidence from the literature that these developments in systems thinking are known within the OT field. For example, a book like *Rethinking Organization* (Reed and Hughes 1992) is entirely innocent of any awareness of 'soft' systems thinking, even though it is very relevant to themes discussed there, such as hermeneutics and activity theory. This lacuna in OT writings has been pointed out, and regretted, by Checkland (1994b).

For present purposes, however, the main point is that neither OT nor IS literature provides ready-made detailed models of organization upon which IS work could usefully be based. In order to bring more clarity to the IS field, however, it does seem important to declare a defensible concept or model of organization which could underlie its practice. Some taken-as-given model of organization will underlie all IS work, whether or not that model has been thought about with care, and whether or not that model is explicitly expressed. So it is a good idea to take this issue seriously, not least because of the manifest limitations of the orthodox goal-seeking model.

A CONCEPT OF 'ORGANIZATION' FOR IS

In developing a richer concept of organization than that on which most IS work and most of its literature are based, the problem is to capture the tension between the rationality of collectively organizing to achieve declared goals and the ultimate recalcitrance of human beings as members of organizations. If human beings were automata then the conventional rational model would be adequate; but we need a model which incorporates the sheer cussedness and irrationality of human beings as well as their readiness to conform.

The tension referred to is central in the writings of a pioneering sociologist, Ferdinand Tönnies. As Fletcher points out (1971), the very emergence of sociology in the late 19th century can be seen as a response to the disruption of a more stable society in response to the rise of industrial capitalism and a new commercialism. In seeking to understand the transition from agrarian to industrial society, Tönnies, in his major work *Gemeinschaft und Gesellschaft* (1887) (translated as *Community and Association* by Loomis (1955)) constructed models of two 'types' of society or organization. These were on the one hand the natural living community of the family or the tribe (*Gemeinschaft*), the group which you find yourself part of, and on the other the formally created associations (*Gesellschaft*) which men and women join in some complicated contractual sense – as when we choose to become employees of a company or members of a climbing club. This is the basis of a typology for analysis rather than a description of actual organizations. The point is that actual organizations in the world, such as companies, although artificially designed and created, also continue to have some of the natural characteristics of the family or the tribe, thanks to the ultimate autonomy and unpredictability of human beings: no *Gesellschaft* is ever simply a rational machine whose members willingly combine together totally to pursue organizational goals. Perhaps the test of a general model of organization is its ability to encompass the idea of the person who is genuinely a member of the organization but who is subversive and is trying to destroy it.

In trying to build here a picture of 'organization' capable of better supporting IS work, we first assume that the word always refers to a social unit, or collectivity. Robinson Crusoe on his desert island cannot be regarded as an 'organization', though once he has seen the footprint of another in the sand, and met up with Man Friday, the two of them could create an organization of which they were the members. This would involve discourse between them. Out of that discourse could emerge a number of things: some measure of declared agreement on purposes which might be actual agreement; social processes to pursue those purposes (which will entail some constraint and control of individuals); and criteria by which they would know whether or not the purposes were being achieved. This could lead to their defining organizational *roles*, as it certainly would in an organization of any size undertaking complex tasks beyond those which individuals could do on their own. There would be expectations of behaviour in role, so-called *norms*, and *values* by which such observed behaviour was judged to be 'good' or 'bad' in the organization. These roles, norms and values would not be fixed, but would be continually redefined in the organizational discourse about its experience. (Exploration of roles, norms and values is in fact part of the 'cultural' strand of analysis in soft systems methodology (Checkland and Scholes 1990a, pages 44–53).

In the present analysis, an organization is clearly an abstraction: it is a social collectivity concerned with some collective action, and there are associated social practices which relate to this. But what causes it, as an entity, to exist? The answer can only be: the *readiness* of some people, usually large numbers of people, members and non-members alike, to talk and act *as if* there were a collective entity which could behave like a conscious being, with the ability to decide to do things and then make them happen. Thus, to pick up the example used earlier, the statement 'Shell has decided to build a refinery in Singapore' is taken to be unproblematical and meaningful only because large numbers of people, both members and non-members of the Shell organization, adopt the convention of assuming the existence of a single entity called 'Shell' which can apparently 'decide' to do things and then do them. In more technical language, an organization is a reified social collectivity; it exists as an entity in that act of reification; and the reification enables both members and non-members of the organization to make sense of part of what they observe in the day-to-day world. Their sense making includes their assuming the existence of *person-like social collectivities* called 'organizations'.

This way of thinking about an organization is rather abstract, but it is necessary to make sense of what we all know from observation and experience, namely that members of organizations are not necessarily simply quiescent contributors to the achievement of organizational goals, as the conventional model suggests.

To be a member of an organization is to have a contractual relationship with it, whether a legal contract of employment or a more complex psychological contract, or both. Thus the volunteer middle-class ladies who run the Oxfam charity shop in the High Street truly feel themselves to be members of the organization Oxfam, and no doubt broadly support its aims. Most people would probably not feel comfortable taking part in the social practices of an organization whose core purposes they strongly rejected, and they would in that case probably cease to be members. But a rich model has to leave room for the subversive who remains a true member. Thus, during the heady days of student revolt in the late 1960s and early 1970s some members of universities who were, in the full sense of the term, members of their institutions appeared at the 'teach-ins' fashionable at the time and urged their fellow-students to destroy the institution – usually in order to create a Utopian 'free university' in its place. This kind of thing is a real phenomenon of organizational life, even though it is not commonly as blatant as this! It is a phenomenon excluded from the model which the conventional wisdom provides. It stems from the fact that the carefully designed logic of organizational activity, carried out in pursuit of organizational ends through a role structure, can never fully dominate and coerce the organizational members – which is something for which we should feel grateful if we value the idea that both individuals and hence collectivities can *learn*.

Figures 3.2 and 3.3 are attempts to express this discussion of the nature of an organization pictorially. Figure 3.2 expresses the conventional model which dominates the literature. It is a more elaborate version of the very sparse concept of Figure 3.1. Figure 3.3 enriches the goal-seeking model, covering the aspects just discussed above.

In Figure 3.2 members of an organization in a role structure are simply assumed to share an image of their organization in terms of its context, aims and objectives, its structures, processes and resources, and the measures of performance which indicate whether or not the aims are

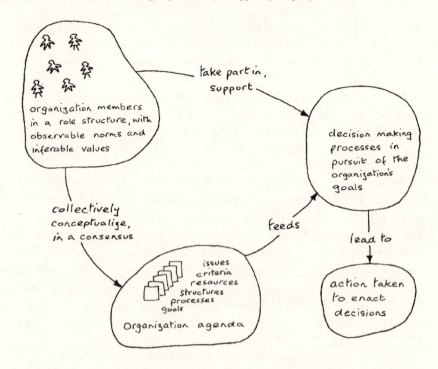

Figure 3.2. *The conventional wisdom model of 'an organization' in much of the IS literature (Figure 3.1 expanded)*

being achieved. Within this framework the members make their contribution to decision making in pursuit of objectives. Philosophically this is a positivistic model, sociologically a functionalist one. This is the model which ignores the features of organizations which make them feel like quasi-families or tribes to their members.

Figure 3.3 takes the concept 'organization' to be much more problematical. In the previous figure the real-world existence of what is modelled is simply taken as given, and the picture offers one description of it. In Figure 3.3 there are two major enrichments of this uncomplicated but naive view.

Firstly, the model includes the condition for the existence of an organization as a unitary entity, namely the readiness of both members and non-members to treat an organization *as if* it were a conscious, person-like entity capable of unitary purposeful action. Acknowledging that this is a linguistic convention rather than an account of 'what is the case' makes it possible to include a richer account of what goes on under the umbrella of that convention.

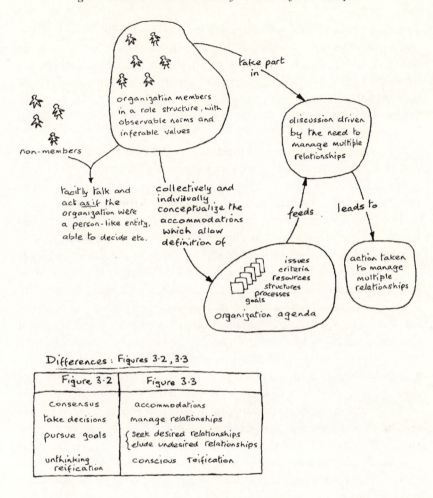

Figure 3.3. *A richer model of the concept 'an organization' than the conventional wisdom of Figure 3.2*

Secondly, then, Figure 3.3 includes an amplification of the idea that what goes on in organizations is rational decision making in pursuit of declared objectives. The first amplification concerns dropping the pretence that there is only one conceptualization, a collective one, of the organization, its context and its aims. Here we have conceptualization based on the interests and agendas of individuals or sub-groups within the organization as well as the overall declared, public, 'official' account of the organization. The two will rarely map each other exactly. The existence of these different interests and agendas means that the organization as a whole, the collectivity, has constantly to seek *accommodations* between conflicting interests upon which action can be based. It cannot simply assume consensus. And, following Vickers, the action is here expressed more richly as managing a (changing) set of relationships, rather than taking rational decisions to achieve goals. Philosophically this is a phenomenological model, sociologically an interpretive one.

These amplifications do not make Figure 3.3 simply an alternative to Figure 3.2. Rather, the enriched picture includes the simpler one, which is a special case of it. In principle, the multiple ways of thinking about an organization, its context and its activity could in particular circumstances collapse into a unitary view, the accommodations could become a consensus and the managing of multiple relationships could reduce to decision making in rational pursuit of declared goals. So the model in Figure 3.3, in principle, subsumes that in Figure 3.2. Whether the latter could ever in fact provide an adequate account of a real organization is of course a different question. It would require organizational members of an astonishingly servile and quiescent kind! It would be a good model if the negative Utopia of George Orwell's *1984* ever came into being.

At present most of the IS literature either implies or explicitly declares a model of organization like that in Figure 3.2. If the richer concept of Figure 3.3 is to inform IS work then that work will have to pay great attention to the organizational discourse in which concepts of the organization, its context, and its appropriate activity are continually debated and recreated. This discourse will depend very much upon 'information', and 'information systems', and in the next chapter we examine the notion of 'information'. It is at least as slippery a concept as 'organization' has turned out to be!

Chapter Four

Information in Support of Action

INTRODUCTION

In the last chapter we examined the context in which most work on IS is done – organizations – and found the idea of 'an organization' to be more subtle than we usually bother to acknowledge as we experience day-to-day organizational life. An orthodoxy was found in the literature, namely the view that organizations are social units whose members collectively pursue declared objectives. Given this, the basic organizational process is seen as rational decision making in pursuit of the explicit aims. This simple notion apparently provides a clear definition of the role of an IS: it is to provide the information which supports the decision making at various levels from the strategic to the operational.

However, the simple model is also simplistic, and IS literature (like that on organization theory) also provides a fledgling strand of thinking which sees organizations in more subtle terms. This strand sees them as cultural processes in which social reality is continually defined and re-defined in both the talk and action which carries and expresses the multiple agendas of both organization members and significant non-members outside the organization.

The simple model was expressed in Figure 3.2, the more subtle one in Figure 3.3, with Figure 3.3 containing the goal-seeking model as something to which the more elaborate model may sometimes reduce. This may seem rather abstruse when set out in this rather po-faced way, but it is really not; it is a recognition of the mixed nature of organizations as we all experience them as members. What we all recognize about organizations from our own involvement in them was recently neatly put by the Vice-Chancellor of Manchester University in the UK (Harris 1994):

> A university, like any other complex social structure, is made up of many special interest groups and forceful individuals with agendas of their own, who need often to be reminded that others are contributing to the success of the collective enterprise.

The broader concept of Figure 3.3 makes it possible to capture that image in a way that Figure 3.2 does not. Its processes can capture both collective activity in pursuit of corporate aims and the existence of personal (maybe hidden) agendas.

Against this background we are now in a position to examine the concept of 'information', treating this as something needed in support of the purposeful action which goes on in organizations; needed, that is, if the action is to be defensible, well-informed, better than simply playing hunches or randomly thrashing about. 'Information' is less complex a concept than 'organization' but it is, again, a subtle one, and one on which there is by no means complete agreement in the literature. We will examine this aspect first, before we develop a concept of 'information in support of action' which is rich enough to match the concept of organization in Figure 3.3.

DATA, CAPTA, INFORMATION AND KNOWLEDGE

Making sense of the field of IS requires a very clear concept of what 'information' is, but given the present confused state of the field it is perhaps not surprising that there is at present no well-defined definition of such terms as 'data' and 'information' upon which there is general agreement. It is noteworthy that a current encyclopaedia of software engineering (Morris and Tamm 1993) contains no entries for either 'data' or 'information'. Indeed one entry asserts that

> Computer programming is concerned with the processing of information *or* data. (present authors' emphasis added). (page 87)

If there were general agreement on the meaning of 'data' and 'information', the terms could be taken as given. Without such agreement, some analysis is necessary.

Anderton (1991) gives some useful examples which illustrate that there are subtleties associated with the idea of information and its communication to others.

a) A motorist is travelling at 30km/hr. The speedometer indicates 30km/hr. Does the motorist have information about his speed? Apparently, yes. But actually the mechanism is stuck and although the indication happens to be correct, *the driver receives no information.*

b) A traveller plans to fly to another country but can do so only if she is free from smallpox. She has some medical tests in the afternoon and arranges with her doctor that if the results are positive the airport desk will be called before 5pm. At 5pm she checks with the desk and finds that no message has been received. She thus receives the information that she is free of smallpox. Yet *no physical event has occurred*: nothing, apparently, has carried the information.

c) A newspaper arrives at a football supporter's house. In it he reads the score: England 1 Italy 2. The supporter has the information that Italy has won the game. Five minutes later a friend arrives with a Xerox copy of the newspaper report. The supporter *receives no information about the game*; he knew the result already. His brother, incidentally, who has not seen the newspaper, receives the information from the Xerox that England played Italy yesterday, a fact he had not previously known. (page 57)

To these instructive cameos we may add a further real but somewhat bizarre example.

At a conference held at Edinburgh University, one of the authors of this book occupied a room in the Pollack Halls of Residence. From the room there was a good view of some of the rock faces known as Salisbury Crags in Holyrood Park. These have attracted rock climbers for many years, and details of 20 climbs here were published as long ago as 1896. It was therefore amusing to read in the present rock climbing guide, which describes 50 climbs in detail, that

at present climbing on any cliff in the park is strictly illegal and anyone caught doing so is likely to be prosecuted. The route descriptions in this section of the guide are reproduced purely for their historical interest . . .

Now, to any red-blooded climber the message conveyed is perfectly clear, though it is not what the words say. To a rock climber, the guidebook is saying: here are descriptions of some good climbs, go and enjoy them, but be discrete, keep a low profile, and have a good story ready! In other words the information the guidebook conveys is virtually the opposite of what the text actually says! Clearly, creating and conveying information is not a simple business.

We need to find an account of 'data', 'information' and the relation between them which will make sense of examples such as these. This will need a careful use of language beyond that in normal everyday conversation. And the exploration should not start from the words themselves, such as 'data' and 'information', asking: what do they mean? Rather, we should take Popper's advice (1972):

> One should never quarrel about words, and never get involved in questions of terminology . . . What we are really interested in, our real problems, . . . are problems of theories and their truth. (page 310)

Popper suggests that if you find yourself arguing about the meaning of words, always a fruitless exercise, the thing to do is to accept your opponent's definitions and get down to arguing about the real problem! Here the problem is to develop at least a skeleton theory of *what distinctions it is useful to make* in order to understand the business of arriving at 'knowledge', the theory including an account of what the process is which leads us to make use of the words which mark the distinctions, such words as 'data', 'information' and 'knowledge'. In the words of Winograd and Flores (1986): 'As observers we generate distinctions in a consensual domain' (page 50), that is to say, a cognitive domain in which knowledge can be shared. Let us see what distinctions it may be useful to make in order to understand IS.

From data to capta

We can start by accepting the obvious: that there are myriad facts about the world. It is fact that the authors of this book were born in Birmingham, England and Melbourne, Australia, and that they are both, at the time of writing, working at Lancaster University. Such facts are in principle checkable; if disputed, evidence can be produced to support or refute them. There is a plethora of such facts, some agreed by all, some disputed, some accepted as meaningful by all, some private to an individual or group who defines them as a result of particular interests. Consider an example of this latter category. There must in principle exist the following fact: the number of octogenarian widows living alone in Wigan. This is a meaningful concept, though it may be the case that no-one has ever ascertained the actual number of such widows. Most people would not want to know this fact anyway; but it could be a significant fact to which attention is paid by a researcher examining the operation of geriatric support services in Wigan.

This suggests that there is a distinction to be made between the great mass of facts and the sub-set of them which we select for attention, those to which we pay heed. The obvious word for the mass of acts is 'data', from the Latin *dare*, meaning 'to give'. But there is no ready-made word for the small fraction of the available data which we know about or pay attention to, or create. At Lancaster during the action research programme which has seen the development of SSM, we have found it useful in discussion to refer specifically to that data which we have decided is relevant and which we therefore know we want to collect. We refer to such data as 'capta', from the Latin *capere*, meaning 'to take' (Checkland 1982) and that is the word we shall use here.

Data are a starting point in our mental processing. Capta are the result of selecting some for attention, or creating some new category – such as 'the number of octogenarian widows living alone in Wigan' in the example above – or being so surprised by some items of data which pass across our gaze that we begin to pay them attention. In the first of the earlier examples from Anderton, (a) above, the position of the speed-ometer needle at 30km/hr is an item of data; it becomes part of the driver's capta when he pays attention to it – though that example also reminds us that we may need to check that the apparent facts of the situation are what they seem to be.

Turning data into capta is a very familiar mental process, so familiar in fact that it has become completely transparent to us: we do it all the time without noticing the process occurring, which is presumably why we have here found it necessary to make up the word 'capta'. Also, it is by no means the end of our mental processing.

From capta to information and knowledge

Having selected, paid attention to, or created some data, thereby turning it into capta, we enrich it. We relate it to other things, we put it in context, we see it as a part of a larger whole which causes it to gain in significance (Holwell 1989). The phrase which best captures this is probably 'meaning attribution'. The attribution of meaning in context converts capta into something different, for which another word is appropriate: the word 'information' will serve here, this definition being close to the way the word is often used in everyday language.

This process, which can be both individual and/or collective, by which data is selected and converted into meaningful information, can itself lead to larger structures of related information for which another word is needed; we may use the word 'knowledge'. Such structures of information may be expected to have greater longevity than many items of information which are only ephemerally meaningful and relevant. For example, at a particular point in time in a home furnishing company, managers might select as *capta*, from all their sales *data*, the figures concerning the sales of a new expensive kitchen chair, aggregated separately for each sales area over the last three months. In the context of introducing this new product, these capta would yield *information* concerning, for example, the readiness of people in different geographical areas, classified socio-economically, to buy a basic but expensive product. This would itself contribute to updating the company's larger-scale slower-moving *knowledge* of the home furnishing market.

The process by which data are turned into knowledge is shown in Figure 4.1. It is suggested that in this process it is useful to mark or highlight three distinctions created by our actions of: selecting data; attributing meaning to this selected data; and building larger structures of meaningful data. And it is further suggested that we use the words data, capta, information and knowledge to describe the four products defined by making these three distinctions.

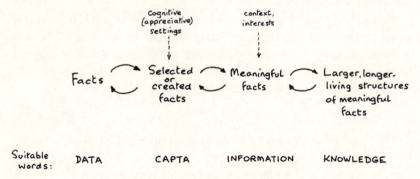

Figure 4.1. *The links between data, capta, information and knowledge*

The scheme of Figure 4.1 allows us to make sense of Anderton's intriguing examples quoted above. The first one (in which the speedometer is stuck) reminds us that apparent facts are not necessarily true: there is in principle a need to have available processes by means of which we can try to check the accuracy of data. In the second example, (b) above, the absence of any message conveys information to the traveller, so that nothing, apparently, has carried the information. This emphasizes the importance of context in acquiring information from data. The arrangement made by the traveller with the doctor establishes a context in which the *absence* of any message before 5pm itself conveys meaningful information. In the third example the existence of the match and the final score are part of the football supporter's capta, and he will no doubt convert the score into information of interest to him – such as, perhaps, England's prospects of qualifying for the World Cup. Neither the existence of the match nor the score were part of his brother's capta. The score tells the brother who won the match but also that the match itself had taken place, a new item of capta for him. Of course, if he is not interested in football he will not attribute the same meaning to it as his football-follower brother, so meaning attribution may be personal or shared.

This illustrates a very important point. The analysis has led us to use the word 'information' to describe 'capta' (itself selected 'data' which gets our attention) to which meaning has been attributed in a context which may be any or all of *cognitive, spatial* and *temporal*.

In the final example above, in which the anonymous writer of the rock climbing guide to Salisbury Crags manages to convey a message which is virtually the complete opposite of what the words say, we have a very subtle situation. It is another example of the important part which *context* plays in creating information. Many people glancing at the guide would of course accept at face value the statement about the illegality of climbing in Holyrood Park. But the writer, being embedded in the culture of rock climbing, knows its knowledge base, its attitudes and its values. He knows that fellow climbers will get the message; what is more, if challenged at the crag he or she will no doubt adopt an air of injured innocence! This example is the equivalent on paper of situations familiar enough in everyday life: situations in which information (in the full sense of the word) can be passed between knowing members of a particular culture by no more than a tone of voice, the gesture of a hand or a wink.

The most important feature of this analysis of data, capta, information and knowledge is that the act of creating information is a *human* act, not one which a machine can accomplish. It is the human being who can attribute meaning to the selected data which has been highlighted for attention, this being done in a context which may well be shared by many people but may also be unique to an individual. Of course the *designer* of a system which processes focused-on data (ie capta) into a more useful form will have the aim of making the processed capta correspond to some obvious categories of information which will be meaningful to many different people. But attributing meaning to the processed data is a human ability, and a particular attribution may be unique to one individual. No designer can *guarantee* that his or her *intended* attributions of meaning will be universally accepted. In the house furnishing example discussed above, the geographically-tabulated capta concerning the sales of the new chair in the three months after launch will yield different information to different people. The salesman will gain information about his bonus payments; the managing director will learn something relevant perhaps to the strategic future of the company; the production planner may take from it the need to recruit more process workers or obtain more raw materials for the furniture factory.

This emphasizes that the phrases in common usage, 'information system', or 'management information system', are ill-chosen. What such systems cannot do, in a strict sense, is provide unequivocal information; what they can do is process capta (selected data) into useful forms which can *imply* certain categories of information. They cannot, however, guarantee that the capta will be interpreted in this way by people making use of the system's outputs. In fact the phrases in common use in the early days of computers, namely 'data processing (DP) system' or 'electronic data processing (EDP) system', were more accurate than the phrases which have unfortunately replaced them both in everyday speech and in the professional field of IS. It would be a good idea to return to the earlier language, but this is unlikely to be achieved. After all, people working in IT will probably wish the word 'management', as in 'management information system', to be associated with their activity since it implies a higher level activity and maybe better career prospects!

DATA AND INFORMATION IN THE IS LITERATURE

The analysis carried out in the previous section was necessary because there is no agreement in the literature on the words needed to describe the processes by which human beings create knowledge.

Students coming to the IS field for the first time often imagine, as they begin to read the literature, that what the books refer to as 'information theory' must be relevant to their concerns. They are then puzzled that the statistical considerations of that theory seem to bear no relation at all to what we understand by 'information' in common usage. The point is that 'information theory' is grotesquely mis-named (Checkland 1981, pages 88-92, 1988b, pages 240–241).

During the 1940s the statistician Fisher, the mathematician Wiener and the communications engineer Shannon all worked independently on a quantitative statistically-based theory of 'information' transmission. They built on the work of communications engineers such as Nyquist and Hartley who, in the 1920s, established the basic way of conceptualizing message transmission: a 'message' is encoded into a 'signal' which is transmitted via a 'channel' before being decoded to recover the original message. Engineers viewing such a process are interested in measuring what is transmitted and its degree of distortion, and the great achievement of the theory was to define a quantitative measure of what is transmitted. Shannon's 'information theory' did this, and he deduced several theorems which are fundamental to the design of communication systems. The mistake, however, was to refer to what is clearly, in plain language, *'signal transmission theory'* as 'information theory'! This was recognized by Weaver whose early paper discussing the issue was reprinted together with Shannon's classic paper of 1948, in 1949. Weaver writes:

> The concept of information developed in [Shannon's] theory at first seems disappointing and bizarre – disappointing because it has nothing to do with meaning, and bizarre because it deals not with a single message but with the statistical nature of a whole ensemble of messages. (In Shannon and Weaver, 1949)

The point is that the content of what is transmitted, to which the word 'information' would seem to draw attention, is irrelevant to the engineering problems tackled by what is really 'signal transmission theory'. Such a theory, as used by an engineer, finds any 100 words of a prose message as interesting as any other 100 words. The theory does not distinguish between a message: 'I have just changed my socks' and another: 'I have just planted a bomb'. It is such differences of semantic content which are likely to concern those interested in IS. (Progress towards a genuine semantic theory of information has been very slow since Shannon's time – see, for example, Bar–Hillel (1964) – but Dretske (1981), does try to build upon Shannon's concept in developing a theory of perception and cognition.)

Within the IS field there are no sharp definitions of such words as 'data', 'information' and 'knowledge' which are generally accepted (Liebenau and Backhouse 1990) but there is a clustering of ideas concerning 'data' and 'information' which is compatible with the analysis developed here. Table 4.1 collects some definitions of 'data' from the literature as examples, these illustrating the range found by Aiba (1993) in 50 such definitions. The most common element was that 'data' refers to 'raw facts' or 'raw material' or 'elements'. More thoughtfully, Hirschheim et al (1995) refer to data as 'invariances' (page 12). Certainly, to someone who sees something as a fact, that something is to them invariant; and there are myriad invariances about which no one would bother to argue. Hirschheim et al see such invariances as having *potential* meaning to someone who can interpret them. In general 'data' refers to

Table 4.1. *Some literature definitions of 'data'*

Avison and Fitzgerald (1995)	Data represent unstructured facts. (page 12)
Clare and Loucopoulos (1987)	Facts collected from observations or recordings about events, objects, or people. (page 2)
Galland (1982)	Facts, concepts or derivatives in a form that can be communicated and interpreted. (page 57)
Hicks (3rd edition, 1993)	A representation of facts, concepts or instructions in a formalized manner suitable for communication, interpretation, or processing by humans or by automatic means. (page 668)
Knight and Silk (1990)	Numbers representing an observable object or event (fact). (page 22)
Laudon and Laudon (1991)	Raw facts that can be shaped and formed to create information. (page 14)
Maddison (ed) (1989)	Natural language: facts given, from which others may be deduced, inferred. Info. processing and computer science: signs or symbols, especially as for transmission in communication systems and for processing in computer systems; usually but not always representing information (sic), agreed facts or assumed knowledge; and represented using agreed characters, codes, syntax and structure. (page 168)
Martin and Powell (1992)	The raw material of organizational life; it consists of disconnected numbers, words, symbols and syllables relating to the events and processes of the business. (page 10)

Table 4.2. *Some literature definitions of 'information' (after Aiba 1993)*

Avison and Fitzgerald (1995)	Information has a meaning . . . (it) comes from selecting data, summarizing it and presenting it in such a way that it is useful to the recipient. (page 12)
Clare and Loucopoulos (1987)	A pre-requisite for a decision to be taken. Information is the product of the meaningful processing of data. (page 2)
Galland (1982)	Information is that which results when some human mental activity (observation, analysis) is successfully applied to data to reveal its meaning or significance (page 127)
Hicks (3rd edition, 1993)	Data that has been processed so that it is meaningful to a decision maker to use in a particular decision. (page 675)
Knight and Silk (1990)	Human significance associated with an observable object or event. (page 22)
Laudon and Laudon (1991)	Data that have been shaped or formed by humans into a meaningful and useful form. (page 14)
Maddison (ed) (1989)	Understandable useful relevant communication at an appropriate time; any kind of knowledge about things and concepts in a universe of discourse that is exchangeable between users; it is the meaning that matters, not the representation. (page 174)
Martin and Powell (1992)	Information comes from data that has been processed to make it useful in management decision making. (page 10)

something taken to be invariant which can be, but has not yet been processed.

The process yields, in the textbook view, 'information'. A similar exercise to that carried out for 'data' found virtually all definitions of 'information' using the word 'data' to describe the starting material out of which information is created. Out of 50 definitions 30 included words like 'shape', 'interpret', 'transform', 'process', 'assemble'; 29 used words like 'meaning', 'value', 'useful', 'relevant', and 21 indicated that it is a *person* to whom the processed data is meaningful (Aiba 1993). Table 4.2 collects some typical definitions as examples.

Many of these definitions could be challenged individually; and in any case they are mostly based on the unquestioned assumptions that organizations are goal-seeking social units and that management is synonymous with decision making – the very assumptions which were challenged in Chapter Three. Nevertheless, they represent at least a partial consensus that data is transformed into information when meaning is attributed to it. Most of them do not cover the clear possibility that different people may attribute different meanings to the same data, or, indeed, different meanings at different times, since that meaning attribution is something done by people, not machines (though that is implicit in some of the textbook definitions). The biggest lack, however, in terms of our analysis, is that no distinction is ever made between the gigantic mass of data which could be selected for processing and the tiny amount which actually gets selected. The field would benefit conceptually by acknowledging the process which turns data into capta, not least because fundamentally what IS do is to *process capta*; a prior selection process to distinguish some capta from the mass of data is unavoidable.

Tables 4.1 and 4.2 illustrate definitions which come mainly from texts which are written, essentially, for a student audience, and which therefore set out the conventional wisdom. Our definitions of data, information and knowledge match those of Kasabov (1996) in his book on neural networks, fuzzy logic and knowledge engineering. For him, and us, data is the factual raw material which becomes information, defined as 'structured data which have contextual meaning', while knowledge is 'high level structured information' whose density gives a 'presentation of previous experience'. Kasabov starts his book with these definitions; ours were developed in the analysis given above, and it is good to find them agreeing with those of a computer scientist. (Kasabov, for his purposes, does not need the concept of capta.) More important from our point of view, however, is that our analysis is itself consistent with that strand of the organization and IS literature which takes a more humanistic view of organizations and their IS support than is presented in the conventional texts. Previously referred to in Chapters Two and Three, this is the strand whose approach centres on the idea that human beings continuously create and recreate social reality in social interaction, especially in conversation – see, for example, Boland (1987), Daft and Weick (1984), Goldkuhl and Lyytinen (1982), Stamper (1987 and 1991), Winograd and Flores (1986).

Thus, Boland (1987) argues that

> We all know that information is the meaning or inward-forming of a person that results from engagement with data. Yet we consistently avoid the problem of meaning in our information systems research. (page 363)

He usefully explores the way in which Herbert Simon's influential metaphors ('organizations are decisions' etc (Boland, page 368)) have allowed data to be substituted for information in IS work.

Daft and Weick (1984) argue that we should take organizations to be 'interpretation systems' in which members scan their world, collecting data about it (which we would call capta) which is given meaning (interpreted) so that action can be taken and learning achieved.

Goldkuhl (1987) and Goldkuhl and Lyytinen (1982) base their approach to IS development on speech act theory (Searle 1969), focusing on the inter-subjective creation of a meaningful language which the IS formally embodies, meaningful that is for a particular group of people in a particular situation. Winograd and Flores (1986) similarly see the use of language as

> . . . a form of social action, directed towards the creation . . . of ' mutual orientation' . . . (which) exists as a consensual domain. (page 76)

The speech acts generate commitments on the part of those who take part in the conversations, and organizations are seen as 'networks of commitments' (ibid, page 150).

Working with similar ideas, Stamper (1987 and 1991) sees semiotics, the science of signs as a crucial base discipline for IS, especially a neglected part of it: semantics, concerned with the relationship between signs and what they purport to represent. He also advocates a focus on the social process in which shared meanings are attributed to selected data, and would base IS development upon a study of the social norms which entail meaning attribution:

> Meanings belong to the human agents . . . If only we can keep track of those agents and what they do, we shall devise a new semantics that can be applied successfully to business, legal and other social information systems. (1987, page 48)

The strand of literature exemplified here, though expressed in rather more abstruse language than our analysis, is clearly compatible with it. It is all based, like our analysis, on seeing the attribution of meaning to create information as a uniquely human (and often a social) act. A more pragmatic model of what we mean by an information system, that of Land (1985), is also compatible with our analysis.

In Land's model (of which Figure 4.2 is a re-drawn version), an IS will always include people using and interacting with the physical artefact, and will contain both formal and informal processing. The information user, having memory, knowledge and values, perceives the world outside himself or herself through a cognitive filter which will 'select, amplify, reject, attenuate or distort' messages – hence 'even simple messages may be interpreted differently by different individuals' (page 212). Action will

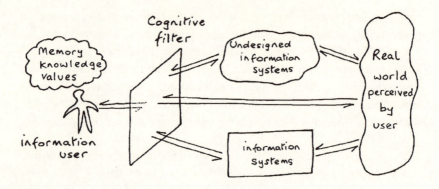

Figure 4.2. *The context of the concept 'information system' (after Land 1985)*

be determined by the association of messages received (whether from a formal IS or from informal sources or from the real world itself) with knowledge stored in a person's memory. Although the model does not distinguish explicitly between data and information, the modifying effect of the cognitive filter is clearly a process which converts signals from outside the user's mind into something meaningful to the user. Land's conclusion from a consideration of this model in relation to different types of information (descriptive, qualitative etc.) is that

> an information system is a social system which has embedded in it infor-
> mation technology . . . it is not possible to design a robust, effective
> information system incorporating significant amounts of the technology
> without treating it as *a social system.* (page 215, emphasis added)

Given the four concepts data, capta, information, knowledge, and the idea that the transformations from data into knowledge are brought about by human beings, we have a clear and simple way of thinking about 'information'. With that clarification established, we can now continue the quest to establish a rich concept of 'information in support of action' by examining the processes which so-called 'information systems' support.

THE PROCESSES WHICH INFORMATION SYSTEMS SUPPORT

Given three things: the broad concept of what we mean by 'an organization', expressed in Figure 3.3; the idea of 'information' as selected data

(or capta) to which meaning has been attributed in a particular context; and the basic premise from Chapter Two that IS exist to serve and support people taking purposeful action, we can now begin to enrich the concept of what is conventionally referred to as 'an information system'. This we shall do by exploring the nature of the processes which go on within organizations and between different organizations, processes in which information will play an important role.

The intention is to build a concept which is rich enough both to make sense of, and to guide work within the IS field, irrespective of whether that work is practical or conceptual. Such a concept needs to be at the same time broad enough to encompass a range of ideas about organizations and their information support, and sharp enough to provide guidelines which are usable in practice.

The personal process

Consider first ourselves as individuals in the world, having self-consciousness. We are all conscious of a world outside ourselves; we are also conscious of ourselves and others as part of that world. To be aware of that means that we have already performed the remarkable mental trick – which we do so often that we pay it no attention – of thinking about ourselves thinking about the world (Checkland and Scholes 1990a, Chapter 1). The trick is 'remarkable' in that it seems to be a uniquely human skill. To explain all the observed behaviour of cats and cuckoos, barn owls and badgers, you have to assume only that they are programmed to cat-like, cuckoo-like, owl-like and badger-like behaviour, not that they are conscious of their own relation to the world, of which they are themselves a part. The fact that we *are* conscious in this way, however, means that we can think about the world in different ways, relate these concepts to our experience of the world and so form judgements which can affect our intentions and, ultimately, our actions.

This line of thought suggests a basic model for the active human agent in the world. In this model we are able to perceive parts of the world, attribute meanings to what we perceive, make judgements about our perceptions, form intentions to take particular actions, and carry out those actions. These change the perceived world, however slightly, so that the process begins again, becoming a cycle.

However, this simple model requires two amplifications. Firstly, we always *selectively* perceive parts of the world, as a result of our interests

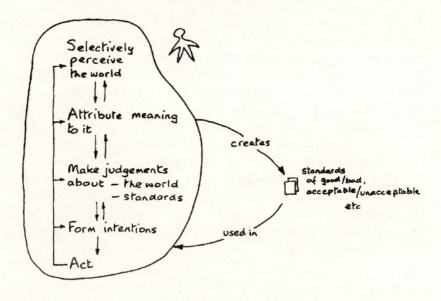

Figure 4.3. *A process model of the active human agent in the world*

and previous history. Rock climbers visiting the island of Lundy in the Bristol Channel will tend to see it as a set of granite crags, and their eyes will at once begin to scan for the climbable routes. They would probably not notice an unprepossessing plant, the Lundy Cabbage which is in fact unique to the island, and which might be the very reason for a visit by a botanist. The rock climber and the botanist each have a framework derived from their interests and experience which structures their perceptions. They create different capta, and hence different information and knowledge.

Secondly, the act of attributing meaning and making judgements implies the existence of standards against which comparisons can be made, standards of good/bad, important/unimportant, etc. Finally, the source of the standards, for which there is normally no ultimate authority, can only be the previous history of the very process we are describing, and the standards will themselves change over time as new experience accumulates – that is Vickers' crucial insight in formulating his notion of appreciative systems (1965) of which the present model is a version. Taking these considerations into account yields the picture in Figure 4.3, which is a process model of the active human agent in the world.

It will be noticed that there are multiple pathways available within the process illustrated. This is because of the great flexibility of the human mind. Thus, for example, the mere fact of making the judgement 'botanically interesting' about the island of Lundy will cause subsequent perceptions and attributions of meaning to be different from those which would have been made in the absence of that judgement. Note also that the judgements made may concern either what is perceived or the standards by which what is perceived is judged: we may begin to notice as significant something we have hitherto passed by, or we may begin to judge differently something we have always paid some attention to.

The model in Figure 4.3 applies to an individual who selectively perceives his or her world, judges it, and takes intentional (purposeful) action in the light of those perceptions and judgements. The model has to allow for the visions and actions which ultimately belong to an autonomous individual, for individuals do not *have* to conform to the perceptions, meaning attributions and judgements which are common, even though there may be great social and/or political pressure to do so, even though we are a social animal. (We are, ultimately, simultaneously both autonomous and gregarious, which is one reason why human affairs are so complex – and interesting.)

In general, the thinking and actions of the individual may have negligible or profound effects on others: sometimes what is initially the vision of an individual becomes that of very many people. An example of this is the reaction to the publication of Rachel Carson's famous book *Silent Spring* in 1962. Her perception, not at all common at the time, was that the excessive use of chemical pesticides was having seriously bad effects on the environment. She was noticing as significant, and attributing new meaning to observations which were in general not much noticed at that time. And she was judging them by standards which were not at all usual at the time, 'the environment' not being perceived as 'a problem' in the early 1960s. Thirty years later we can see that Rachel Carson's act in publishing her persuasive book was one of the earliest and most significant steps in the rise of the 'environmental movement' (Hynes 1989). This has seen the gradual establishment of an influential ecological ethic, one very different from that which previously dominated western culture, namely an ethic grounded in 'exploiting nature'.

The social process

What has just been described is an example of an individual's thinking and action having a profound effect on the mind set and actions of a very large number of people, and of their governments. Nevertheless, we can be sure that, though Carson wrote the book which acted as such a powerful trigger, she would no doubt agree that she had developed her ideas in dialogue with others. Although each human being retains at least the potential selectively to perceive and interpret the world in their own unique way, running the risk of being regarded as 'weird', the norm for a social animal with sophisticated language is that our perceptions of the world, our meaning attributions and our judgements of it will all be strongly conditioned by our exchanges with others. The most obvious characteristic of group life for a social animal with highly-developed language is the never-ending dialogue, discussion, debate and discourse in which we all try to affect each others perceptions, judgements, intentions and actions. This means that we can assume that while Figure 4.3 continues to apply to the individual, the social situation will be that much of the process will be carried out inter-subjectively in discourse – which is the word we adopt here to cover all communications, verbal and written, between individuals, between individuals and institutions, and between institutions, the purpose of which is to affect the thinking and actions of at least one other party. To cover this we need the modified form of Figure 4.3 shown in Figure 4.4; this is the inter-

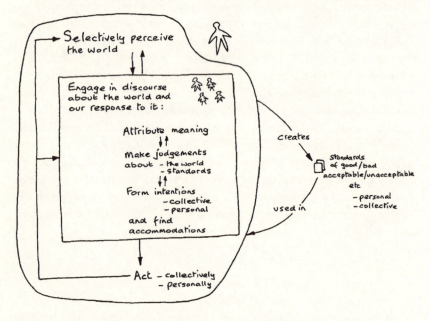

Figure 4.4. *A process model of active human agents in the world*

subjective, or social version of the previous figure. In it, previously personal cognitive acts are now embedded in discourse. Thus, Robinson Crusoe and Man Friday could enact their own versions of Figure 4.3; but once they have met and started to communicate, they will, in general, have to construct through communication a version of Figure 4.4, with the most extreme possible version of that 'communication' being the complete domination of one by the other.

In the example just given, Rachel Carson's act in publishing *Silent Spring* became the subject of much discourse. It turned out to be very persuasive, something which could not have been precisely predicted: we now know, with hindsight, that it did in fact affect, on a grand scale, the mental states of many many people who took part in the discourse or were affected by its course and products. It helped to change what Vicker's calls the 'appreciative settings' which we bring to the discourse, whether as individuals or as groups. Since taking part in this process is the very essence of being human, Vickers (1972) finds it very remarkable that our language deals with it in such a poverty-stricken way. He writes:

> . . . we have not even a name for this state of affairs in our heads which is the fruit of past communication and which is both the target and the interpreter of present communication. This nameless state accounts for nearly everything which we and others do – and, more important, are. Our assumptions about it are basic to nearly all our explanations of the feelings, thoughts and doings of ourselves and our fellows . . . I have taken to calling it an appreciative system, because the word *appreciation*, as we use it when we speak of appreciating a situation, seems to me to carry with it those linked connotations of interest, discrimination and valuation which we bring to the exercise of judgement and which tacitly determine what we shall notice, how we shall discriminate *situations* from the general confusion of ongoing event, and how we shall regard them . . . I call it a system because these categories and criteria are mutually related; a change in one is likely to affect others. (Vickers, 1972, page 98)

Our model of the social process which leads to purposeful or intentional action, then, is one in which appreciative settings lead to particular features of situations (as well as 'the situations' themselves) being noticed and judged in particular ways by standards built up from previous experience. As a result of the discourse which ensues, accommodations may be reached which lead to action being taken. Equally, the appreciative settings and the standards by which judgements are made may well be changed. They will certainly change through time as our personal and social history unfolds: there is no permanent 'social reality' except at the broadest possible level, immune from the events and ideas which, in the normal social process, continually change it.

The organizational process

The idea of appreciative settings is not restricted to individuals. Our personal settings may well be unique, since we all have a unique experience of the world, but often they will overlap with those of people with whom we are closely associated or who have had similar experiences. Indeed, appreciative settings may be attributed to a group of people – to members of a team, for instance, or members of a department of an organization – though we must remember that there will never be complete congruence between individual and (attributed) group settings. We can also attribute appreciative settings to that larger abstraction, the organization as a whole. Indeed, the conventional wisdom on organizations discussed in Chapter Three can be seen as a rather naive assumption that all members of an organization share the same settings, those which lead them unambiguously to collaborate together in decision making in pursuit of organizational (corporate) goals. The reality, as argued in Chapters Two and Three, will be more complex. The model of organization developed in Chapter Three and expressed in Figure 3.3, is of a kind which emphasizes that though the idea of 'the (attributed) appreciative settings of an organization as a whole' is a usable concept, the content of those settings, whatever attributions are made, will never be completely static. Changes both internal and external to the organization will change individual and group perceptions and judgements, leading to new accommodations related to evolving intentions and purposes.

Given this concept of organization, and the concepts of data, capta, information and knowledge developed earlier, together with the accounts of the processes, individual and social, which work done in the IS field will support (the process shown in Figures 4.3 and 4.4), we are now in a position to give an account of the overall organizational process in which the design and implementation of so-called 'information systems' (which, more precisely, are systems which process capta) have a part to play.

The process will be one in which the data-rich world outside is perceived selectively by individuals and by groups of individuals. The selectivity will be the result of our predisposition to 'select, amplify, reject, attenuate or distort' (Land 1985, page 212) as a result of previous experience, and individuals will interact with the world not only as individuals but also through their simultaneous membership of multiple groups, some formally organized (such as a department in an organization) some informal, such as a group of friends. Perceptions will be exchanged, shared, challenged, argued over, in a discourse which will consist of the inter-subjective creation of capta and meanings. Those meanings will create information and knowledge which will lead to accommodations being made, intentions being formed and purposeful action undertaken. Both the thinking and the action will change the perceived world, and may change the appreciative settings which filter our perceptions. Thus the process will be cyclic and never ending: it is a process of continuous learning, and will be richer if more people take part in it.

Adjunct to this process will be another in which the IS needed to support the action will be defined and realised using, usually, appropriate IT and telecommunications, the role of IT-based IS being to serve and support people taking purposeful action in their situations.

The whole process envisaged is shown in Figure 4.5. It is a model which relates to the *processes* in which *organization meanings* are created: the POM model. Element 1 consists of the people as individuals and as group members, element 2 the data-rich world they perceive selectively through their various taken-as-given assumptions. In the language being used here these are 'appreciative settings'; they play the role of Land's 'cognitive filters' in Figure 4.2. The organizational discourse (element 3) is the arena in which meaning is created inter-subjectively, leading to the attributions of meaning which yield information and knowledge, element 4. This is a very complex social process in which persuasion and/ or coercion is attempted, battles are fought and scores settled – the whole process embodying politics as well as, perhaps, rational instrumental decision taking! Organizations have to be able to encourage but at the same time contain such a process to survive. They have to enable assemblies of related meanings, intentions and accommodations between conflicting interests to emerge (element 5) so that purposeful action (element 6) (best thought of and expressed as a managing of relationships) can be taken. Formally organized information systems (element 7a) based on IT and telecommunications (element 7b) support organization members in conceptualizing their world, finding accommodations, forming intentions and taking action (elements 5 and 6). The technology (element 7b) will also require the availability of professional knowledge

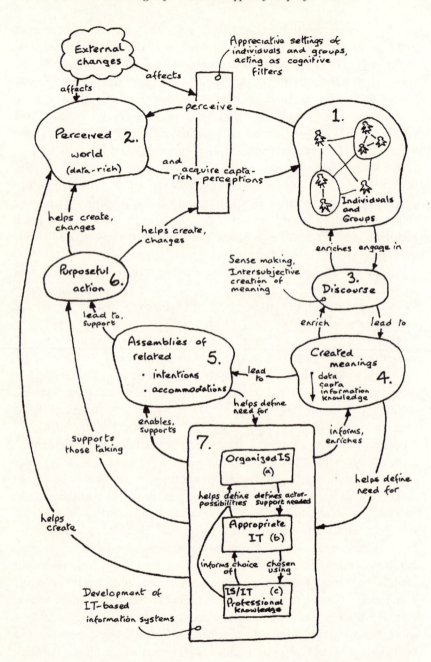

Figure 4.5. *The 'organizational' form of the model of the social process in which meanings are established and lead to information support for people undertaking purposeful action: the 'processes for organization meanings' (POM) model*

of the technology and its possibilities so that suitable configurations can be proposed. This professional know-how will also include the knowledge needed to operate, maintain and, if necessary, modify the technology. This knowledge constitutes element 7c in Figure 4.5.

Sometimes the 'support' the technology offers may include, or comprise, taking over and carrying out, by making use of technology, actions previously in the hands of people – such as doing calculations or drawing graphs. This kind of automation is an obvious radical kind of 'support'; but the more subtle aspects of support are likely to reside in the provision of processed capta which enable the users to modify the way they think about their world – that is to say, help both to sustain and to change the perceived world (element 2).

Several broad features of this model, the POM model, are worthy of comment.

1. It cannot be overemphasized that, like most of the models in this book, it does not purport to be a descriptive account of *the* organizational process. What it does purport to be is a defensible device with a structure and language which can be used *to make sense of* life in real organizations and their provision of information systems (Weick 1995). Real life itself is always richer and more complex than any of our images of it. Thus, though we could argue that Figure 4.5 broadly represents aspects we can observe and analyse, the detailed reality will always be less clear-cut than the model; a terrain is never the same as a map which relates to it. After Checkland and Casar (1986) had represented Vickers' writings in the form of a model of what he meant by 'an appreciative system', Casar 'tested' the model in the company in which he worked in Mexico City (Casar 1990). This was a financial services company, and Casar's professional task at that time was to set up a strategic planning function. As he did that Casar kept a detailed diary of what happened and used the 'appreciative system' model to try to make sense of his experience. He found that the model was very useful for that purpose (and hence helped him to plan and monitor what he was doing) but that the real-world happenings represented an incredibly complex flux in which many appreciative systems, both individual and group, were operating simultaneously and interactively. The complexity derived from the fact that many different appreciative systems, operating simultaneously, were doing so both over different

timescales (from within an hour to over several months) and at different levels, from the tactical to the strategic. Such experience provides useful reminders to us to beware of reifying what are bound to be rather simple models when compared with complex real life!

2. In connection with the first point, it is important not to think of the model as implying a particular set of *structures*. Its elements define a set of connected *processes*. In a real situation these would have to be somehow embodied in structures, but many different structures could be chosen to encapsulate the set of fundamental processes in the model. In terms of the old question from biology: does form follow function or does function follow form? (a real chicken-and-egg question) it is clear that as far as purposeful organizations are concerned, function (i.e. process) is prime, not form (i.e. structure). (The fact that in everyday life in organizations more attention is devoted to structure than process is probably due to two things: ways of thinking about process (such as by building activity models) are unfamiliar to many managers; and in any case forming particular structures is usually a part of political power play in organizations, and hence receives a disproportionate amount of attention. In everyday life, form is 'sexier' than function.)

3. It is worth noting that because the model is cyclic, with pathways which link all elements with each other, there is no clear starting point for use of the model. In a particular situation the initial focus might, for example, be on action (element 6). It might be found to be inadequately supported by the IS in element 7a, or it might be found that some boring action previously taken by people could now be automated. In another situation a new development in IT (elements 7b and 7c), such as, for example, the development of groupware (Grudin 1991) might cause a re-think of possible knowledge (element 4), intentions (element 5), and action (element 6). In general the cycle of Figure 4.5 might be dominated, in particular circumstances, by changes in (or changed perceptions of) any of the elements in the model.

4. The process in Figure 4.5 can encompass any way of conceptualizing an organization. It is certainly not necessarily linked to the conventional wisdom. It could encompass it, however, just as it could encompass treating the organization as a political arena, as an organism, or according to any other organizational

metaphor which seems appropriate in a particular case, whether drawn from Morgan's proposed menu of such metaphors (1986) or freshly coined.

5. Finally, we may note that the model enables us to define what the phrase 'an information system' refers to (or ought to refer to) as well as implying that the process to develop information systems ought to exhibit certain features which may or may not be present in the current processes by which IS are developed. We shall examine this aspect in the final section of this chapter.

CONCLUSION: RICHER CONCEPTS OF 'INFORMATION SYSTEM' AND 'INFORMATION SYSTEMS DEVELOPMENT'

The concept 'information system'

In this and the previous chapter we have examined the ideas of 'an organization' and 'an information system' at a fundamental level. It has been necessary to do this, given the degree of confusion in the literature and the consequent absence of agreed, well-defined concepts. At the end of this path we can now provide, based on Figure 4.5, a richer concept of an 'information system' in the context developed in Chapters Three and Four, and also suggest some necessary basic features of the information system development process implied by that account. These both turn out to be rather different from the definitions implicit in much current practice. That this is so is another indication of the fact that the IS field is still in a rather primitive state.

Figure 4.5 can be seen to contain three parts which are in a particular kind of relationship with each other. Elements 1–5 describe the organizational context in which people create meanings and intentions; this leads to purposeful action being taken (element 6). Element 7 provides what would usually be described as 'information support'. (Using words more carefully we could describe it as providing support either in the form of relevant processed capta or in the form of *processing* selected capta, this latter covering the option of automating actions previously carried out by people such as compiling lists or drawing graphs.) Thus we have a process (elements 1–5) and a form of support (element 7) for a main outcome of that process, namely the purposeful action which people take as a result of the process. Figure 4.6 shows this structure.

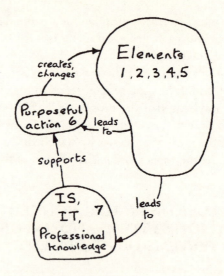

Figure 4.6. *The core structure of Figure 4.5, the POM model*

Formally organized 'information systems' will exist to support directly those taking the action which results from the formed intentions (the link 7 to 6 of Figure 4.5) though we should also note in that figure that the very existence of an organized system of this kind will also have its affects on both the information and knowledge created in the organization (element 4) and the image of the perceived world of organization members (element 2). The main role of an information system, however, is that of a support function; such systems do not exist for their own sake (Bacon and Fitzgerald 1997).

This may seem an unexceptional remark, but an important consequence follows from it, a consequence which is much neglected in current IS thinking.

First we may enrich the remark that the nature of an information system is that it is a function supporting people taking purposeful action by indicating that the purposeful action can itself be expressed via activity models in the form of SSM's 'human activity systems'; similarly, the function of providing 'information support' is always thought of as 'a system', one containing a data storage element and a data processing element as well as people to maintain, operate and modify it. Thus any and every 'information system' can always be thought about as entailing a pair of systems, one a system which is served (the people taking the action), the other a system which does the serving (namely, the capta

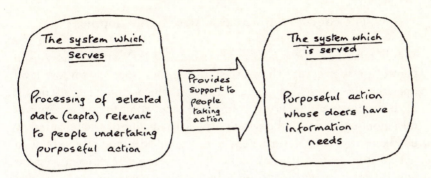

Figure 4.7. *Two linked systems which are entailed in the concept 'an information system*

processing) as in Figure 4.7. This is as true of a system based on group-ware as it is of a system to record resource use in a production process. (The argument here is partially developed in Checkland 1981, Checkland and Scholes 1990a, Checkland and Holwell 1993, Winter, Brown and Checkland 1995.)

Now, whenever one system serves or supports another, it is a very basic principle of systems thinking that the necessary features of the system which serves can be worked out only on the basis of a *prior* account of the system served. This must be so because the nature of the system served – the way *it* is thought about – will dictate what counts as 'service', and hence what functions the system which provides that service must contain (Checkland 1981, page 237). Thus, an information system strategy concerning support to a company manufacturing wheel-barrows can be coherently designed and set up only on the basis of a clear concept of the company. If we think of it as existing to make full use of an existing wheelbarrow-manufacturing capacity, a production-oriented view, this will require IT support different from that which would be appropriate if we think of the company as existing to try to meet a perceived market need for wheelbarrows. This is true not only for the IS strategy of the company as a whole but also for the thinking concerning each detailed system created within that strategy.

This seems an obvious idea, but it has significant implications for the process of 'information system development' (ISD). That process needs to start not, as is so often the case at present, with attention quickly, even immediately focused on data and technology, but with a focus on the action served by the intended system. Given that principle, we can now indicate the broad features of the ISD process implied by Figure 4.5. This account draws on Winter, Brown and Checkland (1995).

The concept 'information systems development'

We describe here the *general* requirements for ISD which follow from Figure 4.5. We accept that in a specific case, and especially for low-level operational systems – for example a system which simply records details of all customers and their orders in a mail order company – the purposeful action supported by the system may be so uncontroversial that it may be taken as given. Nevertheless, it is a good idea not to accept such 'givens' too readily. It is not difficult to develop very efficient systems which later turn out not to meet user requirements. Examples of that happening are legion.

In the general case, then, the first requirement of a good ISD process is a thorough examination of the ways in which people in the organization perceive their world (elements 1 and 2 in Figure 4.5). It is necessary to get a grasp of those perceptions as they lead to the particular assumptions about meanings and purposes which cause certain purposeful action to be regarded as both necessary and in need of capta-processing support. We need to understand why, among these people, certain data are (or could be) selected and treated as relevant capta. Referring back to Figure 4.5, we need the richest appreciation we can get of, first, elements 1–2 in that model, then elements 1–5, in order to get the best possible definitions of accepted purposes and the intentional action which follows from pursuing them. These purposes could be those attributed to the organization as a whole, or to some part of it (such as a department), or they could refer to action which the organization has to achieve even if the action in question is not institutionalized in a section or department. (For example, in many organizations such an action might be something like: 'Decide on resource allocation between competing departments.)' The examination of meanings and purposes should be broadly based, and its richness will be greater the larger the number of people who take part in it. The examination, wide ranging at first, should try to home in on the question: if we wanted to pursue this purpose, which seems meaningful to us, what would we have to do and how could we do it? The aim is to define plausible purposes and ways in which it would be possible to pursue them, remembering the many relationships which they will entail. We must not expect such debate to be entirely dispassionate and rational! Acknowledging what has been said above about the rarity of complete consensus, what are sought are the *accommodations* which enable energy to be enlisted in undertaking action relevant to plausible purposes.

The accommodations sought are necessary not for their own sake (though their very existence will at least signal that the law of the jungle does not entirely prevail in the organization!), but in order that deliberate intentional action can be taken, including action in the name of the organization, or some part of it, as a whole. It is this intentional action, some of it corporate, for which people undertaking it will require information support. And the purpose of the initial exploration and debate is to define it within realizable accommodations between (or achieved consensus among) the people and groups who make up the organization. (Using SSM is one way of conducting this process of exploration and debate, and in the UK in recent years it has been interesting to see the government's Central Computing and Telecommunications Agency (CCTA) working to try to formalize the use of SSM in the early stages of studies which will eventually design data processing systems using the well-known SSADM (Structured Systems Analysis and Design Methodology, CCTA, 1990). This work is described in the references CCTA (1989) and CCTA (1993), where a rather mechanistic approach to SSM is taken.) No matter how the exploration and debate are conducted, however (and no matter which system design methodology it is intended to use), the key point is that a rich initial study of *meanings and purposes* is essential in order to arrive at an account of the right-hand 'system' in Figure 4.7: the served system which the data/capta processing will support.

Once the action to be supported has been decided and described, which can usefully be done using activity models, it can be examined in order to decide whether support should take the form of either or both of the following: automating action which is currently being carried out by people; or providing 'informational' support to people as they carry out their tasks. In the case of the latter, two kinds of informational support need to be thought about: information which will help people who take the desired action, and, especially, information which will help them to monitor it and take control action with respect to it if desired outcomes are not emerging. This monitoring and control needs to be thought about carefully in terms of declared measures of performance which will derive from how the purposeful activity is conceptualized. (One of the reasons that SSM's 'human activity system' models are useful is that they are structured in the form of two sub-systems, one containing the activities which pursue the purpose, one monitoring and controlling those activities in the light of declared performance criteria. Examples will illustrate this in later chapters, where more will be said about SSM as an approach to this kind of analysis.)

The key feature of the ISD process implied by Figure 4.5 is now clear. From an analysis of the information support appropriate for whoever is concerned with taking the intentional action, it is now – and only now – legitimate to turn attention to the system which will provide that support, a system which in the 1990s is usually a computer-based data/capta processing system. This is not to deny that on occasion new emerging technical possibilities may make possible new intentional action. But, before any system which provides informational support can be constructed, there has to be a clear account of, first, the action supported, and then the information relevant to people carrying out the action. The point is that the account of the information relevant to the 'system to be served' will define which data items are the relevant capta and how they need to be processed if they are to provide the information needed by those who carry out the intentional action and monitor and control it.

We can think of the data/capta processing system as containing, in general, a data processing element and a data storage element as well as those who operate, maintain and modify it. This simple model can then accommodate various hardware and software configurations and the selection of a suitable one becomes an issue calling for the expertize of the IT professional. All the tools of computer systems analysis can of course be used in realizing the data/capta processing system, for example data flow modelling (Gane and Sarson 1977, DeMarco 1978) entity relationship modelling/normalization (Codd 1970, Chen 1976, Benyon 1990) and database design (McFadden and Hoffer 1994).

This completes the elaboration of the concept of 'an information system' in Figures 4.5 and 4.6, the logic of which is that the human activity systems describing the purposeful action (the served system) are logically prime, since they in the end dictate the required form and content of the data/capta processing system which serves them. Before moving on, however, it may be useful to point out that the concepts of Figure 4.5 cover not only the use of any formal systems design methodology but also a heuristic approach to systems design, such as prototyping, as well as the purchase of off-the-shelf software packages.

It might be thought that the trial-and-error prototyping approach to ISD runs counter to this concept but this is not so. In prototyping, a quick and inexpensive preliminary version of a system is built, knowing that it will be modified in the light of user reaction. Users get the chance to interact with a temporary version of the proposed system, the system developers realizing that the prototype will probably reproduce only a significant fraction of the required functionality of the final system. The final design can embody the learning which comes from the user involvement. Such an approach is common with 'decision support systems' and 'expert systems', and is clearly also relevant to systems which are created on the foundation of a purchased software package. (Prototyping is discussed by, for example, Earl (1978), Gomaa and Scott (1981), Naumann and Jenkins (1982), Alavi (1984), Boar (1984), Cerveny et al (1986), Agresti 1986, Cooprider and Henderson (1990).)

Prototyping does not, however, make the data/capta processing system in Figure 4.5 prime. As a process, prototyping can only be initiated at all if there is at least some rudimentary idea or preliminary account of the action which requires information support; without that there would be no basis at all for the initial version of the system being developed. Prototyping, as a concept, simply implies that from a very preliminary account of the system served, the system which serves is then developed by multiple iterations between the two systems of Figure 4.7, iterations which may change ideas about both systems.

This is to accept a point made by Emery (1987), quoted in Zwass (1992, page 739) that prototyping can 'serve as a vehicle for organizational learning'. But even if the iterations of prototyping are a means, however limited, of exploring something of the meanings and purposes behind the purposeful action which data processing supports, the starting point still has to be *some* definition of the action to be served, however crude that initial definition of it might be. And the final implemented data/capta processing system is one which serves human action even if that action system has been defined in a piecemeal fashion through the iterations of prototyping.

It might also be thought that the creation of a computer-based system by the purchase of existing software packages lies outside the concepts of Figure 4.5 but again this is not so. The figure, remember, is intended not as a prescriptive account but as a sense-making device. In the case of ready-made software packages, they are produced and sold because the software developers and vendors believe that there exist in modern organizations some very general purposes which lead to very common intentional action which can be observed taking place in very many organizations. In the terms of Figure 4.5, software vendors believe that there are a number of common versions of element 6. Hospitals, for example, *have* to keep records of the patients they admit, treat and discharge. Not surprisingly, software vendors will try to convince the hospital managers that the 'patient administration system' they offer is just what the hospital needs. Similarly, the initiative in the UK known as 'LMS' – local management of schools – has immediately led to the offering of data-processing packages claiming to provide support to head teachers who are for the first time trying to manage their own budgets.

Such once-and-for-all systems are intrinsically unlikely to be able to meet all the idiosyncratic requirements of a particular hospital or school, and by definition they are likely to be less appropriate than systems designed in the light of rich analysis of elements 1–5 in Figure 4.5. But they may be cheaper than custom-built systems, and they may be available quicker. The lesson for such situations from the POM model in Figure 4.5 is twofold. Firstly, in order to know whether a proprietary system is appropriate to its needs, an organization must have a very clear understanding, in some detail, of the purposeful action it is carrying out or intends to carry out based on its achievable accommodations. Without such an understanding the organization will not be able to evaluate the systems offered, and it is never a good idea simply to believe what vendors tell you! So an organization looking for informational support systems must in some way think through its intended purposeful action; it must gain its own understanding of elements 1–5 for its circumstances, or be prepared to be frustrated by inadequate systems. Secondly, the developers of packages which purport to fill general needs will be best prepared for the market-place if they can provide an account of the action which their system serves, preferably in the form of an activity

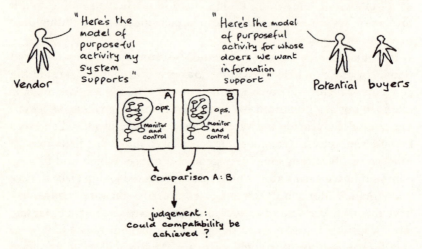

Figure 4.8. *An ideal form of discussion between a system vendor and potential buyers*

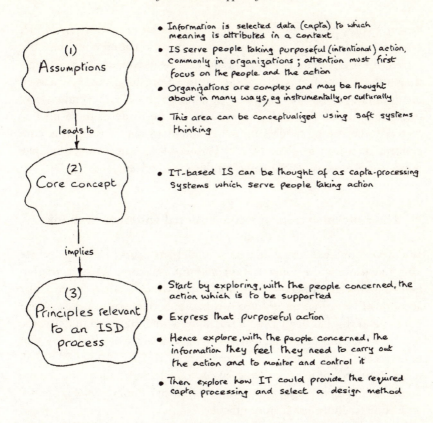

(1)
Assumptions

- Information is selected data (capta) to which meaning is attributed in a context
- IS serve people taking purposeful (intentional) action, commonly in organizations; attention must first focus on the people and the action
- Organizations are complex and may be thought about in many ways, eg instrumentally, or culturally
- This area can be conceptualized using soft systems thinking

leads to

(2)
Core concept

- IT-based IS can be thought of as capta-processing systems which serve people taking action

implies

(3)
Principles relevant to an ISD process

- Start by exploring, with the people concerned, the action which is to be supported
- Express that purposeful action
- Hence explore, with the people concerned, the information they feel they need to carry out the action and to monitor and control it
- Then explore how IT could provide the required capta processing and select a design method

Figure 4.9. *A summary of the argument concerning 'information system' and 'information system development'*

model. Such models would provide a better basis for initial customer-vendor discussion than any documentation of system architecture expressed in the language of IT. In the very best form of dialogue between organizations and vendors the organization's model of the action it wants to support could be compared with the vendor's model of the notional system which their generic system serves. This would enable both sides to judge sensibly whether or not an appropriate customized version could be developed from the basic package. Figure 4.8 illustrates this idea.

Figure 4.9 now summarizes pictorially this discussion of the nature of the concepts 'an information system' and 'information system development'. A set of assumptions (1) lead to a core concept (2) which implies that the ISD process should take a particular form (3). The core concept is of course that of the twin systems of Figure 4.7: the purposeful action served (expressible in the form of activity models) and the system which can serve it by providing 'information' or by automating tasks currently carried out by people, or by doing both. This rests upon basic assumptions about the nature of IS and the nature of organizations, as discussed in this and the previous chapters. In addition there is the higher-level (meta-theoretical) assumption that sense can be made of these phenomena by the use of systems thinking. These assumptions and the core concept then lead to element 3 of Figure 4.9, the necessary principles informing a process of ISD based on this core concept.

The concepts versus the conventional wisdom: textbooks

We have now examined the ideas which in everyday language are captured in the words 'organization' and 'information'. We have tried to build a coherent concept of both of them which leads to a particular account of 'information systems' in the context of 'organizations'. An outcome of this has been a set of principles which ought to underlie the process of creating IS which support real-world action, including that undertaken in the name of an organization. In later chapters we shall relate all this to some of our experiences in real organizations, but before doing that it is interesting to compare the ISD implied by Figure 4.9 with some accounts of current practice.

If we start by comparing the model of IS and the IS development process developed here with the picture presented to students in most current college textbooks, we find the latter all telling the same bland story. We pointed out in Chapter Three that most textbooks take a very instrumental, functional, goal-seeking view of organizations, one which is usually asserted without the authors feeling that any justification is required. Indeed, Aiba (1993), studying the concepts offered to students in textbooks of IS, found that many of the books she examined did not bother to include any definitions of what their authors meant by 'organization', even though it is the context of most work on IS development, and is a concept which is far from unproblematical. When a definition was given, it was of a goal-seeking entity, functionally organized, as shown in Table 3.1. What then follows from that is that the authors, writing about the nature of IS and how they are created in organizations, can duck the problematical issues surrounding the nature of an organization. Taking the idea as given, or at least as unproblematical, they give work on IS the role of supporting the organizational

Table 4.3. *Text book assertions concerning the interaction of IS with organizational activity*

Ahituv and Neumann (3rd edition, 1990)	Decision making is a three-stage process. Each stage requires a different type of information. Therefore, information requirement analysis should begin with an explicit definition of the decision stage to be supported . . . (page 67) A key to the success of the information system function . . . is a comprehensive, effective planning system. (page 229) The information system planning process has to be an integral part of overall organizational planning. (page 230)
Alter (1992)	. . . an information system plan should be consistent with the firm's strategy, goals, and operational plans. . . . information system planning should be an integral part of business planning. Business planning is the process of identifying the firm's goals, objectives, and priorities and developing action plans . . . (page 589)
Lucas (5th edition, 1994)	A key task of top management is formulating corporate strategy. There are three levels of integration of information technology with corporate strategy . . . (page 103)
O'Brien (7th edition, 1994)	A formal information systems planning process that is part of the regular business planning process of the organization is highly desirable. There are typically many opportunities to use information systems to support an organization's end users and its business operations, management decision making, and strategic objectives. (page 356)
Schultheis and Sumner (3rd edition, 1995)	. . . one of the major purposes of information systems planning is to define application development projects that support the strategic goals of the organization. (page 613)
Zwass (1992)	A long-term MIS plan has to be aligned or coordinated with the corporate long-term plan. (page 679) In MIS planning, the strategic business directions set out in the corresponding business plans are reviewed. A long-term MIS plan may be derived directly from an organization's strategic business plan. (page 680)

processes of planning and carrying out operations at various levels. It is, in general, assumed that the organization will have in place a strategic planning system sitting at the top of a hierarchy of planning systems and that the role of the IS function will be to attach itself to those systems. The IS which support both the planning activity and the operations which follow from it can then be developed. The stance adopted is illustrated in Table 4.3 with quotations from a number of textbooks used in the 1990s.

These quotations have a strange 1960s air about them. They might well have been written then, in the heyday of organizational planning, when large organizations were rushing to set up corporate planning departments which would produce the master plan from which various functional operational plans would then be developed in a bureaucratic planning Utopia. Now that such departments have been widely abandoned, it is strange to find IS literature – at least at the textbook level – lagging so far behind.

The intellectual effect of this lag, for the IS textbooks, is that when they move on to accounts of IS development, organizational analysis gets very short shrift indeed. Many of them make use of such ready-made frameworks as the four-cell matrix proposed by McFarlan (1981) and McFarlan and McKenny (1983). This has the strategic impact of existing IS on one axis ('high', or 'low') and the strategic impact of future IS on the other, also 'high' or 'low'. The cells thus created yield four supposed organization types: 'factory', 'support', 'strategic' and 'turnaround'. (Banks, for example, would be in the 'high – high' cell: IT having high impact both with current applications and future planned ones.) Suitable IS for each type can be discussed in general terms. But what is noticeably absent from these current textbook accounts is any kind of deep, specific exploration of organizational situations having problems which IS might help to ease. All these accounts of the conventional wisdom make big assumptions about the nature of organizations and about their having in place planning systems off which the development of IS can feed. They all quickly turn to the problems of the serving or supporting system in Figure 4.7 and simply do not pay situation-specific attention to the system served: the organizational intentional activity.

That this is so is further emphasised by their treatment of the initial stages of developing the required information systems. Table 4.4 collects remarks about the initial moves in IS development from the same texts quoted in Table 4.3. What is most noticeable about them is how quickly they focus on the serving system of Figure 4.7, taking the system served as given. Having declared that IS work can attach itself to the comprehensive business planning system which is assumed to exist in the organization, IS work is assumed to move quickly to consideration of 'the proposed system' (Zwass), the 'new or improved information system' (O'Brien), or 'the problems of the current system' (Schultheis and Sumner).

Currently, however – we note happily – a growing number of books in the IS field, some instructional, some aimed at practitioners, do take a more subtle view of the nature of organizations, and pay more attention to the need to gain a deep understanding of the system served (organizational action) before the system which serves it (the IS) can be

Table 4.4. *Textbook assertions concerning the initial stages of IS development*

Ahituv and Neumann (3rd edition, 1990)	A preliminary analysis is usually conducted. A project can be initiated simply because it is scheduled . . . according to the master plan for information system development, or a nagging information problem may be raised by users. (page 267)
Alter (1992)	Initiation is the process of defining the need for a system, identifying the people who will use it or be affected by it, and describing in general terms what the system will do to meet the need. (page 632)
Lucas (5th edition, 1994)	The idea for a new information system is stimulated by a need to improve existing procedures or to take advantage of a new opportunity. This need leads to a preliminary survey to determine if a system can be developed . . . (page 374)
O'Brien (7th edition, 1994)	Do we have a business problem (or opportunity)? What is causing the problem? Would a new or improved information system help solve the problem? These are the questions that have to be answered in the system investigation stage – the first step in the information system development process. (page 356)
Schultheis and Sumner (3rd edition, 1995)	Problem definition: examination and evaluation of the problems of the current system. (page 623)
Zwass (1992)	The objective of systems analysis is to establish what the system will do in terms of the firm's business functions. In its preliminary phase, the feasibility study, planners analyze the desirability of the proposed system to the organization. (page 723)

developed: see, for example, Jayaratna (1994), Stowell and West (1994), Stowell (1995), Walsham (1993). Tables 4.3 and 4.4, however, deliberately collect accounts of the conventional wisdom as that is encapsulated in the massive college textbooks of nearly 1000 pages. This underpins our wider general argument that there are serious problems for a field in which the conventional story presented to college students is such a long way from the day-to-day reality as professionals experience it.

The concepts versus the conventional wisdom: practice

In fact the rapid concentration in much IS development on data processing, with only scant or superficial attention first paid to the action which will be supported by it, is reinforced if we examine not textbooks but accounts of ISD methodology.

This is done here for two well-known and much-used approaches to information system provision, namely SSADM (Downs et al 1988,

CCTA 1990, Eva 1992, Weaver 1993) and information engineering (Martin 1986).

The structured analysis and design method (SSADM) was developed by consultants for the UK government's Central Computer and Tele-communications Agency (CCTA). CCTA had responsibility for over-seeing the development of computer use in the government service, and became interested in the adoption of a standard approach to ISD. Since 1983, SSADM has been mandatory in UK government projects, and has itself been further developed over the years; Version 4 was launched in 1990. Its provenance gave it a powerful position in the market and it is now very widely used in industry as well as in the government service. Weaver (1993) describes SSADM as occupying 'a dominant market position' (page 5) and Downs et al (1988) say that

> The most distinguishing characteristic of SSADM is its widespread adop-tion by both public and private bodies. That means that it is well proven. (page 142)

Unfortunately this well-established popularity of the method has probably contributed to a disinclination to inspect it closely and to note – in terms of the argument we develop here – some serious limitations. Now, SSADM undoubtedly does well what it sets out to do. Downs et al (ibid) refer to its

> good match between the level of detail in the methodology, and the needs and skills of practitioners. (page 2)

The problem is that it is often not recognized that a study using SSADM starts well down the sequence of events from recognizing an organizational problem situation to implementing an IT-based IS relev-ant to improving that situation. SSADM is concerned only with the analysis and design of the serving system in Figure 4.7, the data/capta processing system.

Its opening feasibility study module, stage 0, is not what those words might imply. The feasibility study 'carries out an assessment of a pro-posed IS system' (Eva 1992, page 28). The aim is to determine whether the system can meet the 'business requirements it is intended to meet.' That is where SSADM starts; the business requirements are assumed to be already established. Eva indicates (page 17) that the use of SSADM *follows* a process of, first, 'strategic planning' and then 'tactical planning', this producing 'a proper specification of a system to meet User Requirements' (page 15) which enables SSADM to be used 'properly'. Downs et al (1988) similarly indicate that a use of SSADM has to be within a context of organizational planning, but are clear about the limitations of the approach:

> Without planning, the development of information systems will lead to systems which are not integrated with each other or the strategic needs of the organization . . . SSADM does not address this area. (page 182)

The very ubiquity of SSADM use often leads to this being overlooked by practitioners. The method is silent on how to conduct the organizational analysis which, in logic, *must* precede design of a system to meet a defined specification. It is ironic that the existence of a near-standard method for system design should encourage neglect of the need to focus first on the intentional action which the IS will serve. The more recent work on the 'front end' of SSADM using SSM (CCTA 1993) is much needed, mechanistic though that initial effort is. Downs et al (1988) point out that surveys in the USA in the mid-1980s (Dickson et al 1984, Hartog and Herbert 1986) point to organizational planning as a major issue of concern for IS managers. This is coming to be realized, and there has been progress in this respect in the last decade, but the need to start with a deep analysis of the system served by the IS (rather than simply assuming that a coherent organizational planning system exists, together with a specification for the IS required) is not yet part of the conventional wisdom.

Information engineering (IE) (Martin 1986) is broader in scope than SSADM. It does work with an explicit model of what an organization is, and uses this to explore the organizational context of the intended IS. Martin describes IE as bringing together models of the enterprise in question, models of the processes needed to run the enterprise, and models of the data needed; these enable the need for data processing systems to be determined. This is a welcome advance on simply taking a comprehensive planning system as given. IE is based, however, on unquestioned acceptance of the simple model of an organization which has been described above as the conventional wisdom: namely, the simplistic model which sees organizations as machine-like, capable of being designed and controlled in order to achieve predetermined goals via rational decision making. Goals are expressed as specific targets to be achieved at a particular time, and lower-level goals derive from those at higher levels, in exactly the manner envisaged in the hard systems thinking of the 1960s. In similar vein, organizational performance requirements relate to what Rockart (1979) termed 'critical success factors', namely those things which have to go right if defined business goals are to be achieved. All this would make difficult any really deep exploration of organizational meanings and purposes, though the recognition of the need for an IS design approach to start from models of organizational processes is welcome.

Neither of these well-established approaches to information systems development, SSADM and IE, embody the kind of in-depth exploration of organizational thinking which is necessary if information requirements are to be richly captured. SSADM version 4 concentrates heavily on the secondary activity of data manipulation. IE includes organizational analysis, but on the basis of a very simple model which can hardly reflect the real complexity of organizational life.

In general, such methods focus very much on the data processing system rather than on the people and processes which that system serves and supports. This itself probably reflects the ubiquity of the step-by-step model of the 'systems development life cycle', which is dealt with at length in the textbooks (for example pages 254–313 in Ahituv and Neumann 1990, pages 620–704 in Schultheis and Sumner 1995). Though different authors use different terminology for the stages in the life cycle model (see Lewis 1994, pages 67–74, for discussion of this), the emphasis is always on the data processing system, not – as it needs to be – on the combination of the organizational action taken by individuals and the IS as the system which serves those people, individually or as a group.

Looking at this in a broader perspective of the thinking about management and organizations which has emerged over a longer period, we can roughly characterize such thinking this century according to the dominant metaphors which have been used for 'organization': first 'machine', then 'organism', then 'process' (Watson 1986, Harrington 1991, Leeuwis 1993, pages 34–36). In these terms it seems that thinking in the IS field is only now struggling to move on from the 'machine' image of organization, with the conventional wisdom still firmly rooted there.

This completes the fundamental examination of the ideas 'organization', 'information' and 'information system' which we started in Chapter Three. We are now in a position to link the concepts and models developed here to experience in real situations.

Part Three

Rhetoric and Reality in the IS Field

Chapter Five

The Information System which Won the War

INTRODUCTION

As we indicated in Chapter One, this book derives from two things which are intimately connected: helping to tackle problem situations in organizations in which information provision is an important feature, and making sense of those experiences by trying to think clearly about relevant concepts related to 'information' and 'information systems'. We pointed out that neither of these two things is prime; each helps create the other. So far, in the first four chapters, we have presented ideas, concepts and arguments which build up a view of IS and IS development which matches some of the more radical current thinking in the field rather than its conventional wisdom. Now, in Part Three, we shall describe some experiences in the real world of IS.

In the interests of readability, the story of the research underlying this book is unfolded more or less logically: first ideas then action. Parts One and Two focused on the ideas and presented a view which Part Three will both illustrate and enrich, leading to the view of the field set out in Part Four. In reality, of course, no research worth doing has this kind of coherence whilst it is underway. In reality, the experiences and the thinking, the happenings and the ideas about them, are all mixed up. But a detailed account of this would be no more than an erratic and in-coherent diary; it would be unreadable as well as very long. What we have tried to do is to tell the story by presenting a defensible argument about the nature of IS which is sufficiently coherent to make sense of the research experiences, some of which are described here. This will pro-vide a base for the enriched view of the field presented in Part Four.

The first account of real-world experience, the subject of this chapter, may seem rather strange. To start with, unlike the rest of Part Three, it is not part of out own experience; indeed, it happened before one of us was born! It is an account of some very significant happenings in the late 1930s which led to the winning of the Battle of Britain during the Second World War, in 1940. This is a well-documented part of history which takes on a new significance when looked at through the lens provided by the concepts in the first four chapters, especially Figure 4.5. For during the summers of the late 1930s, the Royal Air Force's Fighter Command created an 'information system' (though it was not possible to think about it in those terms then: the phrase did not exist) which enabled the German Luftwaffe to be defeated. Faced with Goering's inability to destroy the RAF over southern England – which Goering had promised to do in only four days of fighting – Hitler eventually called off operation 'Sea Lion', the planned invasion of Britain, and turned to the eastern front instead, attacking the USSR in 1941. This failure to defeat Britain in 1940 made it possible for the Western Allies to invade continental Europe from Britain in 1944. This would not have been possible without winning the Battle of Britain; and winning that battle would not have been possible without Fighter Command's information system, which had been created in the late 1930s thanks to the forward thinking of Hugh Dowding and Henry Tizard. So the title of this chapter is not too much of an exaggeration.

Writing of the Battle of Britain, an historian of the Second World War, Arnold-Foster (1973) pays tribute to the young men of several nationalities who flew the Hurricanes and Spitfires which defeated the Luftwaffe:

> The Polish regulars, smaller numbers of Czechoslovakian, British Commonwealth, and American volunteer pilots, the British volunteers and the British regulars worked together more efficiently than the Germans did. Fighter Command squadrons thought for themselves in a way the Germans did not. They wasted neither time nor ammunition. They were not daunted by being out-numbered. (page 66)

It does not diminish the courage of the fighter pilots to point out that what made it possible for them to work efficiently together, to think for themselves and to waste neither time nor ammunition was precisely the existence of Fighter Command's information system. This made it possible to use the information provided by the new technology – radar – to send the fighters to the point in the sky at which they would find the approaching Heinkel, Dornier and Junkers bombers and their escorting Messerschmidt fighters.

One important reason for examining the information system in some detail is that it owes nothing to computers, which did not exist in 1940. It illustrates that fundamental ideas about information systems are not at all dependent upon the particular means through which they are realized. Nowadays computers are normally involved, but that is not really a fundamental part of the basic ideas about information provision. That this is the case makes it clear that IS is not the same as IT.

RADIO DETECTION OF AIRCRAFT

In the early 1930s, the theory of air defence was that fighter aircraft would fly 'standing patrols' in the likely path of raiding bombers, being replaced by other fighters when the first patrol had to land to refuel. The intended replacement for so costly and inefficient a system was the use of fast-climbing 'interceptor' fighters which would take off only when bombers were approaching – but how could this be known, how could the course, height and speed of the approaching enemy be determined in the first place? This was the situation transformed by the invention of radar (Johnson 1978, page 75).

In 1887, Hertz had produced radio waves from sparks, and quickly became aware of how his waves were reflected from solid objects, especially metal objects. In 1934, before any such work had been proposed in Britain, the head of German naval signals research, Dr Kühnold, built radio apparatus which was directed across Kiel harbour to produce a 'picture' of a battleship. Aircraft flying through his radio beams reflected them, giving a serendipitous demonstration of the application of what the US navy later christened 'radar' (Deighton 1977, page 114).

In the UK in 1934, the director of scientific research at the Air Ministry, H.E. Wimperis, proposed that a scientific committee be set up under the physicist H.T. Tizard to consider how science could help with air defence. Wimperis meanwhile took the initiative in investigating every possibility and asked the head of the National Physical Laboratory's Radio Research Laboratory, R. Watson-Watt, whether a radio 'death ray' – beloved by fiction writers – was in fact possible. In reporting that not enough energy could be carried to harm either human beings or machines, Watson–Watt added a note for which he had not been asked but which helped to change the course of history. Ruling out radio *destruction*, he suggested that radio *detection* of aircraft might well be possible. The afterthought had been triggered by the consideration that even if a 'death ray' had been possible you would still have had to know exactly where to aim it to destroy a moving aircraft.

Watson–Watt's report went to the first meeting of Tizard's committee in January 1935; they immediately requested a paper on the subject, and Watson–Watt wrote the historic 'Detection and Location of Aircraft by Radio Methods', submitted in February 1935 (Wood 1969, Chapter 6). A demonstration was called for and later the same month this was arranged at Daventry, the site of a BBC short-wave overseas radio transmitter. At 90 mph, a Heyford bomber (the RAF's last biplane heavy bomber, fabric-covered but with a metal frame) flew a fixed 20-mile course up and down the Daventry beam. In a mobile detector van with a receiving antenna, the watchers saw the green line of a cathode ray tube grow a one inch 'blip' as the bomber passed. According to a probably apocryphal story, Watson–Watt is said to have remarked: 'Britain is once more an island' (Johnson 1978, page 81).

Tizard the scientist, and Dowding the RAF officer who in 1936 was to become Commander-in-chief of Fighter Command, at once appreciated the importance of the demonstration and subsequently fought for government funding for the development of the technology and the establishment, completed by 1939, of a first chain of 20 linked radar stations round the British coast from the Tyne to Southampton.

These were supplemented by the less sophisticated but very important network of 1000 visual observation posts manned by the 30 000 part-time volunteers of the Observer Corps. Before the war the general public liked to make fun of these tin-hatted middle-aged men in their sand-bagged dug-outs who scanned the apparently empty skies and made tea at regular intervals. But they became a crucial part of the system Tizard and Dowding created.

The radar stations could eventually detect an aircraft 40 miles away if it were flying at 5000 feet, 140 miles at 30 000 feet. Later they were supplemented by further stations, working on a shorter wavelength, to detect low-flying aircraft. During the Battle of Britain, the stations in the Isle of Wight or on the Kent coast could watch the Luftwaffe bombers and accompanying fighters forming up over Belgium and France and follow their course across the Channel (Bickers 1990, page 87). A German fighter pilot recalled in the 1970s:

I remember that I was astonished to find that each time we crossed the Channel, there was always an enemy fighter force in position . . . even when we crossed the Channel at very low altitudes the RAF were still ready for us. (Johnson 1978, page 94)

Meanwhile it was the Germans who had maintained a technical lead in radar during the 1930s. The German battleship *Graf Spee* had gun-ranging radar by 1937. When the *Graf Spee* was scuttled after the Battle of the River Plate in 1939, Deighton (1977, page 116) records that a British radar expert took a rowing boat out to the half-submerged ship to inspect its strange aerial. He reported that it was a gun-laying radar, something which no British warship then possessed. By May 1940, a German anti-aircraft battery, using radar, shot down a British bomber it could not see – which caused Goering to make the unwise remark that no enemy aircraft would ever fly across Germany (Deighton 1977, page 116).

Both sides were myopic about enemy developments. The report on the *Graf Spee* radar was filed and forgotten by the British; and, when the Germans captured a British radar set in working order during the advance in France in 1940,

German experts gave it no more than a perfunctory look before declaring it rather primitive by German standards, which it was. (ibid, page 117)

In the event, the fact that the British technology was cruder than that of their enemy did not matter. They won the Battle of Britain because they perceived as a problem, and by 1939 had solved through action research, something to which the Germans paid no attention until much later: how to analyse and act quickly upon the data which the new technology now made available. While German radar operators had often-confusing direct communication through radio telephones with pilots in the air, scientists working with Fighter Command personnel created, during the last summers of peace, the co-ordinated information system which enabled the battle situation to be seen and appraised as a whole. This enabled an outnumbered Fighter Command to deploy its resources so efficiently and effectively that the battle was won.

CREATING THE SYSTEM

Both the Tizard Committee and Dowding, commander-in-chief of Fighter Command from 1936, immediately saw the value of the radar

technology for the air defence of the UK. Most important of all, however, they grasped the need to develop quickly the arrangements by
which the radar observations, combined with the sight-and-sound reports from the Observer Corps – important once the enemy had passed
the two radar chains on the coast – could be collected, integrated and
appraised so that they could be the source of instructions to the fighter
squadrons. This was a considerable problem, since aircraft are very small
fast-moving objects in the immensity of the sky, and the fighters, in
particular, could expect to be in combat for only 15 minutes, with
ammunition for 15 seconds of firing, before having to land to refuel and
re-arm (Wood 1969, page 276). (Equally, Messerschmidt fighters accompanying bombers could spend only a matter of minutes over
London before heading back to base in France.) It was necessary for
appropriately selected squadrons to fly to exactly the right point in the
sky if they were to have any significant chance of destroying the raiders.

The problem of creating the necessary system was solved in the air
defence exercises held in the summers from 1936 to 1939. This was a
unique piece of action research under the aegis of the Tizard Committee. It involved three indispensable groups: the physicists under Watson-
Watt developing radar technology; engineers from the Post Office
seconded to the project because of their skilled knowledge of communication systems; and serving officers of Fighter Command (Kirby and
Capey 1997). The first completed radar station in the chain, at the
Bawdsey research station in Suffolk, was handed over to the RAF in
1937, and during 1938

> radar was transformed from an experimental layout into an operational
> system capable of being used in war. (ibid, page 61)

This 'transformation' entailed solution to the problems of collecting,
analysing, transmitting and presenting information upon which action
could be based. Thanks to Tizard's fertile mind, this work did not have
to wait for the availability of technically good radar equipment. Tizard
had been thinking about the problems of using the radar data for many
months when the 1936 air exercises came round, and he established a
team of scientists and RAF officers at the Biggin Hill fighter station in
Kent to do the necessary 'operational research'. (That phrase had been
used by Watson-Watt at Bawdsey experimental station: he defined it as
'investigation by scientific method on actual operations – current, recent
or impending – and explicitly directed to the better, more effective and

more economical conduct of similar operations in the future' (Deighton 1977, page 120).)

Tizard was unable for security reasons to tell his team about radar. He asked them to suppose that they had information coming to them at regular intervals 'from some mysterious source' (Wood 1969, page 79); this information would tell them the bearing, distance and altitude of approaching enemy aircraft. Their task was to take such information and use it to work out interception courses for the Gauntlet fighters to follow. In the experiments Hawker Hart fighters played the part of bombers, flying in over the Suffolk coast from the North Sea. Since radar signals were not then available, the Harts transmitted a continuous radio signal. Radio stations picked this up and telephoned the necessary information to the Biggin Hill operations room, where the RAF and civilian researchers tackled the problems of interpreting and using it. There were many problems to be solved, and there are several excellent published accounts of this work (those by Wood (1969) and Bickers (1990) being particularly detailed). It is worth recording here one dramatic part of the work, however, since it famously illustrates the joint contributions of the two groups we would now call 'designers' of the system and its 'users'.

The problem was that of quickly bringing two groups of fast aircraft together at the same point in the sky, complicated by the fact that the trackers were always working with slightly out-of-date information and were having to continually recalculate the bombers' course to provide a visual vector on a blackboard. The scientists called this the 'four vector interception problem'; complicated calculating machines were built to try and cope with it. The station commander at Biggin Hill, Wing Commander E.O. Grenfell, an experienced pilot, observing the arguments and exasperation in the operations room suggested he could do better 'by eye'. As Wood describes it:

> To prove the stupidity of the suggestion they suggested that Grenfell try it 'by eye'. Accepting the challenge, he called 'steer seventy degrees' and made further alterations to the fighters' course as he judged necessary. To the amazement of the onlookers he completed a perfect interception. Away to the east the Gauntlets and Harts met. (page 79)

Tizard rationalized what Grenfell had done intuitively in the 'Principle of Equal Angles'. Johnson (1978) summarizes it thus:

> It was based on the assumption that fighters are faster than bombers . . . if one draws a straight line from the bombers to the fighters and makes this

the base of an isosceles triangle, with the angle of the fighters' course made equal to that of the bombers, they will always meet at the triangle's apex. This simple technique, known as 'the Tizzy Angle', became the standard plotting procedure and would remain so until the 1960s, when electronic computers took over in the supersonic age. (page 91)

From the ad hoc operations room at Biggin Hill in 1936 and 1937 was developed the working information system familiar from many films: members of the Women's Auxiliary Air Force (WAAF) in operations rooms plotting incoming raids under the eye of controllers and their aides on a raised platform. These operation rooms were linked, by 1939, with radar stations, Observer Corps posts and fighter airfields in a dedicated telephone and teleprinter network installed by the Post Office. It is time briefly to describe that system. The account which follows draws especially on Wood (1969), Bickers (1990) and Deighton (1977).

THE SYSTEM AND THE BATTLE

It is interesting that the radar 'information system', as we would call it, is not usually described using that generic phrase – which in any case could not have been used at the time the system was created since the phrase did not then exist. Different authors describe it in interestingly different ways:

- Hillary (1942 and 1956): a 'ground control' system (page 77)
- Collier (1962): 'a system of early warning and control' (page 22)
- Wright (1969): a 'communications and control' system (page 63)
- Arnold-Foster (1973): a 'direction and control' system (page 61)
- Deighton (1977): a 'reporting network' (page 122)
- Mosley (1977): an 'early warning network' (page 93)
- Johnson (1978): a 'ground-controlled interception' system (page 90)
- Jones (1978): a 'communications system' (page 66)
- Price (1979): a 'fighter control system' (page 21)
- Ward (1989): an 'early warning defence system' (page 10)
- Bickers (1990): a 'control and reporting' (page 31) and a 'detection and reporting system' (page 33)
- Kirby and Capey (1997): a 'warning and control system' (page 562)

The essence of the system was that a continually-changing stream of data from the two radar chains and the Observer Corps posts was

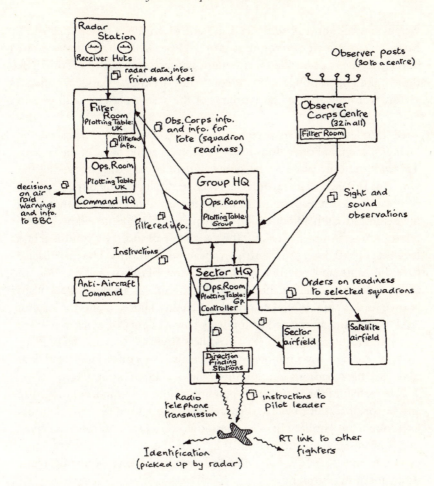

Figure 5.1. *The radar information system used during the Battle of Britain*

collected, integrated and evaluated so that appropriate fighter squadrons could be selected, instructed to take off and then given directions by radio telephone which would enable them to fly on a course bringing them to the bombers and their fighter escorts. After combat the system guided the survivors back to base.

Fighter Command, with headquarters at the mansion Bentley Priory, north of London, was, at the start of the battle, divided into four geographic groups, with the brunt of the fighting borne by 11 Group (200 aircraft) based at Uxbridge under its brilliant commander, Keith Park, a New Zealander. Each group was divided into sectors, each having a sector HQ at one of its airfields. The operations room at Bentley Priory was in overall control, with tactical control within a group area delegated to the operations room at group HQ. When fighters were airborne they were controlled from their own sector operations room. The three linked operations rooms, at command (Bentley Priory), group and sector, were the key to the working of the system, which is shown in Figure 5.1.

At Bentley Priory, in a concrete bunker, Dowding established the Fighter Command operations room which was at the heart of the system. This was the only place in the system where aircraft tracks covering the whole of Britain and its sea approaches were displayed, the display being a physical disposition of counters on a large map. The counters, indicating the height, strength and direction of enemy raids, were moved by WAAF plotters using croupier rakes as if they were in a casino. The controller and his aides looked down on the map from a raised platform. The map display gave the commander and his controller a view of the overall situation. In addition, on the wall of the operations room was a slotted blackboard known as the 'tote' which recorded the enemy raids and also the state of RAF fighter squadrons, indicating via a row of lights whether they were available in 30 minutes, were at readiness (five minutes), at take-off or cockpit readiness (two minutes), or in the air. The commander's task was to deploy his squadrons in response to the overall situation.

The format of the command operations room was duplicated at group and sector operations rooms, the essence of the system design being that everyone from commander-in-chief down to sector controller received the same display of information (but with the group and sector maps covering only their own geographical areas) with changes being made simultaneously throughout.

At the highest level the commander could transfer reinforcements between groups; at group level, the commander deployed his squadrons against raids assigned to him; at sector level controllers guided their own aircraft into combat.

An example of the homogenity of the system is the treatment of time. Each operations room had a clock with five minute periods marked in different colours. A raid designated, say, 'hostile 3', would be displayed by an arrow-shaped counter and changed in colour to match the clock as it advanced. All plots in all operations rooms would show the same colour; a lost or 'forgotten' raid would be picked up because its colour remained unchanged.

A very significant feature of the system at command HQ was the fact that the radar information from the two radar chains (for high and low-level raids) and the Observer Corps information (routed in via group HQ at Uxbridge) were not in fact passed straight to the operations room. First they went to what was called the filter room, with its own map table, and its own clock with colour segments.

The need for the filter room had been established during the air exercises in 1937 and 1938. Its role was to ensure the quality of the wealth of information which it fed to its own operations room (in the room next door to the filter room) and simultaneously to group and sector operations rooms. At the height of the battle, if the sectors in Park's 11 Group were to be used to capacity, accurate plots would be required at the rate of more than 20 a minute if interceptions were to be made, this in addition to the information coming in concerning more distant approaching raids. It was the task of the filter room officers to make sure these plots were of good quality, to filter out disparities and duplication, and to ensure that British fighters did not attack friendly aircraft. This was a job for experienced officers who got to know the characteristics of individual radar stations and operators and could compare, judge and interpret the data they received – very rapidly. They had a crucial role in converting raw data from radar into information for Fighter Command.

At group HQ at Uxbridge, Keith Park received filtered information from Bentley Priory and also, direct, the 'sight and sound' information from Observer Corps posts (which Uxbridge then passed on to command and other groups and sectors). As the counters built up on his map table, Park made his decisions concerning which sectors would deal with which raid, having from his tote board a continuously updated picture of the state of readiness of his squadrons. He would also decide when requests for support from other groups were necessary, which he would pass to command HQ at Bentley Priory.

At the sector operations rooms, usually on the sector's main airfield, the controller issued instructions directly to the fighters. Since their squadrons might already be airborne, there were two units at a sector operations room. One unit established and plotted on the map the exact position of their own fighter planes from their radio transmissions, which were picked up and relayed to the sector by radio direction-finding (DF) stations. The other was a duplication of group operations room with the same map, colour-segment clock and their own 'tote' board, all these elements displaying the same information as that at command and group. It was in the sector operations room during the battle that the Hurricanes and Spitfires were assigned to a particular raid, and continually-updated interception courses were worked out by a deputy controller using compass, ruler, paper and pencil, based on the 'Tizzy angle' approach.

When instructed to do so by group, the sector controller would 'scramble' (order to take off) selected aircraft which were at cockpit readiness. Here was the point in the system at which all the complex coordinated information processing now initiated intentional action: young men of 19 or 20 revved up their Hurricanes or Spitfires and took off to fight, with queasy stomachs. The moment is described by Richard Hillary, a Spitfire pilot, in *The Last Enemy*, the classic account of the pilot's life, which he published in 1942. He was killed in action in 1943.

> Down the loud-speaker came the emotionless voice of the controller: '603 Squadron take off and patrol base; you will receive further orders in the air . . . take off as quickly as you can please'. As I pressed the starter and the engine roared into life, the corporal stepped back and crossed his fingers significantly. I felt the usual sick feeling in the pit of the stomach, as though I were about to row a race, and then I was too busy getting into position to feel anything. (page 6)

Once airborne, the fighters were under the authority of the controller until the enemy were sighted, command then passing to the fighter leader in the air who spoke to his pilots by radio telephone. Conversation between ground and pilots, and between pilots themselves used the special language created within this unique culture: 'Vector 180, angels ten' meant 'Fly due south at 10 000 ft'. 'Bandits three o'clock angels 13' meant 'Enemy are due east at 13 000 ft.' 'Tallyho', from a pilot, meant 'enemy sighted.' The use of this standard vocabulary made it easier for pilots to understand crackling radio messages in a noisy cockpit. (This and other RAF slang quickly entered the national culture in the early 1940s. When schoolboys fell off their bicycles they would describe the accident as a 'wizard prang'.)

Back at sector, the controller listened to the in-air conversation; after combat he resumed command and brought the surviving aircraft back to base.

In achieving its main aim of enabling fighter aircraft to arrive at a point in the sky at which they would find the enemy, the system also maintained links with other relevant services. At Bentley Priory, for example, in the operations room, the commander-in-chief and his RAF staff were joined by officers from the anti-aircraft defences, the Observer Corps, liaison officers from Bomber and Coastal Commands, the Admiralty, and a man from the Ministry of Home Security.

These were all on the raised platform in the operations room, in telephone communication with their organizations – for example, the anti-aircraft liaison officer would order AA sites to cease fire when friendly aircraft entered their area. Dowding had general control over anti-aircraft guns and also the barrage balloons flown to deter low-level attacks (Wood 1969, page 86). Decisions to sound public air-raid alarms and to take BBC transmitters off the air also came from Bentley Priory's operations room, and an Observer Corps liaison officer was present at group HQ which disseminated their 'sight and sound' information.

The staffing of the system shows a number of interesting features. As the system was developed, new roles were being invented for which trained people were not available. Clerks were used to staff operations rooms but, as experience of the system grew, it was appreciated that it was essential for pilots to have complete confidence in their sector controller. To achieve this, experienced ex-pilots were drafted in, people who could identify with the problems the pilots faced. Wood (1969, page 90) points out that during the battle six of the seven sector controllers in the crucial 11 Group were former pilots. This sensible arrangement was achieved in spite of the resentment of the signals branch 'who felt that speaking into microphones and pulling radio switches were their prerogatives' (ibid, page 90). In general the system required personnel of better than average education. Bickers (1990, page 34) describes the WAAF plotters as coming mainly from 'the class that their comrades described as 'boarding school girls'.' Pilots were encouraged to familiarize themselves with the working of the whole system, and were supposed to visit the 'ops room' frequently so that they, from their side, understood the difficulties of the controller's job. Bickers suggests that the presence of the nubile WAAF plotters, known to pilots as 'the beauty chorus', drew the young men to the ops room even if a sense of duty did not (ibid, page 35).

Equally, at the leading edge of the system, where the basic data was captured, another new role had to be defined: that of radar operator. This was a demanding job for the WAAFs sitting in draughty huts peering for long periods at flickering cathode tubes, in locations which made them specific targets for Luftwaffe bombers during the battle. But the young women recruited and trained for this work were equal to the challenge. The official medical history of the RAF during World War II pays fervent tribute to them, in a passage which deliciously reveals some of the social attitudes of the day (Rexford-Welch 1955):

The trade of radar operator demanded patience, intelligence, alertness and appreciation of fine detail. The standard of girls attracted to this trade was high and a good type recruited, with the result that generally they were keener, more able to amuse themselves, maintained higher social and moral standards and had lower rates of venereal disease and illegitimate pregnancy than their contemporaries in other trades . . . (page 667)

This completes the basic account of Fighter Command's radar-based information system. Hillary the Spitfire pilot, based in Scotland before the Battle of Britain, at a time when the Germans were unwise enough to send single bombers across the North Sea from Norway, provides an account of the system's operation in the most favourable possible circumstances:

At this time the Germans were sending over single raiders from Norway, and with six Spitfires between Dyce and Montrose there was little difficulty in shooting them down. Operations would ring through, the corporal at the telephone in the pilots' room would call out 'Red Section scramble base', one of us would fire a red 'Very' light to clear the air of all training aircraft, and within a couple of minutes three machines would be in the air climbing rapidly. The leader, in constant radio touch with the ground, would be given a course on which to fly to intercept the enemy. So good was the ground control that it was not infrequent to make an interception forty miles out to sea. The Section would then carry out a copy-book attack; the bomber would come down in the sea, and her crew, if still alive, would push off in a rubber boat, waving frantically. The Section would radio back the derelict's position, turn for home, and that would be that. (Hillary 1942, page 77)

It was more hectic during the Battle itself! On Sunday 15 September, 1940, the day now celebrated as 'Battle of Britain Day' (though the battle was fought from July to the end of October) British radar detected a large build-up over the Pas de Calais in the morning and 100 Dornier bombers with a mighty escort of Messerschmidt 109s crossed the Kent coast at 11.30am, aiming for London. They were intercepted over Maidstone, squadrons were brought in from all sides and a swirling air battle broke out. On that morning eleven squadrons from 11 Group, one from 10 Group and five from 12 Group were put up. A second attack in three waves came in at 2pm. Thirty-one squadrons from 10, 11 and 12 Groups were in action, 300 fighters in all. Meanwhile there were subsidiary bombing raids on Portland and Southampton.

On that day RAF losses were 27 aircraft, with 13 pilots killed. The Luftwaffe lost 57 aircraft.

This day's fighting illustrates graphically that never in the history of warfare had there been so complex a battle fought at such speeds, and in three dimensions. That the RAF could fight that defensive battle, and, by remaining intact, win it, was made possible by the existence and performance of the radar information system.

It was on 15 September that Britain's war-leader Winston Churchill visited Park's group operations room at Uxbridge; he has left a vivid account of the scene in his war memoirs (1989 edition). Describing the room as 'like a small theatre', he gives an accurate appreciation of what he was witnessing:

> Thousands of messages (from radar and Observer Corps) were . . . received during an action. Several roomfuls of experienced people in other parts of the underground headquarters sifted them with great rapidity, and transmitted the results from minute to minute directly to the plotters seated around the table on the floor and to the officer supervising from the glass stage-box.
>
> I was not unacquainted with the general outlines of the system, having had it explained to me a year before by Dowding when I visited him at Stanmore (Bentley Priory). It had been shaped and refined in constant action, and all was now fused together into a most elaborate instrument of war, the like of which existed nowhere in the world. (page 349–350)

15 September was the day when the Prime Minister saw the lights on the 'tote' board, indicating squadron readiness, go out, heard Park request squadrons from 12 Group to help out, and asked him 'What other reserves have we?' The Air Vice-Marshall replied 'There are none'. Churchill records that according to Park's later account the Prime Minister 'looked grave'; Churchill adds:

> Well I might . . . The odds were great; our margins small; the stakes infinite. (ibid, page 351)

Churchill gives a very good account of his day at Uxbridge, and clearly understood how the system worked, but in the course of it makes a curious misjudgement, when he writes

> All the ascendancy of the Hurricanes and Spitfires would have been fruitless but for this system of underground control centres and telephone

cables, which had been devised and built before the war by the Air Ministry under Dowding's advice and impulse. (ibid, page 349)

The reality is that the Hurricanes and Spitfires did not have any intrinsic ascendancy over the Luftwaffe Messerschmidt 109s. There is general agreement among military writers that the three fighter aircraft were comparable in performance. It is not, as Churchill wrongly thought, that the system allowed the British aircraft to exploit a superiority. Without it, outnumbered as they were, they would not have been able to find and engage the enemy *at all*, given the short time between necessary refuellings. This enhances rather than diminishes our view of the courage shown by the young fighter pilots, a group immortalized in the most famous of all Churchill's flights of wartime rhetoric. Paying tribute to them in the House of Commons he said: 'Never in the field of human conflict was so much owed by so many to so few.' The pilots themselves, hearing this, said 'He must mean mess bills'.

Though the air war over southern England went on into the autumn, petering out at the end of October, it is generally felt that after their reverses on 15 September the Luftwaffe pilots ceased to believe that they could destroy Fighter Command and gain the command of the skies which a sea-borne invasion from the Continent required. The radar-based information system had enabled the defensive battle to be won.

AFTER THE BATTLE

Although they do not concern the radar information system itself, it is worth recording a few events from the periods before and after the Battle of Britain, since they illustrate that every information system, simply because it is a support to human action, will exist within a context of the never-ending political struggles which characterize all human situations. A state of all-out war obviously introduces simplifications into human affairs; it will be relatively easy to achieve an accommodation within which it is taken as given that a top priority is to defeat the enemy at all cost. But that does not eliminate politics.

We know something of the politics of the radar information system from the history books. In the years before the war, the scientific committee in the Air Ministry under Henry Tizard, which had perceived that such a system had to be created if the data from the new technology were to be of use, found itself in difficulties owing to the intransigence of one of its members, Professor Lindemann. Lindemann, who had

Churchill's ear on scientific matters, was reluctant to accept committee decisions and, through his link with Churchill, pressed his own schemes after the committee as a whole had turned them down. (He was particularly keen on the idea of small aerial mines attached to linked parachutes.) After a meeting in July 1936, two important members of the committee, P.M.S. Blackett and A.V. Hill, frustrated, offered their resignations. Lord Swinton, the minister, declined to accept them and solved the political problem he now faced by disbanding the committee; he then re-constituted it with all the original members other than Lindemann: the act of a real professional politician! (See Jones (1978) for a short account of this period, also Clark's biography of Tizard (1965), especially Chapter Five: 'The Political Birth of Radar.')

With the Battle of Britain itself, the main issue lay in disagreements about fighter tactics. Leigh-Mallory, commander of 12 Group (covering the area north of Cambridge) espoused the theory of 'big wings'. This involved assembling large formations of fighters before intercepting big raids, rather than intercepting at squadron or pairs-of-squadrons strength, as Keith Park did in the 11 Group area where most of the action took place and where interception times were very short indeed. Park also felt that, when he requested 12 Group cover for his airfields while his fighters were down to re-fuel and re-arm, their readiness to cooperate was poor. The enmity between Park and Leigh-Mallory was thus considerable. In 1941, 'war game' exercises demolished the 'big wing' theories, but by then Park had gone. Leigh-Mallory had powerful supporters in the Air Ministry, not least the deputy chief of the air staff, Sholto Douglas. After the Battle of Britain, Park was posted to Flying Training Command, and a new commander took over his group – none other than Leigh-Mallory. (See Wood 1969, pages 195–196 and 271–273; also Dowding's biographer, Wright (1969) Chapters 11 and 12.)

Hugh Dowding, an austere man of 'bleak and melancholy countenance' (Bickers 1990, page 107), known as 'Stuffy' Dowding to his pilots, but with the affection reserved for a father figure, was not a political animal. Churchill (1959, page 346) uses the word 'genius' in describing his generalship during the Battle of Britain, but Deighton (1977) points out that he did not have the crucial political skill of leaving his opponents a line of retreat when he defeated them in argument (pages 59–66). Within a month of the end of the Battle of Britain, Dowding was relieved of his command and 'asked to do various mediocre jobs including the investigating of service waste and touring America' (Wood 1969, page 272). Dowding was replaced by Sholto Douglas. (See

Wright 1969, Chapters 10–14, for a detailed account of the treatment of Dowding.)

Henry Tizard, the scientist with the operational research skills which created Dowding's system, had a distinguished career at the interface at which science gives advice to government, but never achieved the eminence which his contribution might be expected to merit. Referring to the period after the Battle of Britain, Sir Solly Zuckerman, himself a distinguished scientific advisor to government, writes of

> the eclipse of Tizard and his committees and the increasing dominance of Lindemann (Lord Cherwell), Sir Winston Churchill's chief wartime advisor on scientific and technical matters.(Clark 1965, page xii)

Unlike Lindemann, Tizard did not go to the House of Lords. His biographer's final judgement is that Tizard was a man of integrity whose overriding concern was that science should benefit society. He made a sharp distinction between science and politics and would not mix the two:

> no man was quicker to pounce on any attempt to smudge the line between right and wrong; no man more suspicious that when science or scientists entered the political arena the fight would rarely be on equal terms. Thus in his attempt to achieve what were really political ends he was handicapped by an unwillingness to use anything which fell within his own clear definition of intrigue, a definition including much that passes as the common coin of political life. (ibid, page 418)

The treatment he received did not make Sir Henry bitter; Clark continues

> He knew that with the passage of years it would become ever clearer that the battle of 'the Few' had been won by the weapon of radar, handed to that bright company almost as the chocks were pulled away.

Thus the two men most responsible for conceptualizing and creating the radar information system – and the third, Keith Park, who used it so brilliantly during the Battle – were, in their political context, judged, condemned and, to different degrees, humiliated. Maybe they paid the price for being too clever in a national culture which suspects cleverness, or for being 'unclubbable' when judged by establishment norms. But they had saved their country.

IS LESSONS FROM THE FIGHTER COMMAND RADAR INFORMATION SYSTEM

Fighter Command's information system at the time of the Battle of Britain is a rich source of general lessons relevant to the development, implementation and use of any information system. These lessons have not been noticed by those concerned with computer-based systems, presumably because the now-primitive technology of the Battle of Britain system has hidden the fact that the system itself was in fact 'an information system'. From its inception that phrase has been associated, wrongly, only with computers, and it is worthwhile to examine here the IS lessons which emerge from the experience of the summer of 1940.

The Nature of the system

Firstly, we should note the importance of the foresight of Tizard and Dowding in spotting the need to create the system if the new radar technology were to be exploited. The need for such a system is obvious with hindsight, but the Germans failed to recognize that need, even though their radar was technically always ahead of that of the British. The very existence of the system, with its well-defined role, was crucial in giving the allies what would now no doubt be described as 'competitive advantage' over their foes in the coming battle. There is a lesson here for people thinking strategically in organizations: information provision is still often treated as a technical in-house service rather than as a potential resource. 'What advantage could we gain from IS?' is a question which should be kept permanently on the agenda.

Secondly, concerning the nature of the Fighter Command system, we hardly need to point out in this case that the information system serves intentional action: here, action to defeat an enemy in war. But, as is always the case, the intentional action can itself be interpreted at a number of different levels. At the level of Fighter Command as a whole, at Dowding's strategic level, the purposeful action served by the IS was defending the UK against the Luftwaffe. The system enabled Dowding to take strategic decisions concerning Fighter Command's resources. Churchill's remark about the 'genius' of Dowding's generalship (1959, page 346) refers to the latter's decision, early in the battle, to withdraw seven squadrons of fighters to rest in and guard the North, so that when Goering, believing he had drawn all the RAF's fighters into the southern battle, attacked north of the Wash on 15 August the Luftwaffe lost 75 aircraft (the RAF 30) and the day became known to the Germans as 'Black Thursday' (Bickers 1990, page 176; Wood 1969 pages 165–170).

It is the system's operational level, however, which provides the richest source of lessons for today's IS professionals, the level at which the intentional action is operational rather than strategic: a 'how' rather than a 'what'. At the operational level, the intentional action served by the IS was the finding and shooting down of enemy bombers and their accompanying fighter escorts. That level will be the one dealt with here, but we should note that, in our general model of an information system in Figure 4.5, the level at which a particular discussion will be held is fixed by *how element 5 is interpreted*, that element being 'assemblies of related intentions and accommodations'. The figure itself is recursive, relevant both to Dowding 'defending the UK' and to Park 'finding and shooting down the enemy'.

At the operational level, it will be useful first to consider the system as a whole and then to consider how it manifests the elements of Figure 4.5.

As a whole the system owes its existence to the development of a new technology, radar, which could generate a new kind of data, data about the location of distant objects. Tizard and Dowding recognized as important *capta* a particular sub-set of that data – that concerning the position in the sky of approaching hostile aircraft. They conceived the need to create the system which would process that capta into meaningful *information*. Thus, the information would be of the kind: 'this particular group of 100 aircraft, approaching at 14 000 feet at 230 miles per hour on a line from Dover to Maidstone, constitutes an attack which requires action by us'. On the basis of that kind of information, the system enabled suitable fighter squadrons to be selected, and interception courses to be worked out and issued as instructions. These instructions triggered the purposeful action of intercepting the enemy which the fighter pilots then carried out. Over time, with the repetition of attacks and the responses to them, the operation of the system yielded a store of *knowledge*, for example concerning the pattern of the attacks, which gave insight into German military thinking. Thus, in August 1940 an operational research study carried out at Bentley Priory

> proved conclusively that the Germans were proceeding to their targets with almost mathematical precision and that the priorities were still airfields and industrial centres . . . the main entry route for then current industrial attacks on Birmingham and Coventry were either Abbeville – Pevensey – Birmingham or Cherbourg – Bournemouth – Birmingham. (Wood 1969, page 194)

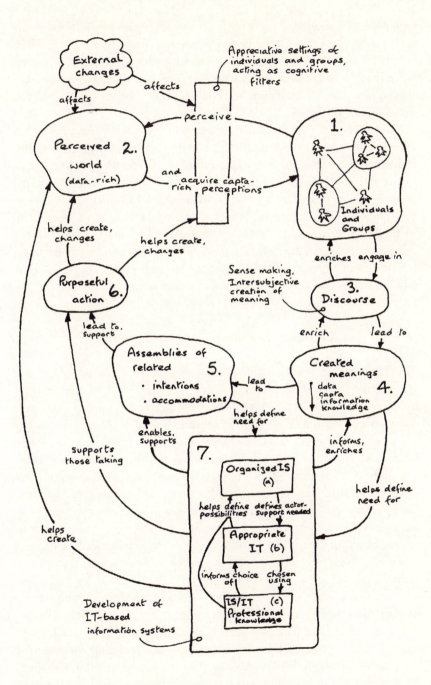

Figure 5.2. *The 'processes for organization meanings' (POM) model*

Thus was knowledge built up from the aggregated operations room raid tracings and the Observer Corps tracks. (Later in the war, when Bomber Command was attacking Germany, this kind of rigid pattern was deliberately avoided: the British bombers flew to targets on dog-leg routes, and diversionary raids were always mounted to try to fool the defences (Middlebrook 1990).)

Having shown that the radar information system illustrates both that information systems serve and support people taking purposeful action, and that they exhibit the data-capta-information-knowledge sequence of Figure 4.1, it is useful to end this section by examining the system in terms of the elements of Figure 4.5, the POM model, which for convenience is here reproduced as Figure 5.2. This will show that the generic figure may be used as a sense-making device; although it does not purport to be a *description* of every information system, it embodies the principles upon which information systems are created, and so its language may be used to give an account of any real-world information system.

Element One: individuals and groups

These are the individuals and groups who have a concern both for purposeful real-world action and for the informational support needed by those carrying out the action. In this case, at the operational level, these groups include both the fighter pilots who took the purposeful action on receiving instructions from sector controllers, and the people whose judgements were needed minute-by-minute as the military situation unfolded: filter room and operations room staff at Bentley Priory, operations room staff at group headquarters, and controllers at sector. Compared with most modern computer-based information systems in less dynamic situations, there was here an unusually close involvement in system functioning by people whose judgements were vital in turning capta from radar into the specific information represented by the instructions issued to sector squadrons. This had to be done continuously, minute by minute, during a raid. In, say, a modern information system in a manufacturing company which collects and analyses sales data so that a sales force can be given instructions, the pace will be much more leisurely and there will be a greater chance of expressing the required judgements about action in rules or formulae, which will allow some automation of that decision making, with only occasional intervention by sales managers, or intervention only at a policy level.

Element two: the perceived world

The outbreak of war introduces a considerable simplification into perceptions of the world. There is now a situation in which, while political in-fighting will not disappear, there will be a general consensus that we must prevent the enemy from defeating us, and must ourselves defeat the enemy. In the late 1930s the perception of the world held by Dowding, Tizard and the people around them was that war would come, that the UK would then come under air attack, and that defence was possible if they could achieve the combination of a 50-squadron Fighter Command equipped with Hurricanes and Spitfires and a means of using the data which a new technology, radar, could provide to direct the fighters on courses which would intercept attacking aircraft. By 1940, the information system had been created, and in that year Dowding also successfully preserved Fighter Command by persuading the politicians, against their inclinations, not to send further fighter squadrons to France as French resistance collapsed (Wright 1969, pages 99–112, Wood 1969, pages 96–101). So the scene was set for the defensive battle, and the perceptions of those who fought it at the operational level were that attacks could be repulsed if the data from radar could be expeditiously converted into instructions to appropriate selected squadrons.

We may note that this is an example of a worldview made possible by the availability of a new development in technology, namely element 7b in Figure 5.2 if we regard radar as an 'information technology'. The new technology made possible a new kind of action, just as long as the information system supporting those taking that action could be created.

Elements three and four: discourse and created meanings

Here the discourse which led to the setting up of the information system, and hence made possible the purposeful action which it supported, took place between operational research scientists and RAF officers during the experiments of 1936–1939. It is those experiments and that discourse which established that it was possible, firstly, to convert blips on radar screens into meaningful statements of the kind: '100 plus raiders are heading for London up the Thames Estuary at 12 000 feet, flying at 220 mph', and secondly to create a stream of responses to such information as the regular output of the installed information system.

Element five: intentions and accommodations

The intentions here were very clear: to deploy appropriate fighter squadrons quickly and economically against in-coming raids. Such intentions among human groups are in general formed in the context of the accommodations which embody the balance of power between individuals and groups. Here again a war situation is a simplifier, and any military organization is specifically constructed to make the power relationships explicit: orders have to be obeyed, and responsibility for giving orders is well-defined. Given that, there might be thought little to say on this element in this particular case; nevertheless, some of the behaviour within Fighter Command during the Battle of Britain did stretch and test the military accommodations which were the foundation upon which the system was created.

The bad feeling between Park, taking the brunt of the onslaught in 11 Group, and Leigh-Mallory, commanding the more northerly 12 Group, has already been mentioned. Leigh-Mallory gave support to his leading pilot, Douglas Bader, even when Bader's behaviour amounted to what Dowding, years later, was to describe as 'insubordination' – a refusal to obey a sector controller's instructions (Wright 1969, page 196). On 27 August, Wood (1969) records, Park wrote an instruction to controllers which thanked 10 Group for their consistent cooperation but added that

> 12 Group had not shown the same desire to cooperate . . . on two occasions when 12 Group had offered assistance and were requested to patrol over (11 Group) aerodromes their squadrons did not in fact patrol over aerodromes. On both these occasions 11 Group aerodromes had been heavily bombed. (page 169)

On 9 September, Bader, asked to protect the 11 Group northerly airfields at North Weald and Hornchurch but, itching to carry the fight to the enemy, flew instead to south-west London (Wright 1969, page 194).

Out of these origins developed the political row which, unjustifiably, was to cost Park and Dowding their jobs.

Alan Deere, a much-decorated pilot in 11 Group during the battle, wrote, in 1959 (quoted in Wright 1969, page 239): 'Dowding and Park won the Battle of Britain but they lost the battle of words which followed'.

This provides a salutary reminder that all information systems operate in a political context, politics being endemic in human affairs. Beneath the official rhetoric will always lie the intrigues and the pursuit of personal agendas which are the stuff of politics. The 'decision-making-in-pursuit-of-corporate-goals' model discussed earlier – the model which, according to the student textbooks, underlies work on IS – is not simply inadequate, it is totally out of touch with the realities of organizational life.

Element six: purposeful action supported by information

No problem here; at the operational level the purposeful action was that of the fighter squadrons who flew the interception courses given them via radio telephone by sector controllers. At this point the information system had completed its task. Wisely, its creators left conduct of the air battle to the section and wing leaders: the system's role was to *enable* them to exercise their deadly skills, not to usurp their fighting role.

Element seven: the IS and its technology

Though the procedures which constituted the information system were sophisticated, as has been described above, its technology was primitive by today's standards. The radar technology itself was crude in the 1940s, as were the devices used by the Observer Corps watchers to try to estimate visually the height of approaching aircraft. Communications were mainly by telephone land lines, and the Tizzy angle had to be worked out on paper with compass, pencil and ruler. But this technology was *good enough* in the circumstances, which is what matters, and the procedures themselves were honed to the minimum necessary to make the judgements, create the information from radar data, and transmit it quickly to sectors.

The professionals whose skilled knowledge enabled them to operate and maintain the system (rather than conduct the discourse in which meaning is created) included many groups: the radar operators in their wooden sheds peering at cathode ray tubes; the WAAF plotters with their croupier rakes in the operations rooms; the airmen who manned the radio direction finding stations; and the Post Office engineers who had to make sure that the telephone and teleprinter network was always intact.

That completes examination of the seven elements in the generic model. The paths between the elements in Figure 5.2 will, in any significant information system, be traced many times, and that will allow learning to be captured. It has already been noted that, in the radar information system, experience from elements 5 and 7 led to knowledge of Luftwaffe routing (yielding an enriched element 2). At a daily operational level, an example of learning comes from the fact that initially the least satisfactory feature of the radar data was the estimate of the altitude of incoming aircraft, which in the early period of the battle tended to be too low. This led controllers to add on height before issuing instructions. Pilots would then add on more since they were always very anxious to attack from above the bombers. The result was that interceptions were missed, and on 7 September Park, with his overview of the situation, issued terse instructions to his controllers about this, indicating that if group ordered a squadron to 16 000 feet but sector and pilots between them turned this into 20 000 feet, bomber formations could slip through at 15 000 feet. Interception could then be made only after bombs had been dropped, something Park always sought to avoid (Wood 1969, pages 215–216).

System Development

Churchill (1959) described the Tizard–Dowding system as 'shaped and refined in constant action' (page 349) and it is the case that the action research carried out jointly by scientists and RAF officers in the immediately-pre-war summers, together with the subsequent refinement of the system during the battle, offers a paradigm case of the successful design, implementation and improvement of an information system. No technical experts 'designed' the system prior to installing it on behalf of 'users'. Potential users and technical experts worked together, and their focus was not on the information system for its own sake, but on the purposeful action which it would support. All the activity of the information system was aimed at realizing the *outputs* from the system which the new radar technology made possible, namely courses which would take the RAF fighters to the enemy. There was none of the current debilitating split between 'users', 'business analysts' and 'IT experts', with too much attention paid to the technology, too little to the intentional action served.

When we consider the rudimentary nature of the technology available in 1940, and the complexity of the task in hand – not least the speed at which action had to be taken – it seems surprising that 50 years later IS provision provides many examples of spectacular failure. Compared with the Fighter Command system, most modern computer-based information systems have a simpler task. For example, a hospital 'case mix' system captures data concerning the flow of patients through a hospital and the treatment they receive. Such systems contain a database which brings together patient data and details of all the medical events which occur in diagnosing and treating them – such as taking X-rays or admitting the patient to a hospital bed for a period. If the treatment records include details of resource use and costs, then the system links resource use and clinical practice in a way which should enable managers and doctors to work together to monitor and improve both. This is a much simpler situation than that facing the RAF in the late 1930s, and yet there are many examples in the NHS of the 1990s of case mix systems being developed and installed without the involvement of the hospital doctors, nurses and managers they serve. In many cases expensive systems were purchased 'off the shelf', set up, and then switched off when they failed to deliver expected benefits, as was found in the evaluation of the NHS £300m 'Resource Management Initiative' (HSMU 1996) which will be further discussed in Chapter Seven.

In the post-war period, when mainframe computers were introduced into organizations, it is not surprising that what can now be seen as an unhealthy degree of attention focused on the intriguing new technology. Also, the computer systems themselves were systems which simply automated transaction processing, something which had previously been done by clerks on paper. Once attention moved on from transaction processing to more sophisticated systems, the technical experts were in place, the language of 'designing' systems for 'users' of them (rather than developing them with potential users) was established, and the thinking involved was taken ready made from the world of engineering projects. Thus a situation was established in which it was simply impossible to notice that the Royal Air Force officers and the Air Ministry scientists had already provided, 20 years previously – a classic demonstration of how to create 'an information system'. The principles so well illustrated by the Battle of Britain system can be succinctly summarized as follows.

- Start from a careful account of the purposeful activity served by the system.

- From that, work out what informational support is required by people carrying out the activity.
- Treat the creation of that support as a collaborative effort between technical experts and those who truly understand the purposeful action served.
- Ensure that both system creation and system use are treated as opportunities for continuous learning.

The legacy of Henry Tizard, Hugh Dowding and Keith Park is even greater than it is usually thought to be.

Chapter Six

Soft Systems Methodology in Action Research

INTRODUCTION

In this short chapter we introduce some accounts of our experiences in IS work. These relate our rhetoric of IS – the language we have used with care in order to clarify its core concepts – to its reality as we have experienced it in real-world situations in organizations. In this introduction we provide a more elaborate account of the thinking and methodology which underpins our work. In previous chapters – especially Chapters One and Three – we briefly introduced soft systems methodology (SSM) as an interpretive approach to organizational problem solving which can be used to provide a structure for action research in which desirable change and organizational learning are the aims. Frequently that change and learning is associated with the design, introduction and use of information systems, though those who developed SSM have never thought of it simply as 'a system development methodology' to put alongside such methods as SSADM or information engineering. It is more general than that: an approach to managing or problem solving whose application area of course includes the problems commonly associated with information provision. (In Hirschheim et al (1995) the authors, in choosing to see SSM as relevant to systems development methodology – as well as a general approach to 'many different kinds of political, social and organizational problems' (page 124) – place it as a 'fifth generation' approach concerned with 'sense making and problem formulation' (page 37) which has provided a basis for more specific methodologies for information systems development such as 'Multiview' (Avison and Wood-Harper 1990) and FAOR (Schäfer et al 1988).) Here we provide a more explicit account of SSM and its use in action research. As described in Chapter One (see Figures 1.7–1.9 especially), the essence of action research – much neglected, alas, in its literature – is the need to make sure that its research findings have a firmer status than mere story telling. This requires us to declare in advance an intellectual framework in terms of which what count as research findings will be expressed. We have tried to use SSM as just such a framework.

This is not intended, however, as a detailed exposition and discussion of SSM; for that, the extensive literature on the approach, both primary and secondary, can be consulted. Here the aim is to provide a general account of the methodology in action just rich enough to make sense of the research experiences in the IS field which are described in later chapters.

Discussion of methodology is not most people's idea of fun, and this is especially true of busy managers whose satisfactions come from action taken rather than simply understanding gained (the latter being often the more limited aim of academic researchers). But if any manager is observed taking deliberate action in response to a perceived problem or problem situation, then there must be some structure of ideas which makes that (deliberate) action meaningful to the manager in question; otherwise, except in unthinking panic, the action would not be taken. That structure of ideas, however rudimentary, represents for that manager some methodological underpinning, whether or not he or she has consciously thought about the ideas or simply acquired them unnoticed from experience. If the taken-as-given structure of ideas *is* thought about carefully, however, it may be possible to pinpoint useful principles which can be tested in further action and – if we are lucky – transferred to a whole range of problematical situations. Well-tested methodology is worth having, in spite of its necessary abstraction.

This makes careful attention to methodology worthwhile, not least because tackling real-world problems is so difficult that any generalized and tested methodology is worth carrying in your intellectual baggage, not to apply slavishly by rote but to use flexibly as a set of guidelines.

FUNDAMENTALS OF SSM

First some general principles underlying SSM will be set out; then its formalized process will be described in the form in which this is usually taught to students and discussed in the primary and secondary literature (though the latter is often flawed by the apparent inability of many commentators to understand the shift of the notion of systemicity in SSM: from assuming that the world contains systems to assuming that the process of inquiry into the world can, with care, be organized as a learning system). Finally the 'internalized' version of the approach will be described; this is how it is used by experienced practitioners who have embedded its principles in their thinking.

Some general principles

1. SSM is not usually concerned with well-defined (often technical) problems in organizations – such as how to maximize the output from a manufacturing facility – but with the ill-structured *problem situations* with which managers of all kinds and at all levels have to cope – such as what to do about researching new products given competitors' innovations, and how to plan, resource, carry out, monitor and control that activity.

2. In the 1970s it was possible to make sense of the experiences which led to the development of SSM only by making the assumption that social reality is not 'out there' as a given, like the physical regularities of the universe which natural science studies. Rather, it was necessary to assume that social reality in human groups is continuously socially created in never-ending social processes, and hence is not an absolute but will change through time, sometimes slowly, sometimes very quickly (see Checkland 1981, Chapter 8). This means that both the persistence of human institutions *and* their change have to be explained. To take an example, the Scout movement recognizably survives through many generations of members; on the other hand girls can now join what used to be 'the Boy Scouts'. Thus, a theory of social institutions would have to develop some dynamic model which covers both phenomena: persistence *and* change.

3. If we were dealing in human affairs with unchanging phenomena, then research could ape the natural sciences and consist of a positivistic testing of hypotheses to destruction. As discussed in Chapters One, Two and Three, this is the assumption made in 'hard' systems thinking, the social world being assumed to consist of systems whose performance can in some sense be 'optimized'. 'Soft' systems thinking, and SSM which embodies it, assumes a

more fluid social world, one which both persists *and* changes. This means that research seeks interpretation and learning rather than optimization. The questions to be answered are of the kind: how do these particular people, with their particular history, currently construe their world? How did they construe it in the past? What leads to some situations being seen as problematical? What would constitute improvements? What accommodations are possible, leading to what actions? How would they be judged? (Adopting this more roomy intellectual stance does of course, in appropriate circumstances, allow the adoption of the more confining assumptions of the 'hard' stance. But that is then done knowingly; it is not taken as an unexamined given. Thus, in this sense, soft systems thinking subsumes hard systems thinking as a special case (Checkland 1983 and 1985).)

4.   These principles mean that in the context of IS work the use of SSM means taking a somewhat radical position. To the authors, their stance seems necessary and defensible rather than radical; it is simply the stance required if they are to make sense of their experiences. They feel very little sympathy with the *MIS Quarterly* Editorial discussed in Chapter Two which declared that acceptable papers had to contain accounts of hypothesis testing. But they note wryly that when Orlikowski and Baroudi (1991) studied the approaches and underlying assumptions in research papers in IS, they found that 95 per cent of the papers studied were in fact based on a positivist epistemology. Such has been the stultifying grip, especially in North America, of the idea that research always consists of hypothesis testing.

The formalized process: 'novice' SSM

5.   SSM's focus of concern is a human situation which at least one person considers problematical. The development of the approach stemmed from the realization that all such situations had at least one thing in common: they contained people, and these people were trying to take *purposeful action* – rather than simply randomly thrashing about (though there will be plenty of that in most human situations!). It was thought that models of purposeful activity would be helpful, not to *describe* such situations but to *explore* them coherently. Methods of building such models were developed. A

systems model of a so-called 'human activity system' consists of two sub-systems: a set of activities linked together according to their dependent relationships so that the whole would be *purposeful*; and a monitoring and control sub-system so that the whole could in principle survive in a changing environment. Building such models normally requires a careful concise description of the purposeful activity, known as a 'root definition' (RD); and guidelines for a well-formulated RD have stood the test of time (Smyth and Checkland 1976). Figure 1.5 (in Chapter One) shows a human activity system built by taking the mission statement of the home furnishing company IKEA as if it were an RD. It contains broad-level activities which are derived from the mission statement and must be present if the mission is to be followed. Each of these could itself be used as a root definition; each activity could then be expanded to provide more detail, and this process can go on to more and more detailed levels if necessary. The status of this model is that it is an account of the purposeful system which, according to instrumental logic, is entailed by the mission statement. It is a concept, a logical machine for pursuing the mission. It is *not* descriptive of real-world IKEA; but it would not be surprising to find something approximating to it manifest in some form or other within IKEA; at least if would if the mission statement is taken seriously by the company!

6. Now, purposeful action can always be interpreted in multiple ways. The Olympic Games, for example, a purposeful event, will be viewed very differently by an athlete, a television advertiser, an athletics fan and someone annoyed to find the television schedules dominated by the games. This means that coherent models relevant to the games have to be based upon an explicitly adopted and declared outlook, world view or *Weltanschauung*. The model which uses the IKEA mission statement as its RD (Figure 1.5) takes as given the world view expressed in it, namely the belief that, in the home furnishing business, products can combine functionality with aesthetics and, moreover, that this can be achieved for a mass market. (That this is such a clear view makes this a rather good mission statement; they are frequently characterized by rather empty 'motherhood and apple pie' rhetoric.)

This need to declare a world view in order to build a model of purposeful activity means that SSM's models of human activity

systems could never be models *of* real–world purposeful action. *The
complexity of real purposeful action will always far exceed the complexity of
our models, however elaborately we formulate them.* But such models
have been found very useful as *devices*. As such they can be used
both to help explore the real–world situation (using the models as
sources of good questions) and to make that questioning an explicit
process which is in principle recoverable by anyone interested
enough to follow the process and see how it led to the conclusions
reached. Thus the models, in a phrase much used by the origina-
tors of the approach, enable us to 'structure a debate'. It is the
debate within which what would count as 'improvement' is defined for a particular group of people in a particular situation with
their unique history and culture, including their politics. It is also
the debate which must define what 'action to improve' is culturally feasible as well as arguably desirable; and it is the debate
which must find its way to the accommodations between individuals and/or groups with different views and interests, which would
enable action to be taken in the situation.

7.   These considerations lead to seeing SSM as a *learning process* whose
      idealized formal structure can be expressed as in Figure 6.1.

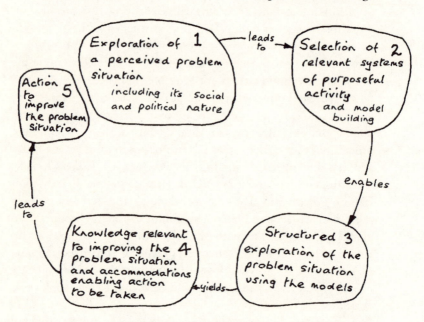

Figure 6.1. *The formalized structure of soft systems methodology as a learning system*

Note that the exploration of the problem situation includes not only finding out about its 'instrumental' features (official public declaration of aims and objectives, existing projects, etc.) but also studying its social and political aspects (Checkland and Scholes 1990a, Chapter 2). This is very important since changes which are both arguably desirable and at the same time culturally feasible are never the result simply of instrumental logic.

In the development of SSM it has been found generally useful to express problem situations in the form of pictures and diagrams as well as in notes, prose and collections of data. This stems from the fact that real-world complexity will always be the result of many interacting relationships; and 'rich pictures' (Checkland and Scholes 1990a, Chapter 2) are a better way to represent relationships than linear prose. They enable both instrumental and cultural relationships to be captured.

Stage 3 of Figure 6.1 can be conducted in many ways, and for different purposes. In our experience, one rich and productive way of using the approach is to get people in the situation to conduct the study themselves in open workshops, with facilitating help if necessary (as is described by Checkland and Scholes (ibid, Chapter 9) in an account of work done in the Shell Group). On the other hand, some professional managers and management consultants, in basing their work on SSM, use it as their private process, and may or may not reveal that process to their clients. Similarly, there are many purposes which a study may serve, and this stems from the many uses to which the models may be put. Suppose, for example, that the model from the IKEA mission statement were being used in that company. The implication of the statement is that the presence or absence of these activities, and these connections between them, could be seriously investigated. The model could help to structure debate about how the mission is being pursued.

Firstly, Stage 3 of the process could explore the real-world manifestations: does this activity exist? How is it done? Who by? How is it judged? What alternatives might be worth considering? etc.

Secondly, the model and its expansions would also allow rational consideration of organizational structure, allowing consideration of possible groupings of similar activities into departments or sections, and defining their links. (Perhaps we should add here that in our experience, real–life organization structures are usually determined at least as much by organizational politics as by rational thinking! Even so, that does not mean that a rational analysis of possible organization structure is not a useful item with which to furnish a debate.)

A third use of SSM's activity models is to inform discussion of management education and training. Such models provide an obvious and straightforward way to think about 'human resource management'. The model and its expansions could be used to define what attitudes and skills would be needed if people were to carry out the activities. These could be compared with current outlooks and skills in order to help define necessary education and training programmes.

Finally, and this is very important in the present context, models of this kind can be helpful in defining what supporting information systems are, in principle, needed, and their nature. This can be done by addressing the question: what informational support would be useful to people carrying out these activities? For example, starting from Figure 1.5 as a parent model, with further models added at more detailed levels of resolution, it would be possible to derive an IS strategy for IKEA, assuming, that is, that they wish to act on the basis of their mission statement. In other words, SSM can be used to guide and enact the IS–related processes in Figure 4.5, and to do so with a focus on the purposeful activity served by IS, rather than on the IT through which the IS will eventually be realized.

8.   It is important to emphasize that SSM, as a methodology – a set of principles of method rather than a precise method – has to be adapted by its users both to the demands of the situation they face and to their own mental modes and casts of mind. Users have to learn their way to versions of the approach with which they are comfortable. No two users will use it in exactly the same way. That this is possible without causing the dissolution of SSM is due to the fact that at its core is the idea of making sense of problematical situations by using, as devices in that process, systems models of purposeful activity. Would-be purposeful activity is ubiquitous in human affairs, and that is the source of the resilience of the approach and its transferability between users and between areas of application, one of which is the field of IS.

The internalized process: 'experienced' SSM

The eight numbered points above have very briefly summarized the principles of SSM and its idealized formal structure (Figure 6.1). Most users, inevitably, start with a step-by-step version of the approach; but once it becomes familiar, and experience with it accumulates, the user can begin to take it as given and can use it more flexibly. Eventually it becomes thoroughly internalized – it becomes an adopted 'way of thinking' which does not itself have to be thought about at all – and then, ironically, it becomes more useful than ever! Describing this 'experienced' use of SSM is not easy, simply because once it has been absorbed as a way of thinking it tends to become 'invisible', like our knowledge of the 'rules' for riding a bicycle or for swimming. But features of it can be recovered by introspection.

Experienced users of SSM are much more problem-situation-oriented than are beginners. The experienced do not start from the methodology, thinking about it and how to 'apply' it; they start from, and remain immersed in the problem situation addressed, letting it speak to them and using SSM to facilitate that process. SSM and its various activities – drawing rich pictures, building models thought relevant to exploring the problem situation, etc. – are then used, not to drive the study but to make sense of the emerging experience. Figure 6.1 itself becomes a device which is used both to grasp what is going on in the study and to define further sensible work.

Once internalized, SSM can be used in a very light-footed way. Sometimes we may see work being done which includes simultaneous action in stages 1, 2 and 3 of Figure 6.1, which is always to be thought of as an iterative self-generating learning cycle, rather than a prescribed sequence. Equally, experienced users of the approach may be found using it simultaneously, in parallel, both to illuminate the process of *carrying out an investigation* of a problematical situation and to deal with the *content* of the situation itself. Thus if, for example, a study is undertaken with the object of creating an information strategy for a particular industrial company, SSM can be used by an experienced practitioner both to help carry out the study and to deal with its substantive content related to the information support needed by people carrying out tasks in the company. In the two uses, which may well be simultaneous and in parallel, relevant models will concern, respectively, the purposeful activity of undertaking the investigation itself and the high-level purposeful activities which are the company's concern in its day-to-day world.

The main characteristic of experienced use of the approach, overall, is the use of the methodology not as a formula to be followed but as a sense-making device, that is to say as a means of helping the process of constructing recoverable and defensible understandings of a complex situation which can lead to action being taken.

In Checkland and Scholes' book (1990a) describing the second decade of development of SSM, a distinction is made between the two ideal types which mark the ends of a spectrum of ways in which the approach can be used (pages 280–284). At one extreme, termed 'mode 1' use, the methodology is taken to be a prescriptive set of stages to be followed in sequence. This is how SSM is usually described in the secondary literature (Forbes 1988) and it is the way most people new to the approach will start to use it. At the other end of the spectrum is a more sophisticated way of using SSM in which the basic model of the methodology (as in Figure 6.1) is used as a sense-making device. Both 'mode 1' and 'mode 2' are concepts, *not* descriptions of actual use; but novices will tend towards mode 1-like uses, more experienced users towards mode 2.

Use of SSM close to the mode 1 end of the spectrum is reasonably clear and explicit. Use nearer to mode 2 is much trickier to describe, and we are in any case reluctant to spell out a prescriptive account of use which is 'close to mode 2' since by definition every use of SSM, and especially uses close to this mode, will be uniquely tailored. Its form and content will be appropriate not only to the particular situation addressed, with its own unique history, but also to the particular investigators involved, with their particular attitudes and experiences. Nevertheless, we feel that it is useful to try to describe in general terms the broad process of inquiry which mode 2-like use of SSM facilitates. This is done below by means of Figure 6.4, which shows investigators moving from taking notice of a problem situation at time t_0 to taking action in the situation at a later time, the process being facilitated by a knowledge of SSM.

All uses of problem-solving methodology ought to be problem-oriented rather than methodology-driven; but since this is especially so for 'internalized' ('mode 2-like') uses of SSM, we first describe some recent work done by a research team of which we were members, and then present Figure 6.4 as a very general model which could apply to this use of SSM as well as to other 'mode 2-like' uses whose specific details would be different from those in the situation described.

An example of use of 'experienced' SSM

For several years a multi-disciplinary research team from the Management School of Lancaster University has been researching in the UK National Health Service (NHS). The work done so far, described in a chapter in Flynn and Williams (1997), has included study of the evolving nature of the new relationship between health authorities who, as 'purchasers', pay for health care services for a given population, and the 'providers' of those services – a typical provider being, for example, an acute hospital or a trust which provides community-based services. (Ham (1992) provides a rich account of the politics and organization of the NHS in the UK, and its frequent reforms.) The relationship between purchaser and provider is in reality complex, and is now changing; but one feature of it was simple and explicit. Purchasers and providers were required to negotiate explicit 'contracts', in which a purchaser paid a provider for a defined service over a defined period. These so-called 'contracts' were not legally binding but were administratively required to be in place.

In the first phase of the Lancaster research, carried out in the very first year of contracting, the aim was to gain a rich understanding of the purchaser–provider relationship as the new roles began to develop, so that themes for later action research could be defined, and collaborating purchasers and providers found. (A possible theme, for example, was the definition of the necessary information support for those negotiating contracts.) This was the initial situation. In order to do the early 'finding out' about 60 interviews were conducted. Both managers and health professionals were interviewed, in purchasing authorities, in general practitioner practices, and in provider organizations which included both acute hospitals and trusts providing community-based services (eg health visiting and district nursing). Since there is no such thing as neutral interviewing, and since in any case we wanted to follow a research process which was explicit and in principle *recoverable* by any interested outsider, the team started by formulating a crude concept of the contracting process. This took the form of one of SSM's models of purposeful activity, the activity here being to undertake the interactions between a purchaser and a provider leading to agreed contracts. Since the team knew little about the process at this stage, the declared world-view making sense of this model was that of *the researchers*. The model simply reflected their interests, which included information support, the financial aspects of contracting and the organizational learning involved in establishing a pattern of contract negotiation. This model is shown in

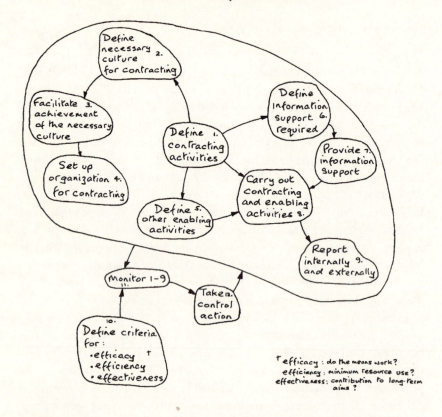

Figure 6.2. *The initial model relevant to 'contracting', reflecting researchers' interests (after Checkland 1997)*

Figure 6.2. It was used as the source of a set of questions about perceptions of contracting which were then used in the semi-structured interviews with NHS personnel. These yielded much information about expectations of the contracting process and also yielded insight into the NHS culture in which the imposed structural and process changes were being absorbed.

The aim was now to extract from the interview material an image of contracting *as it was perceived by the NHS professionals*, not the researchers. The process adopted, which was innovatory within the use of SSM, was to extract from the interview tapes and notes the entities and processes (the nouns and the verbs) used by NHS professionals when they talked about the new contracting process, which they were experiencing for the first time and about which they had various initial views and expectations. Reversing SSM's usual modelling technique (which starts from root definitions) these nouns and verbs were assembled into activity models for each site at which interviews were conducted, whether a purchaser or a provider site. For each site a model of the perception of their role by the people working there was pieced together. From these 'site models', *generic* models of perceived purchaser and provider roles were derived. These were sufficiently coherent eventually to be joined together in a single model relevant to purchaser-provider contracting. This is shown in Figure 6.3. This is an image of contracting teased out from what NHS professionals said about the process as they encountered it for the first time.

Reaching this point brought phase 1 of the team's research to an end. It had become apparent in constructing Figure 6.3 that the type of contract negotiated (block, cost-and-volume, cost-per-case) was not emerging as a main concern. The focus in purchaser-provider discussions was on determining the local pattern of provision of services, with different players (purchasers, providers, general practitioners) placing emphasis on different activities in Figure 6.3 depending on their history and geography. The questions and uncertainties which were surfacing were often of a 'strategic kind', including such issues as: coping with pressures from the centre; involving clinicians in resource-related decisions; improving informational support at all levels; monitoring long-term 'outcomes' as well as short-term 'outputs'; managing relationships with a range of stakeholders, etc. Discussion of such issues, based upon the model, now led to the initiation of several action research projects at particular NHS sites. These constituted phase 2 of the work. (Blacket et al (1993) describe phase 1 of this work, and it is placed in the context of the research as a whole in Checkland (1997).)

During the phase 1 work the eyes of the team were always on the problem situation, not on the methodology, but the latter was used to bring coherence to the research work. Firstly, the exploratory model in Figure 6.2 was used to structure the 'finding out' interviews; later the sense-making model in Figure 6.3 was developed in the process of finding the pattern in what was said by NHS people in the 60-odd interviews. The problem was to see in the interview records (sheaves of notes and audio tapes) an image of contracting as it was perceived by NHS professionals. Since contracting in the NHS is a purposeful process, SSM's models of purposeful activity seemed to provide a way of thinking about and expressing it. In the event, SSM-style modelling was done in the unconventional way described, by corralling entities and processes used by the interviewees, and then using them to create models

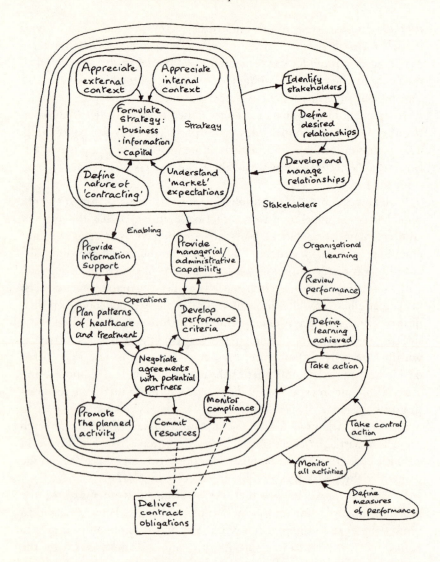

Figure 6.3. *The model relevant to 'contracting' teased out from interviews with NHS professionals, reflecting their interests (after Checkland 1997)*

expressing their worldviews. Those models could then be tested for coherence. This 'backwards' modelling enabled the researchers to shift from their own narrow perceptions of contracting (Figure 6.2) to an image of contacting (in Figure 6.3) which captures the perceptions of NHS professionals as the contracting process was introduced. Finally, we had an account of contracting which made sense in relation to both the

interview material and public discussion of the issues surrounding contracting at the time. Moreover, the process by which the sense-making
model had been derived was recoverable. Any interested observer could
go to the source material and follow the route by which the final image
of the contracting process had been achieved.

This is how methodology works best: not as a prescription to be
followed but as an explicit framework of guidance for sense making,
leading to processes which can be both described and recovered.

A general model of 'experienced' SSM

What has just been described is a specific example of a 'mode 2-like' use
of SSM. It can be regarded as a specific example of the process which is
shown in general terms in Figure 6.4. This is necessarily rather abstract
because the specific content of any 'mode 2-like' use of SSM may well
be unique – even though the specific example just described happens to
be potentially transferable to many situations in which qualitative
research is conducted.

In Figure 6.4, at time t_0, some investigators, having knowledge of SSM
and also some prior knowledge of a problem situation X, together with
prejudices about it and (possibly) some general concepts and/or models
which they use in thinking about the topic area, begin to take notice of X
as a situation requiring intervention. At time t_1 some structuring device,
here described as 'a crude model' is used to engage with the problem
situation. This will yield discoveries about the situation, and so will initiate
the learning process in which more relevant models can be developed, this
process being fed by an increasing understanding not only of the logic of
the problem situation but also of its cultural (including political) aspects.
(In the NHS work described above the initial interviews increased the
team's knowledge not only of the reasonably rational process of agreeing
contracts but also of NHS culture and the politics of the purchaser/
provider split. For example, the notion of an 'internal market' in providing health services, which was strong in the early government rhetoric
when the NHS changes were introduced, quickly came up against political imperatives. It became obvious that no purchaser could undermine the
viability of a local hospital simply because apparently cheaper services were
available 20 miles away. Such closures would have been politically unac-
ceptable; voters care about 'my local hospital'.)

The learning from the use of 'crude models' will enrich the engagement with the problem situation and eventually – at time t_2 in Figure 6.4

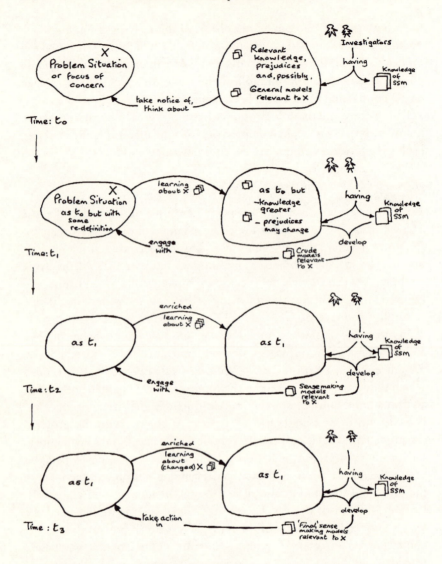

Figure 6.4. *The process of inquiry which 'mode 2' use of SSM facilitates*

– enable rather more relevant models to be developed, ones which are described here as 'sense-making.' The shift from crude to sense-making models, made possible by the lightly-structured (but at the same time well-thought-out) engagement with the situation, is motivated by the desire to move towards action, since this is methodology oriented to action taken rather than simply understanding gained. In the example given, the desired action happened to be the initiation of action research at NHS locations with collaborating organizations, but in general can be thought of as 'action to improve' the original situation. Taking this action (at time t_3 in the figure) will change situation X and the whole (hermeneutic) learning cycle can begin again: ending a soft systems study needs to be seen as an essentially arbitrary act.

Table 6.1 summarizes the mapping between the specific example given and the generalized model of 'mode 2-like' SSM. We have had a number of experiences which could be described using the image provided by Figure 6.4. But we must enter the caveat that it should not be taken as a once-and-for-all definitive account of 'mode-2 like' use of SSM. Because SSM is methodology (the logos of method, principles of method) not *a* method, there will always be room for creative, innovative use of those principles, use which is specific to a particular situation, particular participants and particular users of the methodology. This fatally undermines the generalized assertions about SSM which are often found in the secondary literature.

Table 6.1. *A mapping of Figure 6.4 and a real example of 'mode 2-like' use of soft systems methodology*

Stage and time in Figure 6.4	Manifestation
Stage 1, t_0	A Lancaster University Management School team, experienced in research in the NHS, receive Research Council funding to research 'Managing the Contracting Process in the NHS' under the 'Contracts and Competition' programme (ESRC Award L114251025)
Stage 2, t_1	2.1 A crude activity model of contracting (Figure 6.2) is built, based on researchers' interests.
	2.2 The model is used to define questions for semi-structured interviews at 19 NHS locations.
Stage 3, t_2	3.1 60+ interviews are conducted, covering purchasers, providers (acute and community-based services), general practitioners.
	3.2 Activity models of contracting for each site are teased out from interview and notes and tapes.
	3.3 Activity models for the roles 'purchasers' and 'provider' are derived.
Stage 4, t_3	4.1 Activity models for 'purchasers' and 'providers' are combined in a single model of the contracting process as it is perceived by NHS professionals in the first year of contracting (Figure 6.3).
	4.2 Themes of concern are discussed at interview sites.
	4.3 Agreement is gained for action research projects at 4 NHS sites.
	4.4 Action research projects are initiated.

This completes the brief account of the methodology which informs the fieldwork described in the next chapter. Information systems are there to support people who are trying to take purposeful action. Hence there is a role in the field of IS for an approach based upon the use of models of purposeful activity which can help us to make sense of real-world action before asking what informational support will be helpful to those undertaking it.

Chapter Seven

Experiences in the Field

INTRODUCTION

The intention here is to enrich the material in previous chapters with examples chosen from the work carried out in collaborating organizations during the course of the research. As is indicated in the very first figure in the book (Figure 1.1), the research process has entailed simultaneous work of two kinds, each feeding the other: practical projects in organizations combined with thinking out the ideas expressed in Chapters Two, Three and Four. The research itself struggled with the entwining of the two as each fed, and fed off the other, but in this book they are separated for the sake of clear expression. In reality neither came first, and the final act in the research has been to try to make sense of the lived experiences, both practical and intellectual, in relation to each other. In this chapter we draw on features of the practical projects in order to illustrate the concept of IS which simultaneously fed, and was the ultimate product of those experiences.

The examples described briefly in this chapter come from work in both industry and the public sector, with the emphasis on the latter. This reflects the thrust of the last decade of development of SSM. Initially the action research which produced SSM was carried out in industry because it was industrial managers who realized the need for better, that is to say more holistic ways of tackling the kind of problem situations they had to deal with: situations characterized by multiple stakeholders and interests, problematical objectives and changing circumstances. This industrial focus turned out to be helpful to the development of SSM because, for all their complexity, industrial companies are in one sense simpler organizations than, say, local authorities or acute hospitals. In an industrial company there will be in place some kind of power structure which can cause certain actions to take place and stop others from occurring. This is not unequivocally the case in many public sector organizations. When work using SSM began to be carried out in the National Health Service, the Lancaster University teams involved found that they could not think about the NHS in a unitary way, as is possible to some extent with a manufacturing or commercial company. To make sense of their experiences it was necessary to think of the NHS as a complex network of autonomous and semi-autonomous professional groups through which the delivery of health care emerged, thanks to dedicated professionalism, rather than being routinely 'managed' in a conventional sense. This made it a good arena for the further development of SSM. Another reason why the NHS was an especially suitable arena for work on information systems was that the service had (and still has) a much less developed sense of the importance of IS and IT than is now normally the case in private organizations. That is why the illustrations which follow come mainly from working in the NHS, though the first ones describe work in industrial companies.

INFORMATION SUPPORT FOR RESEARCH SCIENTISTS AND TECHNOLOGISTS

The situation

The work took place in the central research and development laboratories of a multinational science-based group with manufacturing plants in many countries, the laboratories themselves being located in Europe. The laboratories were responsible for carrying out scientific and technological research and development, and their IS/IT professionals were seriously re-thinking the problem of providing those working in the laboratories with appropriate information support for a range of activities. These included such activities as: researching, managing projects, patenting inventions, writing reports and maintaining communications with people in the company's production plants to whom new products and new processes were transferred, or with people in other companies with whom joint ventures were underway.

Work in such sophisticated functions is always complex, and this is for several reasons beyond the intrinsic difficulty of such research and development work in a changing technology. Firstly, there is always a consciousness that such laboratories and pilot plants are very expensive to establish and run; and this goes alongside the fact that there can be no guarantee that they will justify their existence by producing a flow of inventions, processes and products which will generate more wealth than they consume. The uncertainty of this is compounded by the fact that other companies in the same business *may* at any time produce developments which give them competitive advantage. Secondly, there is no known formula for guaranteeing that innovation will occur. For example, ICI's invention of polythene was serendipitous, DuPont's nylon came from giving a brilliant organic chemist a free hand to work on whatever he wished, and the invention of the transistor in Bell Telephone Laboratories came from work dedicated to the understanding of fundamental physical phenomena rather than work aimed at producing a useful device (Large 1980, pages 44-45). In such work, in which the significance of current experiments may become apparent only in, say, five years time, it is extremely important that the information support for those doing the work is very effective. The support needs to ensure that the work uses all appropriate known knowledge as efficiently as possible, so that the company scientists are not re-inventing the wheel, and it needs to capture the knowledge generated in a way that allows it to be securely stored, easily accessed by those with authority to do so, and easily transferred to other appropriate scientists and technologists.

In the laboratories in question, the IS and IT professionals (for they had both, and a few people understood the difference between them) asked for help in a broad systems study of the 'information support problem', using SSM. The work was initiated by the information department rather than by the senior management of the laboratories. This was done in a situation in which the laboratory's scientists and engineers did not hold the information department in high esteem; but the department was anxious to change that.

Information department

The laboratories, which employed 1000 people, were organized into four functions: products research, process research; engineering research; and general administration. The information department (ID), with just over 100 people, and links to a library employing 25, was part of general administration. Within ID were four sections. Three technical sections were concerned with different aspects of IT and telecommunications, and one was concerned with the organization of ID itself and with issues of IS rather than IT. Our work was linked to this latter section, known as ID1, and it was specifically linked to the work of one of its members, Eva, who was temporarily seconded to be the leader of what was known as the 'Reorganization Project', working directly to the head of ID. This project, which had been set up by the department head, was described in an internal document in the following terms:

> The reorganization study is oriented to defining the activities of an ID within the Laboratories, a Department which has and maintains services tuned to changes taking place in the IT environment and as a result within the research organization being serviced. The study will result in recommendations on the activities, expertise and organization of ID1 (sic), and will analyse the role of information providers and users. The analysis is being performed with participation of clients.

The declared focus on the activities, expertise and organization of ID1, rather than the department as a whole, is significant. As the passage quoted clearly indicates, the project being undertaken was really a study of what information support to research scientists and technologists was needed *by the laboratories*. The real question being addressed was: what should be the structures and processes, the role and the expertize, of an information support function for the laboratories? The statement that the study's recommendations would concern merely one of the four sections within one part of the general administration function of the laboratories was a reflection of the reluctance of the head of ID to appear to be treading on the toes of other section heads within ID or, indeed, the managers of sections within the products, process and engineering research functions who were ID's clients. But the implications of the Reorganization Project, launched so diffidently, were clearly implications for the laboratories as a whole. This was a useful early indication that helping to bring about organizational change would not be easy in a company like this one, with a culture strongly committed to the questionable belief that among rational people consensus will always emerge.

Eva's Reorganization Project had been justified on the grounds that many technical developments were currently taking place in IT which suggested the need for re-thinking ID's role. The project 'plan of action' had declared:

> In the area of public information many developments are taking place which allow retrieval of information electronically at one's desk. This is the result of communication networks, on-line data bases and accessibility

to different computing facilities. Future expectations are that new media such as 'voice', CD-ROM and video media will extend the amount of information accessible as well as change the form. Access to Company information will increase as a result of the electronic mail facilities and the RPA Project [Research Project Assistant: a Company-wide project to improve information exchange between research teams and project sponsors]. The amount of information for personal use is also increasing as a result of personally-available PCs.

These considerations led to a list of questions which would be answered in the course of the project:

• What are the presentation requirements for information transfer?
• How should/can integration of information from different sources occur?
• What are the costs of information access, storage and quality?
• What are the possibilities for reducing information?
• What are the required skills of receiver and sender?
• At what rate will changes occur within the laboratories?

There is an ad hoc air about these questions, it being unclear why these particular questions are posed while many other possible questions are omitted. It was at this stage that a systems study was proposed by Eva to the department head, and the present authors were invited to work with Eva in order to provide a contribution from SSM to project thinking. The hope was that there would be a holistic impetus to the Reorganization Project.

The work done

At the initial meeting with the authors, attended by the head of ID, Eva, and other members of the department, it was agreed that the Reorganization Project would make use of workshops to which about 20 of ID's 'clients' from the laboratory's three functional groups would be invited. This was in keeping with the already-declared commitment to 'participation of clients', and it was suggested that the workshops should examine the interaction between ID and researchers in laboratories and on pilot plants, using activity models as a means of structuring the workshops. A basic shared concept of the situation, in which ID give support to the research process, was developed in the shape of the picture shown in Figure 7.1; as shown there, this led to a definition of some relevant roles

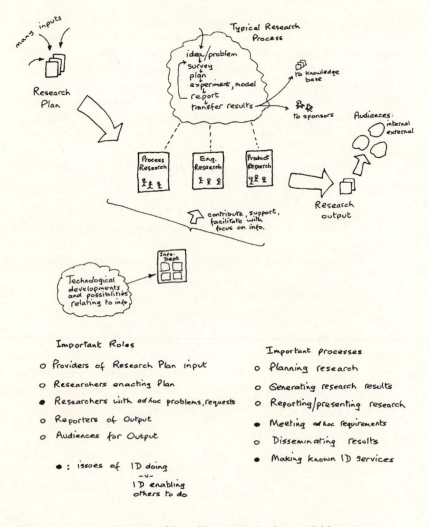

Figure 7.1. *An initial picturing of the problem situation in the research laboratories*

and processes which the Reorganization Project could usefully address. Also developed as a preliminary structuring device was a model based on the official mission statement of ID, which declared it to be concerned with

> the application of information and IT to laboratory activities; and the integration of IT-based information provision into those activities in ways which are innovative and cost effective and are a natural part of research planning, both globally and in detail.

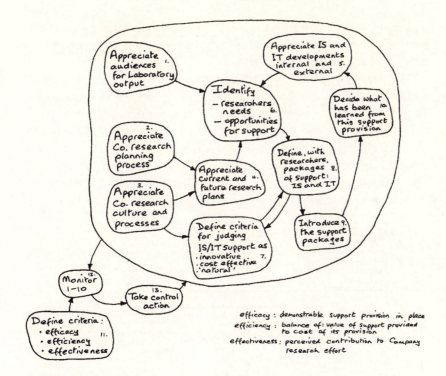

Figure 7.2. *An activity model built from the information department mission statement*

Treating this as an SSM root definition produced the model shown in Figure 7.2, an activity model compatible with the picture in Figure 7.1.

The work using Figures 7.1 and 7.2 was at the same time both a contribution to the next phase of the Reorganization Project and a demonstration of the SSM approach. It led to the design of two one-day workshops in which researchers and ID professionals would discuss the nature of the interaction between them and ways in which it could be developed in the future, including the tricky question of how to strike a continual balance between, on the one hand, ID as a provider of information and publishing services to researchers, and, on the other, ID as a provider of the knowledge and skills necessary to enable the researchers to help themselves. The notion of providing what are described as 'information support' or 'information support packages' (as in Figure 7.2) covers both possibilities, and the balance has to be struck in each specific instance, with an eye on both overall policy and the local context.

It was agreed that any models to be used at the workshops would be tried out first on some researchers, and it is significant that the minutes of a planning meeting prior to the workshops included among the conclusions the point that 'What the researcher needs is more important than how ID wants to use technology.'

The pattern of the first workshop was as follows. First the head of ID and Eva explained the nature of the day, describing the Reorganization Project briefly and emphasizing that its existence signalled an increased 'client orientation' on the part of ID; then the present authors briefly outlined the approach to be taken. Next some models relevant to the laboratories' role in the company, namely carrying out research and development projects in a particular industry within this company's norms, were presented. These models were discussed, argued over,

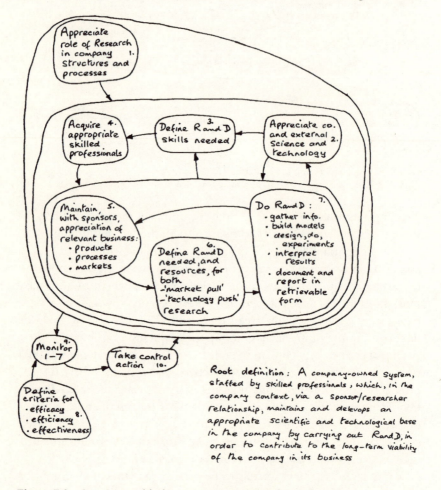

Figure 7.3. *An activity model relevant to carrying out R and D in the company*

modified and commented on, in small groups. This brought us to lunch
time. After lunch, further discussion, again in small groups, turned to
researcher-ID interaction. This was accomplished by focusing on activities in the models which were, or could be, supported by ID. This
provided a framework which enabled views to be expressed, feelings
revealed, hobby horses ridden, scores settled and possible hidden agendas
and constraints on progress revealed. In examining models before lunch,
the groups were asked to start from a particular agenda: identify any
significant activities missed out; indicate any irrelevant activities; adapt
the terminology where this seemed desirable; examine and modify the
links between activities if desirable in the group's view. Later, in discussing researcher-ID interactions, the groups were invited to take activities
which could in principle be supported by ID and ask: should ID *do* this,

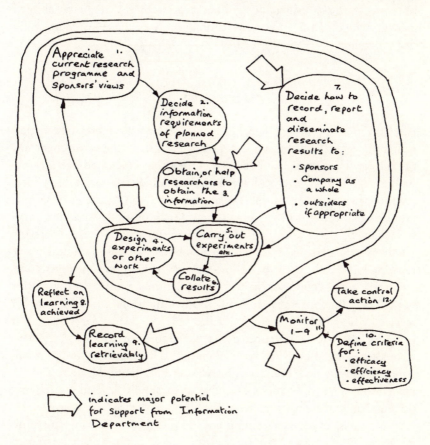

Figure 7.4. *An activity model which expands activity 7 of Figure 7.3*

provide advice, expertise and/or tools relevant to doing it, *provide education and training* or help to *manage* it?

Figures 7.3 and 7.4 show two of the models used: respectively a general high-level model to carry out research and development in this company in its industry, and a model which expands activity 7 of the first model. In the latter figure the fat arrows indicate activities to which the expertise of ID could contribute.

The second workshop, with different researchers invited compared with the first, followed the same general pattern except that after lunch the small groups, in discussing researcher–ID interaction, did so in the light of an account of a number of services which ID could supply, either to provide support to research activity or to help both with report writing and with publication and dissemination of findings. This was a response to the considerable ignorance of what ID might be able to provide which had been revealed among some of the researchers at the first workshop.

Outcomes

After the two workshops had been held, reports were prepared which gathered together all the work done at them. Both the researchers and the ID personnel who had been present felt that much had been learnt, with many issues large and small raised and discussed, at least in a preliminary way. For example, researchers raised the – for them – serious problem that their work generated very much more data and information than was ever included in research reports. Could this material, much of it in personal files and lab notebooks, be captured and made retrievable? Should there be 'ghost-writers' to help good scientists and engineers who were poor writers to report their work? Can literature surveys ever be done adequately by information professionals? For an ID service, where should the balance lie between being responsive and being proactive? etc. At a more general level the workshops had revealed a considerable gap between researchers and ID, in terms of both understanding and, indeed, contact. This was serious, given the increased ID perception, after the workshops, that they simply had to be 'client-driven', had to take 'research needs' as prime, and had to provide support systems, tools, expertise, training and education which were not only understood but actually *used*. (A contribution which had made an impact in the final discussion at the second workshop came from a quiet man who said simply: 'You should visit your clients'.) The general feeling was that since neither the research needs nor the state of development of the technology behind information support would ever be static, there was a need for some *institutionalized* form of on-going dialogue between ID and researchers in which specific support systems could be defined, developed, implemented, monitored, enhanced and, eventually, replaced. But what was culturally feasible in this situation? We modelled a system to provide for such interaction, so that the degree of change entailed in the laboratories' ways of doing things could be explored.

Eva now produced a phased plan for the continuation of the Reorganization Project, and this was discussed at a meeting between Eva, ourselves and one of her senior ID colleagues. The plan involved making changes first within ID1, to ensure that section's capability of filling a broader, more visible and more proactive role, and then within the laboratories as a whole, to realize the new researcher-ID relationship. The work within ID1 involved separating work on analyzing needs and opportunities, and meeting them coherently, from work to support 'publishing', interpreting that concept broadly. The aim was then to make sure that skilled professionals were available for both. The implementation and operation of a new role for ID in the laboratories as a whole would follow, but that was more problematical.

The head of ID was not able to come to this meeting, and his absence may well have been politic. We have already remarked on the low-profile, diffident launch of Eva's project, and its (unlikely) claim that the changes from it would be within one section (ID1) of one part of general administration. It was now very apparent that the head of ID felt less than comfortable with the outcomes that would inevitably bring about changes in parts of the organization outside his own department, though to his credit it was he who had seen the need for the Reorganization Project and had ensured that it got it underway. His determination to proceed with great caution, however, now led to a hiatus in that part of the project work which extended beyond the boundaries of ID, though he did 'test the waters' with an 'away day' meeting of section heads from the research and development functions, arranged in order to discuss with them the findings from the workshops.

In fact nearly a year passed, following the workshops, before a start was made on what was really the institutionalization of the process which the workshops had initiated and illustrated, namely organized dialogue between ID and its clients. The action taken was interesting and, in one sense, very ingenious. It consisted of setting up an 'Information Market' in the headquarters building of the laboratories. This was a physical location at which changing but permanent demonstrations of current IT were displayed. This was not only a magnet to researchers, it provided a location at which, beyond looking at or playing with the latest toys, discussions could take place between individuals or groups of researchers and ID professionals about the researchers' needs and how they might be met using appropriate technology.

The actual launch of the Information Market was an occasion of some style. Speeches were made, tours conducted. The head of the laboratories (whose earlier advice to the head of ID had been: 'Don't focus too soon') described the Market as 'a permanent platform for dialogue', and there was also a little bit of theatre: members of ID assembled polystyrene blocks representing the four functions of the laboratories, so shaped that the whole hung together only when a final piece, labelled 'information' was inserted! (This, it has to be said, provoked a little cynicism from some of the researchers present.) The demonstrations themselves covered such things as: molecular modelling using software which enables the shapes and sizes of new molecules to be worked out before they are synthesized; patent searching on CD-ROM; Beilstein (the organic chemists' bible) on CD-ROM; IT in chemical reaction research; production of tables and spreadsheets direct from recorders on chemical plant; advanced desk-top publishing; text editing, etc.

Two especially interesting remarks were made to us during conversations at this event. A recently-arrived new director of general services, who had returned to the laboratories after a gap spent elsewhere in the company, said how much he welcomed the initiative which the Information Market represented, since on his return to the laboratories he had been dismayed to find everything much as he had left it eight years previously! And commenting on the demonstrations themselves, a visitor made the thought-provoking (or doom-laden?) remark: 'Once you've got some equipment, *then* you can begin to motivate people.' We were glad to be able to discount this remark a little when we discovered that this man worked for a computer vendor! But there is a serious problem for IS behind that casual remark.

Learning from the experience

The work on the Reorganization Project just described yields a number of lessons relevant to making sense of the field of IS. These cover several different areas: methodology; provision of information support for people undertaking purposeful activity; and more general lessons concerning the difficult special role of an information function in an organization.

The learning generated by the project confirmed that it was a much-needed intervention in the company in question. The project thinking, certainly as far as Eva, its leader, was concerned, was sophisticated. She saw clearly that thinking afresh about ID's role had to be built upon first being clear about the purposeful activity which ID was there to support – in this case research and development in a science-based business. She looked for help in that from SSM, and its role in this example of its use was to help structure the rethinking, thus making a contribution to the coherence of the work.

In terms of IS, the situation in the laboratories can be seen as a dysfunctional version of the system which has been built up in earlier chapters and is shown in the POM model (Figure 4.5). In the language of that diagram, elements 1–6 (communication between individuals and groups; the perceived world; discourse; meanings established in discourse; intentions and accommodations; purposeful action) might be taken to cover the research and development work carried out in the context of international science-based industry; the three parts of element 7 (IS; appropriate IT and telecommunications; IS/IT professional knowledge) might then be thought of as capturing the work of ID. But it cannot be overemphasized, as was pointed out in Chapter Four, that the POM model should not be thought of as representing real-world structures. Its elements define a set of connected *processes* which can be used to make sense of real-world attempts to see the world in a meaningful way, form intentions, carry out actions, and support people undertaking those actions with appropriate information. The existence of IS/IT professional knowledge as element 7c (so that technical expertise is available) in no way implies that IS/IT professionals, as organization members, are excluded from the main processes in the model. Indeed, as full members of the organization, those IS/IT professionals must also be involved in the discourse in which meanings are created, intentions formed and action taken (elements 1, 3, 4, 5 and 6). In the laboratories, the system was dysfunctional because the information professionals were only weakly involved in the organizational discourse. The links between elements 1, 2 and 3 on the one hand and element 7 on the other were here rather weak; hence the contributions which 7 could make to 5 (intentions, accommodations) 6 (action) and 2 (their world as perceived by people within the laboratories) were inevitably much weaker than they needed to be. And it also followed from that that ID's role in the IS development process (as the latter is described in Figure 4.9) was not in a well-developed state. The workshops were an attempt to initiate and illustrate the kind of ID-researcher discourse which was needed; the Information Market was an attempt to ensure that that richer ID-researcher interaction would become permanent within the laboratories.

We might note here that in terms of the kind of IT networks which are now common, the working out of the desired intentions and pur-poseful action (elements 5 and 6) might now occur concurrently with element 7 (IS development) in the kind of interactions which take place using 'groupware' in the development of 'computer supported coopera-tive work' (Grudin 1991). The existence of the Information Market could catalyse such developments.

Finally, the most subtle lessons from the experience concerned the organizational role of a support function focused on IS and IT. It is generally accepted that in any organization, in order to carry out its primary tasks, other *enabling* tasks have to be accomplished. These latter include such things as providing buildings, capital and appropriately-skilled people to carry out the primary tasks. A common pattern, which applies equally to a manufacturer making lawn mowers, a charity helping the homeless, a university educating students or an acute hospital treat-ing patients, is to support these primary tasks through several enabling *functions*. These normally include at least two very basic ones, concerned with money ('finance and accounting') and with people ('personnel' or, in the modish current phrase 'human resource management'). Now, a good case can be made that such support functions in all but very simple organizations ought also to include an IS function, ensuring that the vital enabling resource of information is made available via efficient IT-based systems; and such a function should be headed by someone at a senior management level. But this rarely happens. Frequently we come across IS/IT functions with the status of Cinderella, reporting to a finance director who knows little about IT and certainly does not understand the difference between IS and IT. Why should this be so? We suspect because there is at least an uneasy feeling, a usually unarticulated half-understanding, that such a function, being concerned with information, that is to say with *the creation of meaning* is at the very heart of an organization. Any organization's most central activity of all, which is not usually institutionalized in the structure, is its creation and modification of a view of the world which makes sense of its intentions and actions, and which is meaningful for it in its context. This makes a competent IS/ IT function potentially very powerful indeed. Not surprisingly, most senior managers would rather treat such a function as a technical adjunct to organization activities, so that it can be prevented from becoming a threat to more traditional power bases.

In the project in the laboratories, the head of ID was certainly a careful, cautious manager rather than a bold charismatic one, but in our view his extreme diffidence about the project reflected an understanding that a powerful pro-active IS/IT function could so easily be perceived as a threat.

In any lively organization which is to remain viable, the process in which its view of the world is continuously created and re-created ought to bring in a very wide range of voices. This means that such an organization needs to find ways of both making sure that the fundamental IS work (elements 3, 4, 5, 7a in the POM model) is done, and making it widely known, accepting that the embodiment of appropriate information systems in IT will also call for specific technical expertise.

REORGANIZATION OF A SERVICE FUNCTION

The situation and lessons learnt

In the intervention just described, before we were brought in, Eva had already come to the conclusion that she could not advance the 'Reorganization Project' by simply posing questions related to IS and IT. How ID should be reorganized clearly depended upon the view taken of the research and development activities of the laboratories. We found we had no need to argue that point, though we were ready to if necessary. Prior to this involvement we had already had a number of earlier experiences which sharply illustrated the need to begin work on IS and IT by focusing on the purposeful action which will be supported by IT-based IS (as required by the 'two system' concept of Figure 4.7). One dramatic example in particular has already been described in detail in Chapter 9 of Checkland and Scholes (1990a), where it is described as 'a mature use of SSM . . . in the late 1980s' (page 235). The work involved a participative systems study using SSM, aimed at the reorganization of a head office function in the Shell Group, namely the manufacturing function (MF), a department of nearly 600 people located in The Hague. That project will not be described again here. This is only a brief reminder of its role in illustrating the need for good ways of thinking about, conceptualizing and exploring purposeful activity if work on IS/IT is to be truly relevant.

When the study was established there were several possibilities concerning what form it might take. Shell has well-established internal methods of tackling strategic questions; these could have been used. An 'information systems study' was also a possibility. In the event the workshop-based participative study using SSM (in which all 600 members of MF were involved to some degree) led to a new concept of MF; it was newly perceived as an internal 'service business' serving defined groups of 'customers' in the Shell Group, which could be, say, a group of 'operating companies' or could be the main board of the company, for whom the MF professionals were the appropriate people to propose and discuss options for the group's manufacturing strategy. But it was interesting to observe that the definition of that new concept also made sharp – for the first time for many of the managers involved – the *old* concept of MF which had simply been taken as given in the past: namely the assumption that the function was a collection of technological skill pools. It was very apparent in this study that had a conventional 'information systems study' of MF been the means of re-thinking its role, that project could easily have set about establishing the information support needed by the earlier, *unexamined* concept of MF which the actual study considerably modified.

On the other hand, as the IS support for the 'service business-oriented' MF was put in place, there were voices ready to insist or remind that MF, while taking on its modified role, still had to be a repository of world-class technological skills. This is a useful reminder that in the kind of cyclic learning systems developed in Figures 4.2, 4.3, 4.4 and 4.5 no static position will ever be reached. These systems derive learning from engagement with a perceived world – or, to be more precise, a *selectively* perceived world, thanks to Land's 'cognitive filters' or Vickers' 'appreciative settings'. That learning may itself be a source of changes to the perception of the world. (Thus in the Shell study the learning which created the 'new' concept of MF also leads to a new recognition of the 'old' concept and an appreciation of its virtues which also need to be preserved.) In addition the (selectively) perceived world will at the same time be changed continually by happenings completely external to the learning system itself – as when, for example, competitors to the company with the central research laboratories in the previous example develop a new process or a new product which requires a change of research direction by the company.

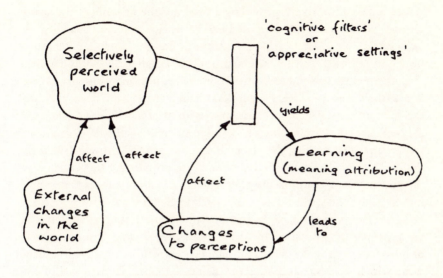

Figure 7.5. *The cycle of perceiving and attributing meaning to perceptions*

Figure 7.5 illustrates this dynamic nature of perception, learning, and meaning attribution, this latter being information creation if we use the word 'information' in its true sense.

This means that the concept 'information strategy' should never be thought of as something to be 'defined' once and for all and then 'implemented'. Rather, an information strategy needs to be thought of as the current position in a process which is on-going. The most important feature for an organization which is to remain viable is not that it has *a* set of meanings which it attributes to its world, and hence *an* information strategy and *a* set of information systems, but rather that it has a constantly-attended-to *process*, integrated into organizational activity, by which it adjusts to its changing world. Finding ways of institutionalizing that constant adaptation is something which few organizations do well.

EVALUATING A CLINICAL INFORMATION SYSTEM

The situation, general: the NHS

The core findings of several experiences of researching in the National Health Service (NHS) will now be described. This general introduction is relevant to all of them, providing a brief outline of some of the many changes which have been imposed on the service in recent years.

The NHS is one of the most popular institutions in the UK. Established by the reforming government which took office after the Second World War, it has always been funded from direct taxation, and so its services are free at the point of delivery regardless of the patients' ability to pay. It is the largest employer in the country, with nearly a million staff, and although spending on health has declined since the early 1970s as a fraction of national income, the absolute amount of public money spent on the NHS annually has continued to rise – to around £40 000 million in the mid-1990s. The innocent belief when it was founded was that spending on the NHS would actually decline as the population became healthier. However, many factors conspire against this, including: the greater expectations raised by the existence of a 'free' comprehensive health service; the ever-increasing range of expensive medical interventions which become available; the increase in the average age of the population. The effect of these outweighs some other changes which tend to reduce expenditure, such as carrying out 'day surgery' instead of keeping people in hospital as in-patients.

The NHS is thus always 'in crisis' over its funding, especially at a time when national policy is to try to contain or reduce public expenditure; many successive governments have sought to improve the efficiency and effectiveness of the service. Usually this has been by imposing *structural* changes. We may doubt whether such changes will induce desired behavioural, attitudinal and procedural changes, but the structure is the feature which government can change most easily. (Ham (1992) gives an insightful account of *Health Policy in Britain* in a book of that name now in its third edition. In a recent commentary (1996) the same author argues that 'the obsession with structural change that has dominated health policy in recent years has (now) given way to a focus on how staff and services can be developed for the benefit of patients and the public.' Butler (1994) gives an insightful account of the changes which began with the setting up of a government working party in 1988, in a collection which discusses evaluating the reforms, edited by Robinson and Le Grand.)

The Griffiths Report (1983), accepted by the government, found the NHS under-managed, and introduced a tiered structure with managers who were 'charged with the general management function and overall responsibility for management's performance' (page 5). In England, below the level of regional health authorities (which have since been abolished!), 192 district health authorities were each headed by a district general manager (DGM). Those in this new role had to decide the management structure for their district, get it approved, and appoint their unit general managers (UGM) in the next tier. A typical pattern in a district might be one in which there were three units for a population of around 200–300 000 people: an acute hospital, a chronic unit and a unit providing community-based services (such as health visitors and district nurses). The UGMs would report to the DGM, who was responsible to the relevant region.

This structure was dramatically changed following publication of the government white paper 'Working for Patients' in 1989. The rhetoric of the new policy was strong: changes would be made which would introduce a form of 'internal market' into the NHS, with general practitioners (family doctors) able to hold independent budgets, hospitals and community units able to become autonomous Trusts, as 'providers' of health services, and the old districts filling a new role in which they became 'purchasers' for health care services for their local population. Purchasers and providers would be linked by negotiated 'contracts' of the form: 'these services . . . will be provided for this amount of money . . . for this period . . . ' (usually one year). It was hoped that this arrangement would bring pressure for greater efficiency, though the so-called 'contracts' were not made legally binding, which weakens the usual connotations of the idea of a 'contract'.

In fact, after several years' experience of purchaser-provider contracting the rhetoric has calmed down considerably. Where an NHS Executive document of 1993 declares: 'There certainly needs to be a creative tension and robust negotiations between purchasers and providers', the 1996/97 *Priorities and Planning Guidance for the NHS* speaks of: 'the need to reinforce and realise the commitment in the NHS to partnership, collaboration and teamwork'.

The introduction of the purchaser/provider split is only the latest in a long series of changes to the NHS. The service has been in turmoil for some years now, not least because the cumulative effects of the changes have required, and continue to require, considerable shifts away from traditional attitudes on the part of both hospital clinicians, family doctors and those who provide community-based services. It is less than ever possible to behave *as if* required resources will always be available, with medical decisions taken on exclusively medical grounds. Doctors, nurses and the other health professionals have now to find ways of thinking like managers, as well as thinking as clinicians. This, in any field, entails deciding priorities and the criteria by which judgements of priority are made. Health is no exception (Maynard 1996, Dixon and New 1997).

Several years after making his contribution to changes in the Health Service, Sir Roy Griffiths, in a public lecture (1987), neatly encapsulated NHS history in the sentence:

> The triumph of the 1940s was the vision to create the NHS. The triumph of the 1980s and 1990s will be to create the wealth to secure it and the will to manage it.

In the mid-1990s the questions of funding and how better to manage it still dominate the debate about the NHS.

The situation, specific: the Huddersfield clinical information system

Huddersfield District Health Authority was one of the 192 such authorities in England set up following the government's acceptance of the Griffiths Report. One of its 'units' was a large acute hospital, Huddersfield Royal Infirmary. In this hospital a pioneering 'clinical information system' was developed, and this section describes briefly an evaluation of that project by a research team from Lancaster University Management School. What exactly is meant by the phrase 'clinical information system' is by no means obvious, and it was the way this was interpreted as well as the way in which the system was developed which made this a pioneering project, as will become clear below.

The Huddersfield project was itself one of six national pilot projects which constituted the opening phase of an NHS programme known as the 'Resource Management Initiative'. This was launched on behalf of what was then the Management Board of the NHS (later to become the NHS Executive) in Health Notice 86(34) from the then Department of Health and Social Security in November 1986, entitled 'Resource Management (Management Budgeting) in Health Authorities'. In fact, in the case of Huddersfield District Health Authority, the work which became one of the national pilot projects had been underway for some time – this being another aspect in which the Huddersfield work was ahead of the conventional thinking at the time.

Nationally, the Resource Management (RM) Initiative stemmed from the surprise felt by Ian Mills, seconded to the NHS Management

Board as director of finance from the well-known accountants Price Waterhouse, when he discovered how little hospitals knew about their resource use and the costs associated with various medical treatments (Mills 1995). When Health Notice 86(34) was sent out, attempts to introduce 'management budgeting' into the NHS were already under-way. RM was to be 'a new phase of development of management budgets' (DHSS 1986, page 2). Recognizing that the initial technical work on accounting systems was not enough, the health notice argued that doctors and nurses had to become involved:

> . . . if medical and nursing managers, and other professionals, are to welcome better financial information and use it positively, the informa-tion must be perceived by them as relevant to their work and must illuminate the key choices about how resources might best be deployed. Thus doctors and nurses must be centrally involved in specifying the information requirements of the new systems (page 2)

To reflect this wider aim 'the term "resource management" is used in preference to "management budgeting" to describe the strategy as a whole' (page 3). It was certainly the case at the time that the attitudes of clinicians were such that 'management budgeting' was not a doctor-or-nurse-friendly phrase, the automatic response to the word 'budgeting' being, at that time: 'nothing to do with us'.

At Huddersfield, work towards a clinical information system carried out jointly by IS experts and four consultants from Huddersfield Royal Infirmary had already been underway for several years when it became one of the RM pilot sites. Initiated by a very pro-active and inter-ventionist chairman, Peter Wood, the project accepted from the start that the 'clinical information system' (CIS) should proceed in the dir-ection, and at the pace dictated by the readiness of the four collaborat-ing consultants in Huddersfield Royal Infirmary to 'own' the project. The view taken was that without real ownership by clinicians there was no point in trying to create a CIS. In any case, the shape of such a system was unclear. The work was thus an exploratory exercise, learn-ing as it went along, rather than the pursuit of well-defined objective defined in advance. We were asked to appraise and evaluate the work done, the shape of which was not easy to discern for those immersed in it from week to week and month to month. They felt the need for a view from the outside as to what exactly was emerging from their work on a CIS.

The work done and the outcomes

It is never easy to evaluate complex interventions which bring about significant change in complex organizations, as is evidenced by the astonishingly rapid growth of the 'evaluation industry' among academics in recent years, with the emergence of a plethora of books, journals, societies and conferences. Since organizational interventions and social programmes are examples of would-be purposeful action, it is not surprising that SSM has been used in evaluation studies (see, for example, Checkland et al (1990), HSMU (1993), Haynes et al (1995), HSMU (1996). Normally in evaluation studies SSM is used in 'near-mode 2' form to construct an inquiry process appropriate to the particular situation being appraised.

In the case of the Huddersfield CIS, at the time the work was done, the system existed as a prototype in 'lash-up' and demonstration form, with the main database under construction by Peat Marwick McLintock, brought in to do that work. The Lancaster team found two main difficulties in grasping the nature of the CIS.

The first problem for us as evaluators was that the phrase 'the CIS Project' had the normal connotations which go with the word 'project' – after all there was a very active 'project manager' in post and a designated project team. But we discovered that none of the usual documentation generated by a project existed: no minutes of project-team meetings, no action plans, no critical path diagrams. Gradually the irrelevance of our models of 'project', thought of in a generic sense, led us to the appreciation that the work being done was a real action research collaboration (one seeking action, not simply knowledge) between the 'project team' and the hospital consultants, a collaboration whose direction and pace were dictated by the readiness of the consultants to move on with something they saw as both useful to them in their professional capacity and capable of assimilation into their working practices. A process approach was being adopted, the focus being on function rather than form, consideration of which was postponed until later. Everything which had evolved during the work done so far met those conditions. (Other RM pilots started the other way round, creating new hospital structures, such as 'clinical directorates' led by senior doctors. Directorates came much later at Huddersfield, where form followed function.)

The second problem for the evaluators was that we had assumed at the start that in order to understand something called a CIS, relevant models would be ones whose *operational* activities consisted of those entailed in being a hospital consultant: updating knowledge, arranging to see patients referred to them by general practitioners (GPs), seeing them, deciding and giving treatment, informing GPs, etc. But we found that the screens created in the CIS were best thought of as being relevant not to operational activities but to activities concerned with *monitoring and controlling*. On the other hand, the monitoring and controlling *intentions* were in no sense generated by the system. This was not an 'expert system' which, by following inference patterns, might, in principle, replace human judgement-forming and decision-making, this being the false hope behind many such systems. Rather, the CIS was one which supported the hospital consultants as *they* made judgements which led to their monitoring and controlling their professional activity. Far from usurping their responsibility for using their professional skill to make medical judgements about diagnosis and treatment, the system supported them in exercising that professional judgement and enabled them to exercise it in a broader context. The system which was emerging, in giving them that support in fact enabled them to better exercise their professional judgement as a result of accumulated learning. It enabled them to do more than simply make diagnoses and treat a sequence of individual patients. It enabled them to make connections between their judgements in individual cases so that over time, thanks to the system, they could learn; their stream of patients became a research object enabling them to hone their professionalism.

The system's procedures were as follows. For a given diagnosis of a medical condition (eg 'uterine fibroids') the collaborating consultants, on the basis of their existing knowledge and experience, made a description of an expected 'norm' in terms of likely symptoms, possible complications, range of expected length of stay, if hospitalization was involved, treatments/procedures likely to be used, and anticipated outcomes. These descriptions were known as 'profiles of care' and were held in the computer. Each profile had a unique code, and for this the Read Clinical Classification was adopted. (Being developed by a GP, the Read codes were rooted in medical practice at the individual patient level, unlike some of the other possible classification systems developed for costing purposes.) Given such a profile, based on purely medical knowledge, it was then enriched by managers who added to it the costs of all the resource use anticipated in the profile – the costs of taking X-rays, performing pathology lab tests, having patients occupying hospital beds, carrying out surgery, etc. Thus the system's database held the expectations of consultants and managers for both action and resource use required by medical conditions as described using the Read Index.

Actual treatments of patients then generated further data concerning diagnosis, treatment and outcomes which matched categories in the profiles of care and could be compared with them. The very act of creating a profile of care provided a conceptual framework which could be used to review individual cases, or a set of such cases, in discussion with colleagues or juniors. Reviewing cases provided rapid feedback about the resource implications of clinical decisions; and ready access to data via the CIS could also be used to support sundry other activities such as, for example, production of letters to GPs. In the longer term, of course, the system accumulated data and information which allowed trends to be spotted and the profiles of care themselves to be reviewed and if necessary modified in the light of experience. (Later, a woman with appropriate intellectual and inter-personal skills was appointed to hold regular discussions with individuals and groups of doctors about the patterns of resource use and medical outcomes which were emerging from the CIS. The question which could be addressed was: what health gains are we getting for what resource use?) This was a true learning system, helpful to consultants exercising their clinical judgement, and generating believable information on both resource use and patterns of resource use, for joint discussion by clinicians and managers. Although the technology of the prototype of the system was soon out of date, being superseded by computers more convenient to use, the concept of the Huddersfield CIS is still well ahead of those which inform most systems to be found in today's NHS hospitals. (Structurally, the core of the system at Huddersfield was a relational database on a central mini computer updated principally by file transfer from departmental computers already in use for other purposes. The database was interrogated via procedures written locally using report-writer software. User stations were micros running terminal emulation software which were also used in stand-alone mode for word processing and other applications.)

Our work sought to understand and display what had been achieved in the action research which had created the prototype CIS. This was done in five reports covering: the CIS in its context; its structure; the needed management education and development; issues of 'going live' with such a system; and the transferability of the system to other hospitals. (The main point of this last report was that what was transferable from such a development strategy was not necessarily the final system achieved, but rather the *process* by which it had been achieved (Hardy et al 1988).)

Learning from the experience

The CIS was aimed, ultimately, at generating knowledge about medical outcomes for patients at Huddersfield Royal Infirmary in relation to the medical practice and resource use entailed in achieving those outcomes. It thus provides a very good example of the role of IS in making the link between data and knowledge via capta and information. Out of the myriad items of data concerning the medical condition of people who may be referred for hospital treatment, a sub-set became capta for the CIS, namely data of this kind concerning people referred, usually by local family doctors, for treatment at Huddersfield's acute hospital. A stored set of such capta for patient X becomes, in that context, information about the medical condition of that patient. Details of items in the episode of care, meaningful as information defining a 'treatment' for that patient, are also stored, together with outcomes, and can later be compared with a relevant profile of care. The profiles themselves can be thought of as *postulated* information derived from the capta yielded by the consultants experience and the relevant medical literature. When comparisons are made between profiles and actual happenings, larger structures of knowledge are created which can later be searched for significant patterns of various kinds, both medical and in terms of resource use.

Two other features of the Huddersfield experience link back to material presented in Chapter Five of this book. The joint development of the system by consultants and IS experts is very like the joint, research-oriented development of the Fighter Command radar information system by RAF officers and operational researchers. Finally, a very interesting similarity exists between the institutionalized discussions about what was being learnt from the CIS, and the kind of discussions about experience which took place in Fighter Command during the Battle of Britain. At Huddersfield the appointment of the woman whose job it was to have regular discussions with doctors and managers about what was being learnt from the CIS was a move to ensure that learning from experience was a consciously-organized process. Though time-scales and urgency were different, there are similarities with the post-action discussions at various levels which took place in Fighter Command: between sector controllers and pilots; between 11 Group command, Uxbridge, and sector stations (the commander of 11 Group, Keith Park, sending a stream of directions during the Battle based upon his analysis of recent experience in discussion with his Sector commanders); and between Park and Dowding, his commander-in-chief at Bentley Priory.

Since information embodies meaning, and meanings in human situations are never static for long; every good installation of an IS will include organized arrangements for ensuring that learning arising from the use of the system is captured and can be acted upon. That this so rarely happens is probably due to a general failure to think of IS as processes which construct knowledge.

EVALUATING A NATIONAL PROGRAMME

The situation

At the national level, the creation of the clinical information system at Huddersfield Royal Infirmary just described, together with the work done at the other five Resource Management pilot sites, was aimed at 'demonstrating the value of the approach' (DHSS 1986, page 4), after which implementation in other acute hospitals would follow. The RM Health Notice spoke optimistically of the pilot sites being able

> to release at least 1 per cent of annual expenditure for redeployment on patient services through the operation of the new resource management approach. (page 6)

This was to be 'a key criterion for judging whether and when the approach should be extended' (page 6). In the event, RM became swept up in the major changes proposed in the January 1989 white paper 'Working for Patients'. Although it was too early to show whether or not the 'key criterion' had been met, the white paper indicated that the RM Initiative would be extended to all acute hospitals with more than 250 beds. This meant that 260 acute hospitals became 'RM sites' by the end of 1992, and this extension of the programme was managed chronologically in four waves. It constituted a huge experiment in bringing about organizational change, here carried out in a very complex shifting situation in a giant organization.

In early 1995, as the intervention came to an end, the NHS Executive commissioned an evaluation of the RM programme in England. Following a tendering process, the work went to a consortium led by the Health Services Management Unit, University of Manchester. The consortium linked management consultancies focused on organization development, accounting, and computing; Peter Checkland was included with a responsibility for methodology.

It is not the intention here to describe the evaluation and its conclusions in any detail; they are described in the more than 200 pages of the final report (HSMU 1996). For our purposes here two aspects of the evaluation are relevant: the shape of the methodology developed for the evaluation, which made flexible use of soft systems methodology; and the general picture it provided of information systems and organizational development in an organization which, as has already been indicated, was not yet a very sophisticated user of IT.

The evaluation methodology

The holistic concept behind the RM initiative was that two linked areas of change had to be managed together in each acute hospital or community-services unit – there were a few – at which an RM project was executed; the two areas were those of organizational change (which is always a heady mix of procedural, structural and attitudinal change) and changes to information provision aimed at meeting the needs of both clinicians and managers. This made RM a bold and complex initiative which had to be evaluated at national, regional and site levels. Also, many different facets had to be investigated, including: organization development; IS and IT; project management, examined both at the centre and at sites; outcomes and benefits realization; finance; and, finally, the relevance of RM to the purchaser/provider split which was introduced during the lifetime of the initiative. Thus, a complicated matrix of evaluation activities at different levels and with different time spans had to be managed. In order to ensure that they were linked into a coherent whole, the different evaluation activities were developed on the basis of a number of activity models relevant to the RM concept.

Taking the health notice which launched RM as a core statement concerning it, three SSM-style activity models were built. (We were here taking Health Notice HN 86/34 as what in SSM is called a 'root definition' – in this case a 12-page definition!) The first model was of a purposeful activity system to set up and execute an RM project at an NHS site, incorporating all the facets of the initiative as described in HN 86/34. A second model expanded at a more detailed level the activity which in the first model is simply the bald: 'Manage the project'. Finally, a third model covered RM activity at regional level, the regions being the route through which RM projects were funded and monitored. These models, together with much knowledge of the NHS gained by the consortium partners as a result of previous work within the service, enabled a coherent set of questions to be defined. Answering those questions then provided, in a recoverable process, a picture of the course of the RM initiative which enabled the evaluation team to make mature judgements about it. The questions were used in a number of different ways in different parts of the evaluation. They underpinned interviews with more than 30 people concerned with RM at a national level. They provided an intellectual base for site reviews of RM projects carried out over several days by small teams of evaluators at 16 acute hospitals and four community units, these having been selected to provide a defensible selection of sites (covering different regions, range of services/ specialities, level of local 'competition', etc). Finally, they underpinned development of a survey questionnaire sent to the chief executive of all participating sites; this generated well over 100 returns.

The interviews, site reviews and the site survey produced a mass of material all of which was potentially relevant to making judgements about the RM intervention. In order to try to see the patterns in this richness of material, another model was used. This pictured what characteristics an NHS site would have following whole-hearted and successful adoption of RM as described in the original health notice. Using this model, a judgement could be made about how close the sites reviewed or surveyed were to the Utopia represented by the model of 'an RM'd site'. A modified version of this model is shown in Figure 7.6. It will be noticed that in order to make it unique within the study it is expressed differently from normal models within SSM, in which elements which are activities are linked by arrows which show functional dependencies between activities. Such models are independent of any particular structures through which the activities may be carried out in real situations. In Figure 7.6, however, some of the real-world arrangements in the NHS are taken as given, and the activities in the model are carried on arrows linking the elements of the model, which are here a set of entities. These entities may be either concrete, such as 'doctors and nurses', or abstract, such as 'RM concept'.

Use of this model allowed rapid holistic judgements to be made about the extent to which a particular site had moved towards the state which the initiative intended to reach. The purpose in this part of the evaluation was not to make detailed judgements about individual sites but to assemble a picture which enabled overall patterns to be seen.

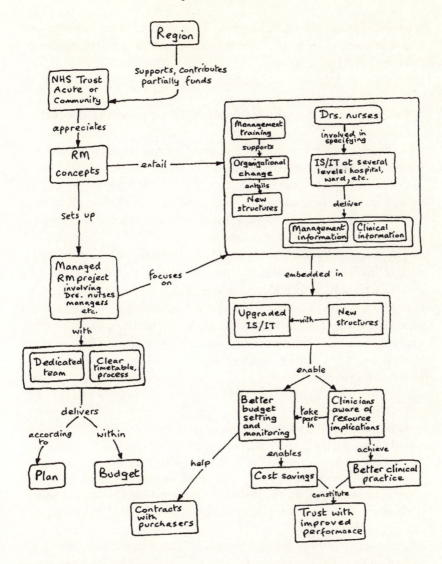

Figure 7.6. *A model showing how full adoption of the declared principles of Resource Management (RM) would affect an NHS Trust in a purchaser-provider relationship (after HSMU 1996)*

Following the analysis based on results from sites reviewed or surveyed, the material was then re-examined in terms of five different aspects of RM. Task teams pulled together the material concerning benefits realization, IS/IT, finance, organization issues and the impact of RM on purchaser-provider interaction. (This latter was important because although the purchaser-provider split was not envisaged when the initiative was launched, the systems it introduced were subsequently found in many cases to be extremely important in enabling purchaser-provider contracts to be agreed.)

The picture of IS and organization development in the NHS

As indicated above, it is not the intention here to summarize or discuss the detailed findings on RM in the NHS, which are presented in full in the evaluation report and its extensive appendices (HSMU 1995). Relevant here is the general picture which emerged of the introduction of IS in the NHS and the organizational change which is always associated with changes to information provision.

The introduction of RM took place at a time of great attitudinal change in the NHS. It was the period in which clinicians gradually accepted (mainly with reluctance) that resources for health care were limited in relation to demand, and that it was no longer possible to hold on to the myth that all medical decisions can be taken on exclusively medical grounds. Clinicians were increasingly accepting that they are also managers of resources. Interesting external evidence of this comes from the founding, in 1991, of the British Association of Medical Managers (BAMM). The association's brochure declares that it was formed

> in response to demand from doctors in clinical management roles in the UK. Many doctors found themselves in management positions, as clinical directors, medical directors or as head of a service, both in acute and non-acute sectors, with little or no management education . . . BAMM's aims are quite straightforward – to support and develop doctors in their management and leadership roles in delivering health care. (BAMM Brochure)

Such an organization would not have been formed even five years earlier, and it is significant that a document entitled 'The Involvement of Clinical Staff in the Management of NHS Trusts', described on its cover as 'supported by the NHS Executive', is endorsed jointly by BAMM, the British Medical Association, the Institute of Health Service Management and the Royal College of Nursing (BAMM 1996).

The RM evaluation found that much organizational development activity had taken place at RM sites, with a rich mixture of developmental activity. Historically, the readiness for this stemmed partly from the Griffiths Report's introduction of general management roles into the

NHS; but management training was not then routinely embedded in the professional training of clinicians. The most common organizational change associated with RM projects was the introduction of a management structure of 'clinical directorates' headed by a hospital consultant. Not surprisingly, the success of an organizational development programme was found to be very dependent upon energetic support by the chief executive of a Trust.

As regards IS and IT, the expectation was that improved use of resources, leading ultimately to better patient care, would result from investment in case mix management systems and in systems to support provision of nursing care. The former would contain a database fed from departmental systems which collected details of patients, their diagnoses and treatments (including costs), and made it possible for the individual patient data to be grouped in clinically meaningful ways. The Huddersfield clinical information system described in the previous section was just such a system, but with the added emphasis, via the prior definition of expected 'profiles of care', on the system's ability to encourage steady learning. Nursing systems were less well-defined but would support preparation and analysis of patients' nursing care plans, comparison of nursing workloads with needs, nurse rostering and the planning of staffing levels. Since this was an immature market, with development work necessary by suppliers, there was earmarked funding within the initiative at the level of £350 000 per site for procurement of case mix systems and £100 000 for nursing systems, with £50 000 for upgrading local infrastructure.

Results in this area were in general disappointing: many systems were late in implementation, failed to produce expected outputs and, in some cases, were switched off (the site questionnaire revealing, for example, 46 of 143 sites with 'full installation' of case mix systems, 15 'switched off', and seven 'procured but not installed'). Also, although the RM projects left many sites with enhanced experience and skills with regard to IS and IT provision, doctors and nurses had often had little effective involvement in specifying system requirements, especially where regional authorities had actually prescribed particular systems, rather like Henry Ford's original insistence that buyers could have any colour of Ford car they wanted as long as it was black.

Perhaps the most significant feature of the picture of IS work in the NHS which was revealed by the evaluation, related back to the original concept of RM in Health Notice 86(34) (DHSS 1986). This required IS and IT developments which were *linked to* parallel organizational development which involved 'from the outset management develop-ment and training programmes' (page 3). (Figure 7.6 makes clear this feature of RM.) Much good OD work was done at RM sites, and some good systems were implemented, but it was exceptionally rare to come across a site where the RM project entailed parallel strands of OD and IS/IT work which were integrated. This was the most important broad finding from the national evaluation of RM, and it has been confirmed in simultaneous work by a management consultant, Mike Haynes (1997) in helping RM sites achieve their 'sign-off' reports, using a workbook designed earlier for that purpose (Haynes et al 1995).

Learning from the experience

The synthesis of the arguments in Chapters Two, Three and Four leads to the POM model (Figure 4.5) as an account of the holistic process in which people form intentions in line with their perceptions of the world and take purposeful action to realize those intentions supported by relev-ant information and knowledge. For convenience, a simplified version of Figure 4.5 is repeated here as Figure 7.7.

In the Figure we have a learning system which embeds IS and IT within the human process of taking purposeful action, and gives IS/IT work a clear role. Above all, the process in Figure 7.7 is a single process in which each element plays a part; the learning the system achieves (either from within itself or because external happenings abruptly change element 2, the perceived world) is a product of the whole.

In these terms the evaluation of the RM initiative revealed what was on the whole a dysfunctional version of this system in the NHS in the first half of the 1990s. This is perhaps hardly surprising given the amount of change to which the service has been subjected and its relative inno-cence concerning IS and IT compared with the position in industry by the 1990s. This gloomy general picture contrasts with the functioning version of the process in Figure 7.7 which was observed in Huddersfield Royal Infirmary, at least during the development of the prototype clini-cal information system there.

The implementation of the Griffiths Report in the NHS began to change the perceived world of clinicians and managers (element 2 in Figure 7.7). This changed elements 1, 3, 4 and 5 as the acceptance of the need to get the best possible health care for patients from limited re-sources gradually increased. The nature of the intentional action of

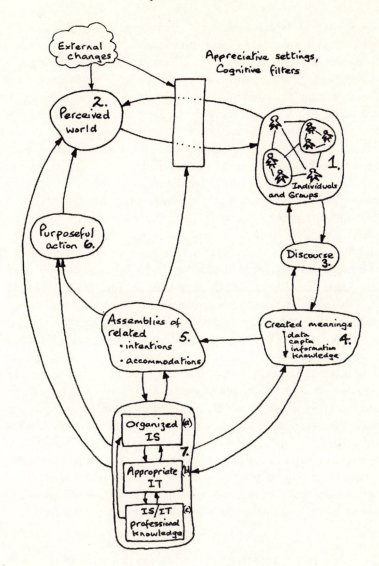

Figure 7.7. *A simplified representation of the 'processes for organization meanings' (POM) model, (Figure 4.5)*

providing health care services in acute hospitals (element 5) changed as the need to manage the achievement of maximum 'health gain' from available resources became part of clinicians' thinking. New accommodations (within element 5) became necessary: clinicians accept the need to think like managers while managers accept that their task has to be defined in a way which accepts the ultimate professional autonomy of hospital consultants, who cannot be made to take action they feel is against their professional judgement. These changes were leading to new interpretations of the purposeful action of providing hospital services (element 6) which implied more sophisticated requirements for informational support. In principle there was a clear need to move gradually to more evidence-based clinical interventions, together with a careful monitoring of resource use. Unfortunately the real situation showed very poor links between, on the one hand, elements 1 to 6, to which the OD work at RM sites was relevant, and on the other, element 7, the provision of information support. This was undertaken by IS/IT professionals and, although project teams frequently contained a doctor and a nurse as members, there was very little evidence of clinicians being 'centrally involved in specifying the information requirements of the new systems' as called for in Health Notice 86(34) (DHSS 1986, page 2). There were probably at least three reasons for this. Firstly, most NHS sites at that time simply did not know ways of thinking out information requirements; secondly, there was evidence that when the purchaser-provider split was imposed, the requirement to provide information related to purchaser-provider contracts overtook the aim of generating data which was clinically useful. Thirdly, it was in any case the finding that too much of the RM work flowed from the identification of a single type of systems solution, namely a case mix management system, irrespective of the adequacy of the existing operational systems within an acute hospital. A fundamental feature of the process in Figure 7.7 is that the IS and IT support has to provide the particular support required by the people in a particular organization culture. Even though some generic functional requirements may be defined, the system solutions ought to be tailored to *these* people in *their* particular situation.

RE-THINKING AN IS STRATEGY

The situation

The Royal Victoria Infirmary (RVI) is a large teaching hospital in the centre of Newcastle in the North East of England. Twenty-five miles up the valley of the River Tyne is the small town of Hexham with its own more modest hospital, Hexham General. In the early 1990s the two hospitals were merged, though physically they remained on their separate sites. Steve Clarke, from Hexham, became the Information Officer of the new hospital, and set about re-thinking information needs. An outcome of this was the setting up of a project to re-formulate an information and IT strategy for the combined hospital, what is called an 'IM and T strategy' in NHS-speak. The project has been described in Checkland et al (1996) and will be summarized here.

There was a considerable sense of urgency in the situation, and the project, initiated in March, was required to deliver a new information strategy by September. In spite of this demanding timetable, Steve Clarke was anxious that the work should be done not simply by the IS and IT professionals in the hospital but by representative groups of users from all areas of hospital activity, and he wished to use SSM to achieve this.

Funding for the project was obtained from central sources in the NHS: it was funded as an 'HISS project.' HISS, which stands for hospital information support systems, was a central initiative launched by the Information Management Group of the NHS Executive in December 1988. It was managed independently of the RM initiative, described earlier, and was conceived much more as an IT, rather than an IS project. HISS tackled boldly (many would say too boldly) the problem that most hospital computer systems are not linked; for example, a pathology laboratory system may be quite separate from the patient administration system (PAS), though the pathology lab tests refer to patients whose details are in the PAS. Sixteen different attempts to create fully integrated systems in NHS acute hospitals were funded, at a cost of just over £100m. The initiative has been treated roughly in a report by the National Audit Office (1996) and criticized in apocalyptic language in the trade press ('impossibly ambitious'; 'underestimated the risks of failure, ignored early signs of disaster'; 'exaggerated the benefits', etc) (Collins 1996). However, outside the major projects, which included such items such as £6.8m capital costs for systems of American origin for Greenwich Healthcare Trust, much smaller sums of HISS money became available for useful but more modest projects: Steve Clarke achieved his new information strategy for less than half of one percent of the total of £8.3m spent at Greenwich.

After a tendering process, the contract for the work at Newcastle and Hexham went to a management consultancy unfamiliar with SSM, and Peter Checkland was drafted in to provide methodological help. Luckily the senior management consultant assigned to the project, John Poulter, was one of nature's systems thinkers; he immediately understood and absorbed the principles of SSM, and could assimilate it into his work. (Since the work at the RVI and Hexham was completed, he and Checkland have prepared for the HISS team a document published as: '*Guidelines for the use of Soft Systems Methodology*'. This is based on seven applications within the NHS (Poulter et al 1996) and is one of four 'Facilitator's Guides' from, the HISS Central Team relating to the management of organizational change.)

The work done and the outcomes

The project to redefine the IS strategy was launched at a meeting of more than a hundred people in one of the RVI's tiered lecture theatres. The chief executive of the hospital spoke first, indicating his support for the work and its importance to the Trust in the new situation arising from the NHS reforms. He also said that the project would be carried out with the active participation of some of the doctors, nurses and managers at the RVI and Hexham. How the work would be conducted was then explained, and a basic indication of the nature of the approach to be adopted was given, emphasizing the prior careful definition of would-be purposeful activity as a route to definition of the appropriate information support needed by those undertaking that activity.

Subsequently each hospital nominated 15–20 doctors, nurses and managers to take part in the information analysis process. Each team was asked to examine the purpose, activities, and information needs of some of the functions performed in the hospitals: pathology, theatres, surgery, medicine, business management, finance, human resources, anaesthetics, radiology, nursing, etc. The teams were mixed but functions were selected so that at least one member would be working in a function examined. With help from Steve Clarke and John Poulter, the teams organized themselves to fit in meetings and carry out the work at times convenient to themselves. No team members were relieved of normal duties! Each month a joint workshop was held to review progress. At these meetings Checkland found that his role was essentially to re-articulate the whole process being followed, reminding people where they had come from and where they were going next, and providing ideas to help with the next stage. In addition, the whole study was reviewed by a steering group consisting of directors and senior managers from the RVI and Hexham hospital. With an eye constantly on the clock, the work had to be organized tightly. Activity modelling was

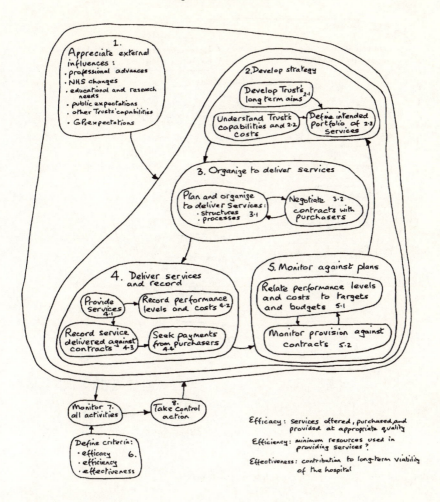

Figure 7.8. *A low-resolution activity model relevant to any acute hospital in a purchaser-provider relationship (after Checkland et al 1996)*

done in the period March–April, information analysis in May–June. Given the September deadline, no strategy-level analysis of the desirable longer term pattern of services provided by the hospitals was undertaken within this study. Given the short time available for the study, the existing pattern was taken as a given base.

Since no one in the teams was familiar with activity modelling, and there was little time to learn, some very basic general models were offered to the teams with the suggestion that they modify them for their own purposes in any way they wished. Figure 7.8 shows a high-level

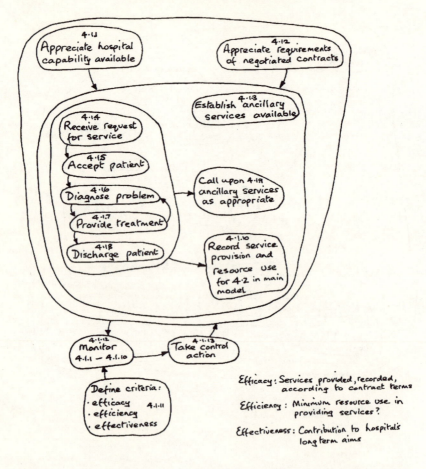

Figure 7.9. *A model which expands activity 4.1 in Figure 7.8 (after Checkland et al 1996)*

model relevant to any provider trust, concerned, in a context of various external influences, to develop its strategy, deliver its services and to monitor outcomes against intentions. One of the activities in that model, activity 4.1: 'Provide services' is then expanded in more detail in Figure 7.9 for a particular clinical service. Generic models of this kind helped teams to understand the nature and purpose of modelling, which was to provide a coherent basis for asking about the information support needed by people carrying out hospital activity, and comparing that with the existing provision. Here the facilitation by IS/IT specialists was especially useful, the object being to identify information gaps and opportunities which the new strategy could address. This review of information needs questioned the IS/IT situation in the hospitals and

Table 7.1. *An activity chart based on Figure 7.9*

Activities from the model	How the activity is done	Measures of performance	Information needed	Information support provided by	Information gaps and opportunities
4.1.4 and 4.1.5 Receive request for service, and accept patient	Letter, phone call	Speed with which the request is handled	Patient's details, clinical condition, and history Contract situation	PAS	Automatic generation of letters to patient and referrer Up-to-date contract situation
4.1.6 Diagnose problem	Consider history Examine patient Conduct investigations	Medical audit	Case notes Results from investigations		Case notes often missing Much duplication of recording of patient's details Delays in receiving test results
4.1.7 Treat patient	Conduct procedures/ operations Prescribe drugs	Medical audit	Availability of facilities (theatres, anaesthetists, etc) Drug effects and interactions	Theatre booking system	Systems not available at ward level
4.1.8 Discharge patient	Discharge summary, discharge letter	Speed with which produced	Post-treatment test results Availability of discharge facilities Coding	PAS	Links to ongoing providers of care Automatic generation of discharge summaries and letters Support for Read coding

identified the gaps/opportunities by using the activity models as a source of questions to put to the real world. For this purpose charts of the kind shown in Table 7.1 were compiled. This example, which is illustrative, rather than descriptive of the situation at Newcastle, uses some of the activities in the model shown in Figure 7.9.

Following work of this kind, options for solutions, in terms of both processes and IT support, were developed and presented to a final joint workshop, followed by presentation to the steering group. The new information strategy was prepared by the September deadline.

Those who took part in the teams' work found it an interesting and, on the whole, rewarding experience. Interviewed a year after the work was completed, team members' recollections of the project were in the main rosy. Many said that, although fitting the team meetings and work-shops into their busy professional lives had not been easy, the experience had given them a different perspective on their own work, a better view of the overall activity to which they made a contribution. It is the case in most large organizations, even those staffed mainly by professionals, that horizons are normally limited by short-term pressures; resolving imme-diate issues and getting through to the end of next week tend to drive out broader considerations. There was thus a welcome for this oppor-tunity to see, for once, the bigger picture.

Learning from the experience

The project was a good demonstration of what can be achieved particip-atively in a short period of time, given the kind of energy and drive shown by Steve Clarke and John Poulter in organizing and facilitating the pro-cess. There were also examples of how a declared methodology can stimulate thinking. A good example of this is worth recording. One of the teams set out to build an activity model relevant to providing nursing services. Now, in advance of model building, SSM questions the concept of the purposeful activity which is being modelled very carefully. One of the questions asked is: who is directly affected by this activity, whether as beneficiaries or victims? (This is the C – for 'customer' – question in the mnemonic 'CATWOE' used to formulate careful statements about pur-poseful activity so that modelling is straightforward; see Smyth and Checkland (1976), Checkland (1981), Checkland and Scholes (1990a).) In considering the provision of nursing services, the team immediately wrote down 'patients' as the answer to the question concerning who is affected by the activity. After all, the fundamental motivation of people who choose to become nurses is that they wish to care for people. But as the team moved on it was pulled back by one of its members who pointed out that, while that used to be the case, it could now be argued that, under the purchaser-provider contract arrangements now in place, the answer was not 'patients' but 'the hospital contracts manager'! The point being made was that in the so-called 'internal market' in the NHS, the nurse's role could now be argued to be to provide that amount and quality of nursing care specified in the contract – and hence paid for. The senior nurse who reported this incident to one of the joint workshops said that this exchange had crystallized for her the unease she felt at the NHS reforms but had not previously articulated. She had had the feeling that her professional responsibility to her patients was being chipped away: now she understood how and why. Certainly models relevant to current practice in providing clinical services have at the moment to include activities concerning purchaser-provider contracts and contract monitoring. In the language developed earlier, the introduction of contracts has created in the NHS many new items of capta which now have to be collected and processed, even though the confrontational aspects of contracting are now being downplayed, and 'contracts' may well become 'service agreements' over longer periods than a year.

In terms of the concepts of data, capta, information, knowledge, IS and IS development, developed in the earlier chapters, this example at the RVI can be seen as an attempt consciously to create a functional version of the processes in the POM model (Figures 4.5 and 7.7). It was argued above that the huge NHS-wide RM initiative, in the way it was realized in specific cases in particular local circumstances, was, on the whole, a dysfunctional version of the process in Figure 4.5. Here, on a much smaller scale, we had an attempt to create participatively a functioning version. In relation to the POM model, the 30–40 hospital professionals who made up the teams, together with the IS and IT experts who joined them, were the 'communicating individuals and groups' creating afresh the meanings underlying their purposeful activity in order to work out what information support was needed by people carrying out the range of hospital activities in the RVI and Hexham General.

In terms of Figure 4.9 (concerning IS development) this experience illustrated, at the level of an IS and IT strategy for the hospital as a whole (rather than the specific design of particular systems), the IS development methodology which follows from the core concepts developed earlier in Chapters Three and Four.

Part Four

A Concept of the Field

Chapter Eight

The Field of Information Systems

INTRODUCTION: THE ARGUMENT REVISITED

As indicated in Chapter One, the work which has led to the writing of this book has included several parallel strands. These include: gaining research experiences in situations in which IS and IT were important factors; reflecting on these experiences and trying to make sense of them in the light of a pragmatic (rather than a philosophical) examination of the process of creating what in everyday language we casually refer to as 'information' and 'knowledge'; and relating both these strands to the confusing literature in this field. Now, in this final chapter, we draw the argument together and describe what in the opening chapter was referred to as: 'an account of the IS field which makes sense of it and hence ought to help in planning and carrying out coherent work within it'.

We will start by reiterating the shape of the argument so far.

1. IS and IT are now ubiquitous in both professional and everyday life, and the concept of 'information' is frequently taken to mark a revolution as important as the Industrial Revolution of the late 18th and early 19th centuries, which focused on 'energy'. Both IS and IT are agents of change: they enable us to do things which would not otherwise be possible, often conquering both time and space; and it is not possible to introduce IS and IT into a human situation without changing that situation significantly. So it is not surprising to find the field of IS/IT emerging as an important area for study, for we need to understand these potent sources of social change.

2. Intellectually, however, the field is still extremely confused. There is no agreement on its history, its reference discipline or its basic concepts. Almost any assertion made in its literature can be matched by a counter assertion; there is a need for fundamental thinking if IS/IT is to emerge as a coherent field.

3. The core concern of the field can be taken to be the orderly provision of accessible information support for people acting purposefully, often, though not exclusively in an organizational context. In order to explore this process, we need to direct attention to the idea of 'an organization' and to the idea of 'information' and the process by which it is created. Both concepts are problematical.

4. 'An organization' is a social collectivity which many people, members and non-members alike, are prepared to treat *as if* it had a unitary consciousness and hence could do such things as obtain resources, make plans, try to implement them, change its mind, etc, even though there is in fact no unitary 'corporate mind' to change. But since much action is taken in the name of organizations, as if the corporate entity were capable of behaving like a person, there is a need to explore the process by which intentions are formed and action is taken at both the individual level and, if accommodations between conflicting views are possible, at the group or social level.

5. As a result of their knowledge and previous experience of the world, individuals acquire in-built readinesses to notice certain features of their situation as significant. Attribution of meaning to these selective perceptions enables judgements to be made and intentions formed, which may lead to purposeful action to try to realise the intentions. The group, or social process, is in general not dissimilar, but exhibits two important extensions of the individual process. Firstly, the perceiving, attributing meaning, judging and forming intentions will be mediated in the complex social process we have described in Chapter Four as 'the never-ending dialogue, discussion, debate and discourse in which we all try to affect each others perceptions, judgements, intentions and actions.' Secondly, in any social situation, and especially in organizations, the actions which get taken – which will probably include cooperative, shared or joint actions – will be within the *accommodations* which can be established among the different views and interests represented in the discourse. (Finding such

accommodations is a condition for the continued existence of the social group, or organization, though in the latter case – for example, in the case of an industrial company or a family – the accommodations which individuals can 'live with' may well be based on asymmetries of power.)

6. Thinking about the idea of information support for people undertaking the intentional action which is the outcome of these processes, whether individual or social, requires a number of distinctions to be made which establish a language of: 'data' (the factual invariances); 'capta' (data selected, created, or to which attention is paid); 'information' (meaningful selected data in a context); and 'knowledge' (larger, longer-living structures of information).

7. These considerations lead to the process for organization meanings (POM) model shown in Figure 4.5 and, in simplified form, in Figure 7.7. This is a process not dependent upon any particular technology, but one whose difficulties have become apparent through the spread of modern computer-based IT. It is a process which any organization with aspirations to survive has to think about seriously, and this applies equally to traditional organizations with well-defined boundaries and to the more open organizations which are now becoming more common. In general, some version of the process will have to be institutionalized in an appropriate form which fits the organizational culture. It is a process which will need to be continuously managed, not least because it will never be wholly under control, given its susceptibility not only to 'maverick' members of the organization but also to external happenings elsewhere which change the perceived world of the organization and the appreciative settings of its members.

8. A consequence of the nature of the process, in which intentions are formed and purposeful action is undertaken by people who are supported by information, is that an 'information system' has to be seen as a service system: one which serves those taking the action. Hence its form and content will have to be dictated by how the action supported is conceptualized. This means that 'information systems development' must start by carefully defining the action to be served, in its specific context, and using that definition to decide what information is needed and how technology can help provide it. (This reverses what often happens

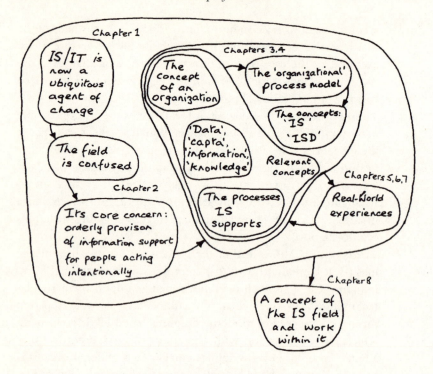

Figure 8.1. *A summary of the book's argument and its structure*

today in organizations – with poor results which then lead to spectacular headlines about 'another IT failure'.)

9.   This process model, POM, together with its implications, have both fed and been fed by many research experiences, some of which have been described here.

This summarizes the argument developed in the first seven chapters of this book. Figure 8.1 provides a reminder of it in drastic summary, and links its parts to the structure of the book.

We now turn to the implications of the argument for IS, and explore the view of the fledgling field which it provides.

THE PROBLEMATICAL CONCEPT 'INFORMATION SYSTEM'

The argument just summarized leaves the notion of 'an information system' as a problematical one. That this is so can be demonstrated by asking ourselves what an *unproblematical* concept of 'information system' would look like, and then realizing that it would be the one implied in the conventional wisdom presented in the student texts. If that conventional view were an adequate account of organizational reality, then organizations would be established as goal-seeking human 'machines' staffed by people wholly committed to the attainment of the organization's explicit well-defined goals. Managing such an organization would consist of explicit decision taking in pursuit of the goals, and, given that, it would be possible to carry out a completely logical analysis of the goals, the network of tasks necessary to achieve them and hence the information support needed by the organization members to whom the tasks are assigned. It would even be possible gradually to build up libraries of 'information requirements' related to common tasks, and IT-based 'solutions' to the problem of supporting the people carrying out these tasks.

But real organizations are staffed by real people, not by the automatons implied in the conventional wisdom! The real world of organizations is very much messier than this – which is actually something we should be grateful for, since although it makes work in IS and IT more complex, it also makes it much more interesting, more human.

The core of the ambiguity in the concept 'information system' lies in the fact that meaning attribution is a human act, and individuals can do it both autonomously and, in groups, inter-subjectively. The individual's attributions of meaning will be his or hers. The assumed meanings created by a group, on the other hand, will obviously be shared by the group to some extent; but that sharing – although it is what makes social life possible – will rarely be complete, except on trivial and uncontroversial matters, and may or may not be in harmony with the meanings owned individually within the group. Individuals simultaneously both remain free and are conditioned by their membership of a group. No wonder meaning attribution is a complex business, and 'information system' a complex concept!

As we have argued in Chapter Three, real organizations are best thought of as simultaneously would-be purposeful 'machines' *and* quasi-families. Real organizations are characterized by permanent debates about aims and how best to achieve them, and are staffed by people whose perceptions of the world never coincide exactly, and certainly not with any notional worldview which is that of the abstraction 'the organization'. (Indeed, the best managers encourage, as well as contain, mavericks whose views cut across the local conventional wisdom, whatever that is, and so encourage debate.) And even if a basic uncontroversial IS is agreed, designed and installed, the *designer's* definition of 'information' (which means his or her definitions of which data need to be capta and which capta need to be processed in a particular way) does not have to be – and, in practice will not be – universally accepted, or accepted in every situation which unfolds. Thus, consider a spreadsheet setting out which course options college students have chosen and what marks they have achieved in their chosen courses. This may well have been logically designed as part of the provision of information for 'student assessment', but it will be eagerly and anxiously perused for other reasons by a lecturer who feels herself to be unfairly over-worked. She will see it as a source of information about the workload and productivity of her – as she sees it – more favoured, or lazier colleagues.

It is because a system designer's definitions of information will be re-interpreted, in multiple ways, by actual users that the NHS Resource Management initiative described in Chapter Seven called for the doctors and nurses in hospitals to be 'centrally involved in specifying the information requirements of the new systems' (DHSS 1986, page 2); it is for the same reason that Mumford has worked steadily over 20 years to develop her approach to IS design, ETHICS (effective technical and human implementation of computer systems) in which the potential users of a system become its designers.

Even if such user participation is achieved, however, it will still be the case that the local meanings which convert capta into information for a particular group of people will change over time as the context changes. And we can be sure that the context *will* change. It will do so not only because of external happenings in the flux of events and ideas in which the intentional action is embedded, but also because IT is a fast-changing technology and changes there will make new possibilities available, re-quiring a continual re-thinking of intentions, actions and the meanings which define relevant information.

All these dynamic factors make 'information system' an ambiguous concept. The POM model (Figures 4.5 and 7.7) provides a picture which makes sense of the shifting situation in which information systems are defined, created, modified or abandoned. It is instructive to ask: what picture of the IS field is implied by it? But first it is useful to appreciate the nature of some real-world responses to the ambiguous status of information systems.

RESPONSES TO THE COMPLEXITY OF THE CONCEPT 'INFORMATION SYSTEM'

Given its complexity and the ambiguity of some of its core concepts, it is not surprising that within the untidiness of the field of IS there are multiple concerns and approaches which are not easy to relate to each other and to the whole. These approaches and concerns come in various forms at various levels and focus on different features and, of course, are not mutually exclusive – many overlaps occur. At a broad level, we can see them as addressing three different kinds of question. At a fundamental level there are questions concerning the different base assumptions made in different kinds of work in the field; assumptions about, for example, the nature of the social world. Such assumptions, whether taken-as-given or carefully thought about, then condition the approach developed. Then there are more pragmatic questions concerning ways of getting things done in organizations – for example, how best to develop successful information systems. Thirdly, there are questions focused on what technological developments are taking place, and what the technology might become in the future: what possibilities will that open up? This third area is not surprising given the astonishing pace of technical development and the fact that, in this field more than most, new technology enables new possibilities for action or structure to be realized.

Fundamental concerns

Examples of a focus on fundamental concerns are Iivari's (1991) 'paradigmatic analysis of contemporary schools of IS development', and the more extensive complementary work by Hirschheim et al (1995), building on Hirschheim and Klein (1989). Iivari finds seven major schools of thought in ISD and examines their fundamental assumptions. The seven are identified through two characteristics: 'institutionalisation of the school in the scientific community' and 'the existence of identifiable founders and followers' (page 250). They comprise: software engineering, database management, management information systems, decision support systems, implementation research, the socio-technical approach, and the infological approach. He offers support for the claim made by Hirschheim and Klein (1989) that there is an identifiable orthodoxy in ISD and suggests that all seven schools adhere to positivism as their underlying epistemology. Only the school of decision support systems is claimed to have 'some anti-positivistic tendencies' (page 263). Hirschheim et al (1995) take rather the opposite approach to Iivari. They, following Burrell and Morgan (1979), define four ways of looking at the social world (functionalism, social relativism, radical structuralism and neo-humanism) and then seek to show 'the influence of these in current approaches to ISD' (page 99). They use their framework to explicate several approaches to both ISD methodologies and data modelling. (For ISD they choose: structured approaches, prototyping, SSM, and the work practices approach (Mathiassen 1981)). For data modelling approaches they identify fact-based approaches – 'the mainstream of the field' (page 172) (e.g. Chen 1981), and rule-based approaches – in which social reality is 'constructed and enacted' (page 198) (eg Stamper 1973, Stamper et al (1988).

Our interest here is not to agree or disagree with the conclusions of Iivari and Hirschheim et al, or indeed to summarize them. Our point is simply to note that one response which the complexity and ambiguity of the IS field has evoked among researchers is to analyse in great detail the fundamental assumptions underlying some of the work in the field.

Pragmatic concerns

A more common response has been to *develop* the many practical approaches to improving organizational activity or solving organizational problems via IS and IT. A few illustrations of pragmatic approaches will be included here; again, they can be seen as different responses to the complexity of a young and rapidly moving field.

We suggest that the many varieties of what we are calling 'pragmatic approaches' can be related to two broad categories: data-oriented approaches and approaches which focus on organizational activities and IT-based support to those who carry them out. (As always with such classifications offered from an observer's stance, it needs to be stated that these are two 'ideal types' in terms of which real examples may be described, rather than themselves being descriptions of categories which exist in the world; and they are not mutually exclusive.)

It is not surprising to find much work devoted to data and how to capture, store, process and retrieve it. Obviously computers are constructed as machines for manipulating a gigantic stream of electrical tokens for data; and dealing with something apparently as basic as data avoids, at least at first sight, some of the complications which occur when the meanings people attribute to data become the focus (though there is still the problem – which may or may not be recognized – of deciding which data should become the capta which are the concern of a particular IS in a particular situation). Hirschheim et al (1996) provide an excellent historical introduction to the idea of knowledge representation (their Chapter 6), and find work on data modelling to be based either on the assumption that 'reality can be defined by independent facts' (page 171) or on the assumption that 'what counts as reality are socially constructed images which emerge in social interaction' (page 171). The former constitutes the mainstream of work, and is captured in many research programmes, a huge literature and regular conferences for those who opt for a data-oriented approach. It is this data-led approach which has produced the idea, formulated during the 1970s, that an organization may be modelled *as*, essentially, its relevant data, which can be collected and stored in databases which may be managed via high-level languages like SQL. The literature contains many proposed data models for this purpose (see, for example, Nijssen 1976).

Most of the effort on data-oriented approaches has been deployed within the 'fact-based' school, which takes a functionalist goal-seeking view of organizations and does not itself address issues concerning how organizational purposes are formulated and how they change. These issues are more relevant to the much-less-developed 'rule-based' school within a 'data' orientation, but they are especially relevant to the approaches which focus pragmatically not on data but on organizational activity and support for the organization and its members. Several examples may be briefly cited to illustrate the spread: the definition of generic activities; prototyping and 'end-user computing'; sociotechnical and worker-focused approaches.

One powerful way of reducing the complexity of human affairs is to try to focus on generic activities which apparently recur in many situations across many organizations, and to develop IS to support these activities. (This is the IS field's equivalent to the argument of classical management science that types of problem situation recur: hence the development of algorithms for 'the queueing problem', 'the depot location problem' or 'the equipment replacement problem'.) In IS it is the approach which leads to vendors developing the kind of 'case mix' systems for hospitals which featured in the NHS's Resource Management Initiative discussed in Chapter Seven, or systems to help with production planning in manufacturing industry, or nurse rostering systems in hospitals. A variant of this is Wilson's advocacy (1984), in any organization, of developing a general 'primary task' model (using SSM's modelling technique) which can be used as a base for discussion of what IS the organization in question needs to support its activity.

Prototyping (Nauman and Jenkins 1982, Alavi 1984) takes an experimental approach to systems design, working with the users to refine an initial crude system until user needs are met, rather than trying to tease out and define those needs at the start of the design process. In its refined form it becomes 'rapid application development' (Martin 1991). In end-user computing (Nelson 1988) support is provided to enable users to develop their own modest systems for accessing data in the organization which is relevant to supporting their activity, often via spreadsheet and database software and query languages. It obviously has its dangers for a coordinated information strategy in an organization, but was ranked as the second most important issue in the IS field in a survey of practitioners and academics conducted in the mid-1980s (Dickson et al, 1984).

Socio-technical theory (Emery and Trist 1960) argues that a technological system cannot be separated from the social system of those involved with it; hence, in the context of ISD, good design and implementation of an IS should focus equally on both technical and human concerns. Such ideas underlie Mumford's ETHICS approach to systems design, with potential users becoming designers. More radical is the approach by some Scandanavian researchers (discussed by Hirschheim et al (1995)) This school sees socio-technical approaches as

> . . . a form of manipulation to reduce worker resistance to systems which served mostly the interests of managers and owners . . . (page 38)

Several projects have produced some tools and principles, rather than a methodology (for example the DEMOS and UTOPIA projects: Ehn 1988), the emphasis being on striving to achieve more democracy in the workplace.

These are enough examples to illustrate something of the range of considerations which drive pragmatic approaches to work in the IS field. Finally, the third such 'driver', the technology, will be briefly considered.

Technological concerns

Whenever a technology is developing rapidly it seems to do so under its own momentum, even though the development is actually in the hands of human beings – hence the phrase 'technological determinism'. The onward march of a technology can provide great satisfaction and excitement for the professionals involved in it, especially when their motivation stems from a desire to do new things or to achieve more from fewer resources. These are very powerful motivations, and it is not surprising that the impression given to outsiders is that, if something is in principle technically possible, then people will try to do it somehow. This means that, when considering a technological orientation within the IS/IT field, we are not referring to an approach or a methodology. What we mean, for our purposes here, is that for many people in the field there is an attitude which gives technology prime status, a propensity to focus on the computer-based IT and to do what the technology allows us to do, almost, it sometimes seems, for its own sake: if the technology is good for spreadsheets, let's use spreadsheets!

Two technology-dependent developments will be noted briefly here: the emergence of computer-supported cooperative work (CSCW) as a sub-field within IS/IT, and the rise and rise of the Internet.

Definitions are still fluid (Grudin 1991) but the terms CSCW and 'groupware' (systems supporting collaborative work) are now common (Ciborra 1996). Kuutti (1995) sees the very name CSCW as

> . . . the antithesis of traditional information systems: instead of automation, support is emphasized; instead of predetermination, active cooperation is emphasized; and instead of a concentration on systems, work is emphasized. (page 182)

Certainly, software products supporting cooperative work are now ubiquitous. A survey of a dozen such products in the trade press in 1994 found 17 functions available, including, for example, e-mail, database, document management, bulletins, conferencing, and group sharing (Mill 1994). Thus these are systems which occupy ground which lies between major organizational systems and single-user applications.

What is interesting in connection with our purpose here is not so much the burgeoning of this new field, or its technical content, but its emergence from practice rather than from academic work. Although academics now flock to this area, and fill large volumes of proceedings from conferences like those organized biannually, since 1988, by the Association for Computing Machinery (ACM), the conceptualization of this area and issues within it has followed rather than led practice. The field exists because of the technical development of 'hardware and software that support and exploit networking, communication, concurrent processing and windowing environments' (Grudin 1991, page 5). The technical developments were not pursued *in order that* CSCW could be created; CSCW has emerged because the confluence of particular technical developments makes it possible.

The case of the Internet is in some ways similar. The Internet exists as a result of the coming together of computer and telecommunication technologies and the consequent development of large networked systems. What happened at the birth of the Internet was that solving a particular problem for those responsible for the defence of the USA required defence-related systems with multiple pathways. This was in order to ensure that damage to a particular part of the system could not put the whole out of action. A project to build the Advanced Research Project Agency Network (ARPANET) saw computers, radio systems and satellite communication systems connected in just such a system. The National Science Foundation built its own network (NSFnet), and the linking of ARPANET and NSFnet started the Internet, which is now expected to have 100 million users by 1998 (Schultheis and Sumner 1995 page 270).

(As a cultural phenomenon the Internet has naturally stimulated a heady literature. This may be sampled via, for example: Strate et al 1996, Ludlow 1996, Shields 1996, Dovey 1996; Randall 1997. Sharply reviewing books in this area, Barbrook (1997) finds plenty of psychobabble, writers who 'have their own peculiar fantasies to project onto the Net', and the 'tired discourses of poststructuralism and postmodernism'. Certainly this is a literature not immune to apocalyptic hyperbole; but Birkerts' beautiful *The Gutenberg Elegies: the fate of reading in an electronic age* (1996) provides a lambent restorative.)

Technically, the Internet seems certain to have a significant effect on IS 'design' and 'development' – if, indeed, those terms continue to retain their old meanings. It provides good examples of the fact that technological development can lead to changes in social thinking and activity.

As we write, a senior manager in IBM has declared that that company

has completely focused its basic business strategies around network computing . . . Software has to provide the technology to enable this shift to network computing and bring about the commercialisation of the Internet. (J. Lawrie, reported by Schofield, 1997)

Technically, this would mean enabling IBM's operating system OS/2 to run applications written in the Java computer language. Java, derived from C++, is an object-oriented programming language developed because of a perceived demand for a platform–independent method of distributing applications as and when users demand them. Small–scale applications known as 'applets', here written using Java, can be stored on a server and accessed remotely by users using a 'Java-enabled' Web browser. When the user selects an application it is down-loaded and started on the user's terminal. But, and this is the point of Java, only then is the program converted into whatever appropriate code is required by the user's particular machine. Java code is written for a 'Java virtual machine' (JVM) and soon every computer's operating system will contain a JVM (Schofield 1997).

This leads to thoughts about the possible IT architecture of organizations in the future. It is probably significant that in the most recent survey of the issues regarded as most significant by IS executives, in the series by Wetherbe and his associates: 'For the first time . . . the key issue framework has taken a technical flavour' (Brancheau et al 1996, page 234). Ranked as the most important issue was: 'Building a responsive IT infrastructure'. With the Internet as an external communication network, many organizations will no doubt set up their own similar Intranets, perhaps with a wide area network and several local area networks for different functions in the organization. Links between the organization's Intranet and the Internet itself would include a so-called 'firewall', a barrier with appropriate protocols to provide security. Users would make use of applications relevant to them, whether developed internally or available externally. Such an architecture will undoubtedly have its effect upon both the thinking of people in the organization and the activity undertaken in the organization's name.

MAKING SENSE OF THE RESPONSES: THE COAT MODEL

In the last few pages we have quickly skimmed through some of the different kinds of activity – theoretical, practical, and a mixture of both – which go on in the IS field. They illustrate the diversity of the field, and may be seen as various responses to the need to tackle important problems in an area which does not have the kind of well-defined shape which quantum theory brings to nuclear physics, or plate tectonics to vulcanology. If we are to find an image which enables us to see a coherent pattern in the confusion of the field – which is our final aim here – then it will have to be one capable of subsuming the different kinds of work in the field; and if it is to be convincing it will have to be one rooted in experience in IS and in the ideas which animate the field. A first candidate for such an image is that captured in the POM model, which is relevant to the social processes – usually embedded in the context of an organization – in which people who form intentions and act purposefully are supported with information: the model of Figures 4.5 and 7.7. This derives from the interaction between the ideas developed in Chapters Three and Four and the experiences described in Chapters Five, Six and Seven. It is presented not as a copper-bottomed *theory* of the field but as a model which can be used to *make sense* of this core process at the heart of IS work, including the examples briefly presented in the previous section.

We can examine these (or many other) examples of work in the field and relate them to the concepts and language of the POM model. Take, for instance, the first example of IS work discussed above, concerned with analysis of the sociological assumptions behind work on approaches to ISD: the work of Iivari (1991) and that of Hirschheim et al (1995). Iivari argues that his analysis will 'promote self-reflection' among researchers and 'open up new research perspectives' (page 249), Hirschheim et al that 'synthesis of . . . existing knowledge is . . . valuable . . . to decrease confusion in the area' (page xi). Both address, implicitly, the processes included in the POM model (Figures 4.5 and 7.7) and what these researchers do can be described (inevitably rather ponderously) in the language of that model, as follows – where figures in brackets refer to elements in the POM model:

> Examination of the fundamental sociological assumptions concerning the perceived world (2) which are embedded in the methodologies of people using professional knowledge (7c) (including, especially, ISD methods) to provide informational support via information systems (7a) based on IT (7b) to individuals and groups (1) undertaking purposeful action (6).

Similarly, the work done in projects based on prototyping can be expressed in terms of the quick assembly of a crude system (7a, 7b, using 7c) and then cycling a number of times round the sequence 1–3–4–5–6–2, checking that the needs of people (1) are being met (by 7) as they undertake their work (6). A modern version of prototyping might make use of rapid application development (RAD) (Martin 1991, Kerr and Hunter 1994, Fulton and Sasse 1996) and include joint application development (JAD) workshops. These are carefully structured workshops attended by users and system developers, with a facilitator who leads and manages the meeting in order to engender commitment to the project, and to achieve sharp definition of requirements to be achieved within immovable 'timeboxes'. JAD workshops are an organized version of element 3 in the POM model, attended by both users and those with IT expertise (7c) in order to achieve more quickly the information-supported purposeful action (6) which is the aim of the processes in POM. The Internet provides, potentially, a ready-made version of element 7b to which people involved in that cycle can attach themselves using suitable IT to make the link.

It would be tedious to describe each example in this way, but some of the tedium is collected in Table 8.1.

Table 8.1. *Some examples of IS work expressed in the language of the POM model (Figures 4.5, 7.7) (Figures in brackets indicate elements in the model)*

Data-oriented pragmatic concerns	Purposeful action (6) in organizations is dependent upon relevant organized data being available. That data and its processing (7a, b, c) can be decided by people in the organization (1) who undertake a functionalist analysis of the perceived world (2) (fact-based school) *or* an analysis of the linguistic practices in the organization among organization members (1) as they construct and enact their social reality (2) (rule-based school).
Activity-oriented pragmatic concerns	The kinds of purposeful action (6) in organizations which require information support for those undertaking them (via 7a, b, c) can be expressed *generically*, so that 'readymade' systems (7a) can be prepared by those with technical knowledge (7c).
Socio-technical approaches to ISD	Designing IT (7b)-based IS (7a) in an organization, needs to bring together technical considerations (7a, b, c) and the nature of the social system (1, 3, 4, 5) which will use the technology. This requires people within (1) who will become users of the systems to be closely involved in their design (7).
End-user computing	It is possible to convey enough knowledge (7c) to people in (1) who will become system users to enable them to develop their own systems (7a, 7b) which enable them to draw upon the resources available in corporate versions of (7a, 7b)
Work-force-oriented approaches (UTOPIA project, Ehn 1988)	A view of the perceived world (2) is taken in which those involved in discourse (1) to create systems (7a, b, c) to support action (6) undertaken by workers *ought* to include the workers themselves as 'drivers' of the system development process, helped by those with technical knowledge (7c).

Now, it might be thought that this kind of analysis establishes the POM model as the sense-making device we seek. It certainly confirms from the literature what we have found from our experiences that such a model is useful for sense making, for seeing a particular episode of IS work, at whatever level, and of whatever kind, in a holistic way. But it is not general enough for our overall purpose, useful though it is. A reason for this is that it is focused on ISD, and although this is the central core of work in the field of IS, it is not the whole of it. It would be useful to move to a higher-level model which *contains* the POM model but is broader in concept.

In order to do that we need to analyse what the essence of the POM model is, and then try to place it in a broader context.

The processes in the POM model occur in the interactions between three different elements. These are, first of all, the people, the human *agents* (A) who interact to create the wholly or partially shared meanings which make sense of their world to individuals and to various groupings of individuals. These interactions take place via various forms of *organization* (O). These may be represented in a real instance by typical structures of the kind found within organizations, such as departments, divisions, project teams, etc; but they may also include any organized patterns of tasks, communications, reporting, etc. In fact, this element of organization represents, in general, any structured pattern of interaction which involves the agents. Thirdly, the processes of the POM model entail *technology* (T) by means of which informational support may be provided. This might, in a real situation, be represented by telephones, teleprinters, hand-written messages and maps, as we saw in Chapter Five; nowadays it will almost always include computers and telecommunication systems. These three elements make possible the processes in the POM model, which means that in any real manifestation they will all be involved and will affect each other. Any change to one will have some affect on the others; the three make up a whole as in Figure 8.2.

When we use the POM model to make sense of any example of work in IS, we are thinking about the elements O, A, T and the relationships between them in a particular case. Put the other way round, we can say that sense making in IS entails *thinking about* the three elements and their relationships. Expressed pictorially, this gives us the 'three dimensional' Figure 8.3 where the 'thinking about' is rendered as the element C, for 'conceptualizing'. The participle form is important: this is a process not a product. It is this COAT model which captures the business of 'making sense of IS': it can be done by *consciously thinking about O, A, T and their*

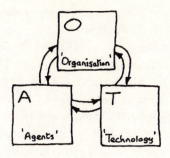

Figure 8.2. *The elements whose interactions enact the processes of the POM model (Figures 4.5 and 7.7)*

links in a particular example of IS work. But the model draws attention, in element C, to the need for that thinking to be done, and done consciously. The specific content of C will be different in different cases. In particular cases, depending on context, it might entail, say, bringing to bear the current ideas about 'virtual organizations', or the ideas of Habermas, or the latest ideas stemming from work on neural networks. The specific content of C will change with context; but for IS work in general we can be sure that O, A, T and their mutual relationships will be relevant. The IS field itself is then the aggregate of different versions of the COAT model; and we could add that some of its confusion stems from the *absence* of C, in frameworks which purport to describe the real

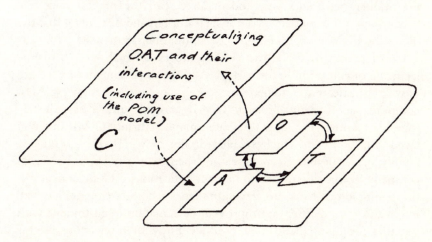

Figure 8.3. *The COAT model*

world, or from the *neglect* of C, which directs attention to the *four* aspects of the lower level: O, A, T, relationships.

It is important to emphasize that element C makes the COAT model different in kind from the myriad frameworks in IS literature, and this is because of its two levels, which contain elements of two different kinds. At first sight the figure might be thought to look like one more of the many frameworks which are scattered across IS literature – Mok (1993) reviews no less than 30 of them. Figure 8.2 does in fact look like Leavitt's (1964) framework of tasks, structure, people and technology, with tasks and structure here subsumed in our broader interpretation of 'organization'. But making sense of IS *entails* the introduction of the second level into the model. The frameworks in the literature are always presented as if they were descriptions of part of the real world.

Where does this leave the POM model? Use of it is *a part of C*, one which we believe will turn out to have some long-term stability and relevance, simply because its focus is on the social processes of meaning attribution which are at the very core of the concept 'information' when we use that word in its full sense, not simply as a synonym for 'data'. The POM model provides one well-tested way of thinking about the relations between O, A and T; it offers one basic way of defining those relations.

If the writing in this section seems laboured, it is because the status of the COAT model is rather subtle. It is not a would-be descriptive model of IS. It is a process model for making sense of IS, one relevant to practitioner, researcher and student alike. But the process itself will depend upon the context. It is not spelt out beyond our saying that the use of the POM model is likely to be an important part of it.

Consider, for example, the kind of situation which faced a manufacturing organization in the early days of the development of what are now sophisticated systems for computer–aided design (CAD), computer-aided manufacturing (CAM) and, in some cases, the altogether grander computer-integrated manufacturing (CIM). Initially, faced with software which enabled design drawings to be produced rapidly on a computer screen, rather than on paper, an engineering company faced a situation with many ramifications. At a strategic level, the technology, thanks to developments of computer graphics, had implications for a different, improved, presentation to customers, with potential for giving them a better service, but with implications also for employment policy: fewer draughtsmen would be needed. At an operational level, the new technology would bring changes to the design process. The distinction between design engineer and draughtsman, previously clear, would tend to become blurred and working practices would be changed, with the work of the draughtsman, previously very public, becoming less transparent. The technology would bring new possibilities both for the storage and modification of engineering drawings, and for calculating material use. There would also be potential opportunities for increased productivity. These and similar factors contribute to a rich socio-technical situation in which O, A and T will all be changing individually and at the same time affecting each other. The organization's managers in such a situation need consciously to conceptualize these elements and their interactions as a whole, if their organization is to absorb the technical, operational and social change successfully. In such a case socio-technical theory would have something to offer, and the changes in O, A and T and in their relationships might well lead in this case to a re-thinking of the overall design, production and marketing system of the company – in which case the POM model, perhaps enriched by SSM-style activity models would be useful too.

The need for organized thinking of this kind applies equally to practitioners, to would-be researchers as they formulate their enquiries, and to students of IS anxious to grasp a subject area in all its interconnected richness. A renewed and enhanced attention to C would seem to be required if the fledgling field of IS is to attain the status of a coherent field of endeavour.

Conclusion

In this book we have presented the story of our attempt to see the IS field whole. It seemed appropriate to do this at book length because the story is itself a whole; each part of the story, whether based on reflection or on carrying out particular projects within organizations, both affects the other parts and is itself affected by them. We like Peter Keen's notion that in the present state of this field 'Books help us find clearings in the forest' (1991, page 36) though in our case the attempt is to see the shape of the forest as a whole and to make sense of the diversity within it. The motivation came from the puzzlements we felt in our professional work. For one of us, heading an IS function in the Australian Government Service, there was a remarkable gap between day-to-day practice and academic writings. For the other, an ex-manager turned academic, carrying out action research in organizations, it seemed strange that a field with the word 'systems' in its title was so untouched by systemic thinking. Those puzzlements set us going.

The work was done within a particular tradition, that of systems work at Lancaster University: working within real situations using a declared intellectual framework and reflecting on the experiences. This is a way of working which puts researchers into the role which Schön (1983) defines as that of the 'reflective practitioner', though we use a more sharply defined framework of ideas than Schön envisages. The outcome is a high-level tool for structuring reflection: the two-level COAT model with its crucial element C for 'conceptualizing'. C itself contains an element we would expect to have a long and respectable life, if the field itself coheres and consolidates: the model of processes in which 'organizational' meanings are generated, the POM model, with O interpreted as including not only formal organizations but also any group of people working together and the regularities that entails. This outcome is not a picture *of* the IS field. It is a process outcome, an intellectual tool which helps furnish a process of inquiry for making sense of the field, a tool available not only to reflective practitioners but to reflective researchers and reflective students as well.

Those who crave a substantive description of the straggling thicket which is the IS field will never get that, except by artificially reducing its diversity and complexity; and it is important to appreciate why this is so.

There are at least two fundamental reasons why the outcome of this research is a sense-making process rather than a substantive account of the IS field. The development of the technology associated with IS will roll on, and, as acknowledged earlier, this is a technology which creates new kinds and patterns of activity, changing the range of things it is now possible for people to do, both in work and play. This is enough to determine a process outcome to the research; but there is an equally cogent second reason, which stems from the core of the concept of 'information'. At the core of the IS field is a particular process, perhaps the most important process there is. We refer of course to the process in which human beings make their perceived world into a social haven comfortable enough for them to live in: the process of meaning attribution, in which perceptions are linked together and built into larger wholes. This is both an individual process and one which goes on in human groups of many kinds – families, organizations, football teams, street gangs, the sisterhood – and there will always be interesting clashes between individual and group perceptions. Yes, we are all constrained in the thoughts we can think, constrained by our genes, by early experiences in our families (when aunts and grandmothers tend to write scripts for us to follow) and by structures of power in formal organizations. But history shows us that those constraints are never total, never totally determining. Part of being human is to have a chance of re-writing the script. And as we follow that chance, meanings will never be totally agreed; they will always be in a state of flux. Hence what counts as 'information' will never be static, or subject to only one definition; it too will be in a state of flux.

With 'meaning' at the core of the concept of information and hence at the core of the IS field, work in that field has to be done *outside* any belief that there is the possibility of a static social world 'out there', with purposeful action defined once-and-for-all and supported by 'information requirements' defined only by instrumental logic. The idea is elegantly caught by Vaclav Havel, the Czech playwright who was imprisoned four times in five years by an oppressive regime, but who then emerged to become President of his country:

> We have to abandon the arrogant belief that the world is merely a puzzle to be solved, a machine with instructions waiting to be discovered, a body of information to be fed into a computer.

References

Adams, G.B., Forester, J. and Catron, B.L. (eds) (1987), *Policymaking, Communication and Social Learning: essays of Sir Geoffrey Vickers*, Transaction Books, New Brunswick, NJ

Agresti, W.W. (ed) (1986), *New Paradigms for Software Development*, IEEE Computer Society Press, Washington

Ahituv, N. and Neumann, S. (1990), *Principles of Information Systems for Management* (3rd Edition), Wm. C. Brown, Dubuque IA

Aiba, H. (1993), The conceptualizing of 'organization' and 'information' in IS work, MSc dissertation, Lancaster University

Alavi, M. (1984), An assessment of the prototyping approach of IS development, *Communications of ACM*, 27, 556–563

Alter, S. (1992), *Information Systems: a management perspective*, Addison-Wesley, Reading, MA

Alvesson, M. and Willmot, H. (eds) (1992), *Critical Management Studies*, Sage, London

Andersen, P.B. (1991), A semiotic approach to construction and assessment of computer systems, in Nissen, Klein and Hirschheim (eds) qv

Anderton, R.H. (1991), Information and Systems, *Journal of Applied Systems Analysis*, 18, 57–60

Anthony, R.A. (1965), *Planning and Control Systems: a framework for analysis*, Harvard University Press, Cambridge, MA

Argyris, C., Putnam, R. and McLain-Smith, D. (1982), *Action Science: concepts methods and skills for research and intervention*, Jossey-Bass, San Francisco

Arnold-Foster, M. (1973), *The World at War*, Collins, London

Avison, D.E. and Wood-Harper, A.T. (1990), *Multiview: an exloration in information systems development*, Blackwell, Oxford

Avison, D.E. and Fitzgerald, G. (1995), *Information Systems Development: methodologies, technologies, tools* (2nd edition), McGraw-Hill, London

Bacon, C.J. and Fitzgerald, B. (1997), The field of IST (submitted for publication; private communication to Peter Checkland)

BAMM (1996), The involvement of clinical staff in the management of NHS Trusts, British Association of Medical Managers, Cheadle, Cheshire

Banville, C. and Landry, M. (1989), Can the IS field be disciplined? In Galliers (ed) (1992a) qv

Barbrook, R. (1997), Fantasy, reality and futures collide on the Net, *Times Higher Educational Supplement*, 14 April 1997

Bar-Hillel, Y. (1964), *Language and Information*, Addison-Wesley, Reading, MA

Barnard, C. (1938), *The Functions of the Executive*, Harvard University Press, Cambridge, MA

Bell, D. (1973), *The Coming of Post-Industrial Society*, Basic Books, New York

Bemelmens, Th.M.A. (ed) (1984), *Beyond Productivity: information systems development for organizational effectiveness*, North-Holland, Amsterdam

Benyon, D. (1990), *Information and Data Modelling*, Blackwell, Oxford

Bickers, R.T. (1990), *The Battle of Britain*, Salamander Books, London

Birkerts, S. (1996), *The Gutenberg Elegies: the fate of reading in an electronic age*, Faber and Faber, London

Blacket, D., Checkland, P. and Martin, S. (eds) (1993), Improving Management of the NHS Contracting Process: SSM in Phase 1 of action research, Lancaster University Management School (Research funded by ESRC Grant No.L114 25 1025)

Blau, P. (1968), The study of formal organizations, in Parsons (ed) (1968) qv

Blum, F.H. (1955), Action research – a scientific approach? *Philosophy of Science*, 22 (1), 1–7

Blumenthal, S.C. (1969), *Management Information Systems: a framework for planning and development*, Prentice-Hall, Englewood Cliffs, NJ

Blunden, M. (1985), Vickers' contribution to management thinking, *Journal of Applied Systems Analysis*, 12, 107–112

Blunden, M. and Dando, M. (eds) (1994), Rethinking Public Policy-Making: essays in honour of Sir Geoffrey Vickers, special edition (38 (1) September-October) of *American Behavioural Scientist*. Also published as a book, 1995, Sage, London

Boar, B.H. (1984), *Application Prototyping: a requirements definition strategy for the eighties*, John Wiley and Sons, New York

Boland, R.J. (1979), Control, causality and information requirements, *Accounting, Organizations and Society* 4 (5), 259–272

Boland, R.J. (1986), Phenomenology: a preferred approach to research on information systems, in Langefors, Verrijn-Stuart and Bracchi (eds) qv

Boland, R.J. (1987), The In-formation of Information Systems, in Boland and Hirschheim (eds) (1987) qv

Boland, R.J. and Hirschheim, R.A. (1985), Series Introduction to the first volume of the Wiley Series on Information Systems

Boland, R.J. and Hirschheim, R.A. (eds) (1987), *Critical Issues in Information Systems Research*, John Wiley and Sons, Chichester

Brancheau, J.C. and Wetherbe, J.C. (1987), Key issues in information systems management, *MIS Quarterly*, 11 (1), 23–45

Brancheau, J.C., Janz, B.D. and Wetherbe, J.C. (1996), Key issues in information systems management: 1994–95 SIM Delphi Results, *MIS Quarterly, 20* (2) 225–242

Brans, J.P. (ed) (1984), *Operational Research '84: Proceedings of the Tenth International Conference on Operational Research*, North-Holland, Amsterdam

Bülow, I. von (1989), The bounding of a problem situation and the concept of a system's boundary in soft systems methodology, *Journal of Applied Systems Analysis*, 16, 35–41

Burrell, G. and Morgan, G. (1979), *Sociologial Paradigms and Organizational Analysis*, Heineman, London

Butler, J. (1994), Origins and Early Development (of NHS reforms) in Robinson and Le Grand (eds) (1994) qv

Carson, R. (1962), *Silent Spring*, Houghton-Mifflin, Boston

Casar, A. (1990), Human Action and Social Process: a systemic perspective, PhD Dissertation, Lancaster University

CCTA (1989), COMPACT Instruction Manual, Version 1.1, Issue 1, CCTA, Norwich

CCTA (1990), SSADM Version 4 Reference Manuals, NCC, Manchester

CCTA (1993), *Applying Soft Systems Methodology to an SSADM Feasibility Study*, HMSO Publications, London

Cerveny, R.P., Garrity, E.J. and Sanders, G.L. (1986), The application of prototyping to systems development: a rationale and model, *Journal of Management Information Systems*, 6 (4), 52–62

Checkland, P. (1972), Towards a systems-based methodology for real-world problem solving, *Journal of Systems Engineering 3* (2), 87–116

Checkland, P. (1979), Techniques in soft systems practice, Part 2: building conceptual models, *Journal of Applied Systems Analysis* 6, 41–49

Checkland P. (1981), *Systems Thinking, Systems Practice*, John Wiley and Sons, Chichester

Checkland, P. (1982), An organized (?) research programme in information systems? Internal Discussion Paper 1/82, Department of Systems, Lancaster University

Checkland, P. (1983), OR and the systems movement: mappings and conflicts, *Journal of the Operational Research Society*, 34 (8), 661–675

Checkland, P. (1984), Systems theory and Information Systems, in Bemelmans (ed) (1984) qv

Checkland, P. (1985), From optimizing to learning: a development of systems thinking for the 1990s, *Journal of the Operational Research Society*, 36 (9), 757–767

Checkland, P. (1988a), The case for 'holon', *Systems Practice*, 1 (3), 235–238

Checkland, P. (1988b), Information systems and systems thinking: time to unite? *International Journal of Information Management*, 8 239–248

Checkland, P. (1991a), From framework through experience to learning: the essential nature of action research, in Nissen, Klein and Hirschheim (eds) (1991) qv

Checkland, P. (1991b), Organisations as Process: the organizational thinking needed for effective groupware, in Hendriks (ed) (1991) qv

Checkland, P. (1994a), Systems theory and management thinking, in Blunden and Dando (1994) qv

Checkland, P. (1994b),Conventional wisdom and conventional ignorance: the revolution organization theory missed, *Organization*, 1 (1), 29–34

Checkland, P. (1997), Rhetoric and reality in contracting: research in and on the NHS, in Flynn and Williams (eds) (1997) qv

Checkland, P. and Casar, A. (1986), Vickers' concept of an appreciative system: a systemic account, *Journal of Applied Systems Analysis*, 13, 3–17

Checkland, P., Clarke, S. and Poulter, J. (1996), The use of Soft Systems Methodology for developing HISS and IM and T strategies in NHS Trusts, in Richards and de Glanville (eds) qv

Checkland, P. Forbes, P. and Martin, S. (1990), Techniques in soft systems practice, Part 3: monitoring and control in conceptual models and in evaluation studies, *Journal of Applied Systems Analysis*, 17, 29–37

Checkland, P. and Griffin, R. (1970), Management information systems: a systems view, *Journal of Systems Engineering*, 1 (2), 29–42

Checkland, P. and Holwell, S. (1992), Information systems: making sense of the field, paper presented to UKSS Meeting on *Information and Information Systems: a reappraisal*, Warwick University

Checkland, P. and Holwell, S. (1993), Information management and organizational processes: an approach through soft systems methodology, *Journal of Information Systems*, 3, 3–16

Checkland, P. and Holwell, S. (1995), Information Systems: what's the big idea? *Systemist*, 17 (1), 7–13

Checkland, P. and Scholes, J. (1990a), *Soft Systems Methodology in Action*, John Wiley and Sons, Chichester

Checkland, P. and Scholes, J. (1990b), Techniques in soft systems practice, Part 4: Conceptual model building revisited, *Journal of Applied Systems Analysis*, 17, 39–43

Chen, P. (1976), The entity-relationship model: toward a unified view of data, *ACM Transactions on Database Systems*, 1 (1) 9–36

Chen, P. (1981), Entity-Relationship Approach to information modelling and analysis, *Proceedings, Second Internatinal Conference on E-R Approach*, Washington

Churchill, W.S. (1989), *The Second World War*, Penguin Books, Harmondsworth (an abridgement of the six-volume history)

Churchman, C.W. and Verhulst, M.C. (eds) (1960) *Management Science Models and Techniques*, Vol 2, Pergamon, Oxford

Ciborra, C.U. (1984), Management information systems: a contractual view, in Bemelmans (ed) (1984) qv

Ciborra, C.U. (1987), Research agenda for a transaction costs approach to information systems, in Boland and Hirschheim, (eds) (1987) qv

Ciborra, C.U. (1996), *Groupware and Teamwork*, John Wiley and Sons, Chichester

Clare, C. and Loucopoulos, P. (1987), *Business Information Systems*, Paradigm, London

Clark, P.A. (1972), *Action Research and Organizational Change*, Harper and Row, London

Clark, R.W. (1965), *Tizard*, Methuen, London

Codd, E.F. (1970), A relational model of data for large shared data banks, *Communications of the ACM*, 13 (6), 377–387

Collier, B. (1962), *The Battle of Britain*, Batsford, London

Collins, A. (1996), NHS ignores IT health warnings, *Computer Weekly*, 25 April, 12

Cooper, R.B. (1988), Review of management information systems research: a management support emphasis, *Information Processing and Management*, 24 (1) 73–102

Cooper, W.W., Leavitt, H.J. and Shelly, M.W. (eds) (1964), *New Perspectives in Organization Research*, John Wiley and Sons, New York

Cooprider, J.G. and Henderson, J.C. (1990), Technology-process fit: perspectives on achieving prototyping effectiveness, *Journal of Management Information Systems*, 7 (3), 67–87

Cotterman, W.W. and Senn, J.A. (eds) (1992), *Challenges and Strategies for Research in Systems Development*, John Wiley and Sons, Chichester

Crowe, M., Beeby, R. and Gammack, J. (1996), *Constructing Systems and Information*, McGraw-Hill, London

Culnan, M.J. and Swanson, E.B. (1986), Research in management information systems, 1980–84, *MIS Quarterly*, 10 (3), 289–302

Daft, R.L. and Weick, K.E. (1984), Toward a model of organizations as interpretation systems, *Academy of Management Review*, 9 (2), 284–295

Dahlbom, B. and Mathiassen, L. (1993), *Computers in Context: the philosophy and practice of systems design*, NCC Blackwell, Oxford

Davis, G.B. (1974), *Management Information Systems: conceptual foundations, structure and development*, McGraw-Hill, New York

Davis, G.B. (1980), The knowledge and skill requirements for the doctorate in MIS, *Proceedings, First International Conference on Information Systems*, Philadelphia, 174–183

Davis, G.B. and Olson, M.H. (1985), Second edition of Davis (1974) qv

Deighton, L. (1977), *Fighter: the true story of the Battle of Britain*, Cape, London

DeMarco, T. (1978), *Structural Analysis and System Specification*, Yourdon, New York

Dennis, A.R., Tyran, C.K., Vogel, D.R and Nunamaker, J.F. (1990), An evaluation of electronic meeting systems to support strategic management, *Proceedings of the 11th International Conference on Information Systems*, Copenhagen, 37–51

DHSS (1986) Health Services Management: Resource Management (Management Budgeting) in Health Authorities, Health Notice HN (86)34, London

Dickson, G.W., Leitheiser, R.L., Nechis, M. and Wetherbe, J.C. (1984), Key information system issues for the 1980s, *MIS Quarterly*, 8 (3), 135–148

Dixon, J. and New, B. (1997), Setting priorities New Zealand style, *British Medical Journal*, *314*, 86–87 (11 January)

Donaldson, L. (1985), *In Defence of Organization Theory*, Cambridge University Press, Cambridge

Dovey, J. (ed) (1996), *Fractal Dreams: new media in a social context*, Lawrence and Wishart, London

Downs, E., Clare, P. and Coe, I. (1988), *Structured Systems Analysis and Design Method (SSADM)*, Prentice-Hall, London

Dretske, F.I. (1981), *Knowledge and the Flow of Information*, Blackwell, Oxford

Earl, M.J. (1978), Prototype systems for accounting information and control, *Accounting, Organizations and Society*, 3 (2), 161–172

Earl, M.J. (1989), *Management for Information Technology*, Prentice-Hall International (UK), Hemel Hempstead

Ehn, P. (1988), *Work-Oriented Design of Computer Artifacts*, Arbetslivscentrum, Stockholm

Ein-Dor, P. and Segev, E. (1978), *Managing Management Information Systems*, D.C. Heath, Lexington, MA

Emery, J.C. (1987), *Management Information Systems: the critical strategic resource*, Oxford University Press, New York

Emery, F.E. and Trist, E.L. (1960), Socio-technical systems, in Churchman and Verhulst (eds) qv

Eva, M. (1992), *SSADM Version 4: a users guide*, McGraw-Hill, London

Farhoomand, A.F. (1987), Scientific progress of management information systems, *Data Base*, 18 (4), 48–56

Fletcher, R. (1971), *The Making of Sociology*, Vol 2, Nelson, London

Floyd, C., Züllighoven, H., Budde, R. and Keil-Slawik, R. (eds) (1992), *Software Development and Reality Construction*, Springer Verlag, Berlin

Flynn, R. and Williams, G. (eds) (1997), *Contracting for Health*, Oxford University Press, London

Forbes, P.E. (1988), The Development and Dissemination of Soft Systems Methodology, PhD dissertation, Lancaster University

Forrester, J.W. (1961), *Industrial Dynamics*, MIT Press, Cambridge, MA

Foster, M. (1972), An introduction to the theory and practice of action research in work organizations, *Human Relations*, 25 (6), 529–556

Friedman, A.L. with Cornford, D.S. (1989), *Computer Systems Development: history, organisation and implementation*, John Wiley and Sons, Chichester

Fulton, D. and Sasse, A. (1996), The impact of the development context on the implementation of Rapid Application Development approaches, *Proceedings, Fourth Conference on Information Systems Methodologies, British Computer Society*, Cork, 395–406

Galland, F.J. (1982), *Dictionary of Computing*, John Wiley and Sons, Chichester

Galliers, R. (ed) (1987), *Information Analysis: selected readings*, Addison-Wesley, Sydney

Galliers, R. (ed) (1992a), *Information Systems Research: issues, methodology and practical guidelines*, Blackwell, Oxford

Galliers, R. (1992b), Choosing information systems research approaches, in Galliers (ed) (1992a) qv

Gane, C. and Sarson, T. (1977), *Structured Systems Analysis: tools and techniques*, IST, New York

Giddens, A. (1979), *Central Problems in Social Theory*, Macmillan, London

Giddens, A. (1984), *The Constitution of Society*, Polity Press, Cambridge

Gilmore, T., Krantz, J. and Ramirez, R. (1985) Action-based modes of inquiry and the host-researcher relationship, *Consultation*, 5 (3), 160–176

Goldkuhl, G. (1987), Information requirements analysis based on a language-action view, in Galliers (ed) (1987) qv

Goldkuhl, G. and Lyytinen, K. (1982), A language action view of information systems, *Proceedings, Third International Conference on Information Systems*, Ann Arbor, 13–30

Goldkuhl, G. and Lyytinen, K. (1984), Information system specification as rule reconstruction, in Bemelmans (ed) (1984) qv

Gomaa, H. and Scott, D.B.H. (1981), Prototyping as a tool in the specification of user requirements, *Proceedings, Fifth International Conference on software engineering*, San Diego, 333–339

Gorry, G.A. and Scott Morton, M.S. (1971), A framework for management information systems, *Sloan Management Review*, 13 (1), 55–70

Griffiths, R. (1983), NHS Management Inquiry – a report to the Secretary of State, HMSO, London

Griffiths, R. (1987), Radcliffe-Maud memorial lecture, quoted in *NHS Management Bulletin*, No.7, August, DHSS

Grudin, J. (1991), Groupware and CSCW: why now?, in Hendricks (ed) (1991) qv

Ham, C. (1992), *Health Policy in Britain*, 3rd edition, Macmillan, London

Ham, C. (1996), The future of the NHS, *British Medical Journal*, 313, 1277–1278 (23 November)

Hardy, J.L.G., Checkland, P. and Goh, K.C. (1988), Resource Management in Huddersfield Health Authority:
1. CIS in its context
2. Structure of CIS
3. Management education and development
4. 'Going live' with CIS
5. Transferability of CIS
ISCOL Ltd, Lancaster University, Lancaster

Harrington, J. (1991), *Organizational Structure and Information Technology*, Prentice-Hall, London

Harris, M. (1994), in a column in *The Times Higher Education Supplement*, 25 February 1994

Hartog, C.F. and Herbert, M. (1986), 1985 opinion survey of MIS managers: key issues, *MIS Quarterly*, 10 (4), 351–361

Haynes, M. (1997), Private communication to the authors

Haynes, M., Checkland, P. and Rose, J. (1995), Resource Management: a review process for achieving project sign-off reports, NHS Executive, Leeds

Hendriks, P.R.H. (ed) (1991), *Groupware '91: the potential of team and organizational computing*, Software Engineering Research Centre, Utrecht, The Netherlands

Hicks, J.O. (1993), *Management Information Systems: a user perspective* (3rd Edition) West Publishing, Minneapolis MN

Hillary, R. (1942), *The Last Enemy*, Macmillan, London (also Pan Books, 1956)

Hirschheim, R.A. (1985), *Office Automation: a social and organizational perspective*, John Wiley and Sons, Chichester

Hirschheim, R.A. (1992), Information systems epistemology: an historical perspective, in Galliers (ed) (1992a) qv

Hirschheim, R.A. and Klein, H.K. (1989), Four paradigms of information systems development, *Communications of the ACM*, 32 (10), 1199–1216

Hirschheim, R.A., Klein, H.K. and Lyytinen, K. (1995), *Information Systems Development and Data Modelling*, Cambridge University Press, Cambridge

Holwell, S. (1989), Planning in Shell: joint learning through action research, MSc dissertation, Lancaster University

HSMU (1993), *Evaluation of the Clwyd Resource Management Project*, Third Report, Health Services Management Unit, University of Manchester (HSMU), Manchester

HSMU (1996), *The Evaluation of the NHS Resource Management Programme in England*, A Report to the NHS Executive by the Health Services Management Unit, University of Manchester,with Dearden Management Consultants, SDC Consulting, Secta Consulting and Prof. Peter Checkland, Lancaster University, The University of Manchester (HSMU), Manchester

Hult, M. and Lennung, S. (1980), Towards a definition of action research: a note and a bibliography, *Journal of Management Studies*, 17 (2), 242–250

Hynes, H.P. (1989), *The Recurring Silent Spring*, Pergamon, New York

Iivari, J. (1991), A paradigmatic analysis of contemporary schools of IS development, *European Journal of Information Systems*, 1 (4), 249–272

Jackson, M.C. (1987), Systems strategies for information management in organizations which are not machines, *International Journal of Information Management*, 7 187–195

Jayaratna, N. (1994), *Understanding and Evaluating Methodologies*, McGraw-Hill, London

Johnson, B. (1978), *The Secret War*, BBC Publications, London

Jones, R.V. (1978), *Most Secret War*, Hamish Hamilton, London

Kaltnekar, Z. and Gricar, J. (eds) (1989), Organization and Information systems, *Proceedings of International Conference*, Bled

Kasabov, N.K. (1996), *Foundations of Neural Networks, Fuzzy Systems and Knowledge Engineering*, MIT Press, Cambridge MA

Kast, F.E. and Rosenzweig, J.E. (eds) (1973), *Contingency Views of Organization and Management*, SRA Inc., Chicago

Keen, P.G.W. (1991), Relevance and rigor in information systems research, in Nissen, Klein and Hirschheim, (eds) (1991), qv

Kempner, T. (1987), *The Penguin Management Handbook*, Penguin Books, Harmondsworth

Kerr, J. and Hunter, R. (1994), *Inside RAD – how to build functional computer systems in 90 days or less*, McGraw-Hill, New York

Kirby, M. and Capey, R. (1997), The air defence of Great Britain 1920–1940: an operational research perspective *Journal of the Operational Research Society*, 48 (6), 555–568

Kling, R. (1987), Defining the boundaries of computing across complex organizations, in Boland and Hirschheim (eds) (1987) qv

Kling, R. and Scacchi, W. (1982), The web of computing: computing technology as social organization, in Youvits (ed) (1982) qv

Knight, A.V. and Silk, D.J. (1990), *Managing Information*, McGraw-Hill, London

Koestler, A. (1967), *The Ghost in the Machine*, Hutchinson, London

Koestler, A. (1978), *Janus: a summing up*, Hutchinson, London

Konsynski, B.R. (1992), Issues in design of interorganizational systems, in Cotterman and Senn (eds) (1992) qv

Kuhn, T.S. (1962), *The Structure of Scientific Revolutions*, Chicago University Press, Chicago

Kuutti, K. (1995), Debates in IS and CSCW research: anticipating system design in post-Fordist work, in Orlikowski et al (eds) qv

Land, F. (1985), Is an information theory enough? *The Computer Journal*, 28 (3), 211–215

Langefors, B., Verrijn-Stuart, A.A., Bracchi, G. (eds) (1986), *Trends in Information Systems*, North Holland, Amsterdam

Large, P. (1980), *The Micro Revolution*, Collins, London

Laudon, K.C. and Laudon, J.P. (1991), *Business Information Systems: a problem solving approach*, Dryden Press, Chicago

Laurence, P.R., Barnes, L.B. and Lorsch, J.W. (eds) (1976), *Organization Behaviour and Administration* (3rd Edition) Richard Irwin Inc., Homewood IL

Leavitt, H.J. and Whisler, T.L. (1958), Management in the 1980s, *Harvard Business Review*, Nov-Dec, 41–48

Leavitt, H.J. (1964), Applied organizational change in industry: structural, technological and humanistic approaches, in Cooper, Leavitt and Shelly (eds) (1964), and in March (ed) (1965) and in Laurence et al (eds) (1976) qv

Leeuwis, C. (1993), *Computers, Myths and Modelling: the social construction of diversity, knowledge, information and communication technologies in Dutch horticulture and agricultural extension* CIP-Data Koninklijke Bibliotheck, The Hague

Lewis, P. (1991), The decision making basis for information systems: the contribution of Vickers' concept of appreciation to a soft systems perspective, *European Journal of Information Systems*, 1 (1), 33–43

Lewis, P. (1994), *Information-Systems Development*, Pitman, London

Liebenau, J. and Backhouse, J. (1990), *Understanding Information*, Macmillan, London

Loomis, C.P. (1955), Translation of Tönnies' *Gemeinschaft und Gesellschaft* (1887), Routledge and Kegan Paul, London

Lucas, H.C. (1994), *Information Systems Concepts for Managers* (5th edition), McGraw-Hill, San Francisco

Ludlow, P. (1996), *High Noon on the Electronic Frontier: conceptual issues in cyberspace*, MIT Press, Cambridge, MA

Lyytinen, K. (1992), Information systems and critical theory, in Alvesson and Willmot (eds) (1992) qv

McFadden, F.R. and Hoffer, J.A. (1994), *Modern Database Management* (4th edition) Addison-Wesley, Reading, MA

McFarlan, F.W. (1981), Portfolio approach to information systems, *Harvard Business Review*, Sept–Oct

McFarlan, F.W. and McKenney, J.L. (1983), *Corporate Information Systems Management*, R.D. Irwin, Homewood IL

Machlup, F. (1962), *The Production and Distribution of Knowledge in the United States*, Princeton University Press, Princeton

Maddison, R. (ed) (1989), *Information Systems Development for Managers*, Paradigm, London

March, J.G. and Simon, H.A. (1958), *Organizations*, John Wiley and Sons, New York

March, J.G. (ed) (1965), *Handbook of Organizations*, Rand McNally, Chicago

Martin, C. and Powell, P. (1992), *Information Systems: a management perspective*, McGraw-Hill, London

Martin, J. (1978), *The Wired Society*, Prentice-Hall, Englewood Cliffs, NJ

Martin, J. (1986), *Information Engineering* Vols. 1, 2, 3, Savant, Carnforth, UK

Martin, J. (1991), *Rapid Application Development*, Prentice-Hall, Englewood Cliffs, NJ

Mathiassen, L. (1981), *Systems Development and Systems Development Method*, DAIMI, pp 8–136, Department of Computer Science, Aarhuis University, Denmark

Maynard, A. (1996), Rationing health care, *British Medical Journal 313* 1499 (14 December)

Mayo, E. (1933), *The Human Problems of an Industrial Civilisation*, Macmillan, New York

Middlebrook, M. (1990), *The Berlin Raids*, Penguin Books, Harmondsworth

Miles, R.K. (1985), Computer systems analysis: the constraint of the 'hard' systems paradigm, *Journal of Applied Systems Analysis*, 12, 55–65

Mill, J. (1994), Talk among yourselves, *Computer Weekly*, 17 March

Mills, I. (1995), Resource Management – a vision for the nineties, *British Journal of Healthcare Computing and Information Management*, 12 (4), 14–15

Mingers, J. and Stowell, F. (eds) (1997), *Information Systems: an emerging discipline?* McGraw-Hill, London

Mok, S-F (1993), Frameworks in IS work, MSc dissertation, Lancaster University

Morgan, G. (ed) (1983), *Beyond Method: strategies for social research,* Sage, Beverly Hills

Morgan, G. (1986), *Images of Organization*, Sage, Beverley Hills

Morris, D. and Tamm, B. (eds) (1993), *Concise Encyclopaedia of Software Engineering*, Pergamon Press, Oxford

Mosley, L. (1977), *Battle of Britain*, Time-Life Books, Alexandria, Virginia

Mumford, E. (1983), *Designing Human Systems – the ETHICS Method*, Manchester Business School, Manchester

Mumford, E. (1996), Designing for freedom in a technical world, in Orlikowski et al (eds) qv

National Audit Office (1996), *The Hospital Information Support Systems Initiative* (HC322), HSMO, London

Nelson, R.R. (ed) (1988), *End-User Computing: concepts, issues and applications*, John Wiley and Sons, New York

NHS Executive (1993), Purchasing for Health: a Framework for Action, NHS Executive, Leeds

NHS Executive (1996), Priorities and Planning Guidance for the NHS: 1996/97, NHS Executive, Leeds

Naisbitt, J. (1982), *Megatrends* Warner Books, New York

Naumann, J. and Jenkins, M. (1982), Prototyping: the new paradigm for systems development *MIS Quarterly* 6 (3), 29–73

Niederman, F., Brancheau, J.C. and Wetherbe, J.C. (1991), Information systems management issues for the 1990s, *MIS Quarterly*, 15 (4), 475–495

Nissen, H-E., Klein, H.K. and Hirschheim, R. (eds) (1991), *Information Systems Research: contemporary approaches and emergent traditions*, Elsevier, Amsterdam

Nijssen, G.M. (1976), A gross architecture for the next generation database management systems, in Nijssen, (ed) qv

Nijssen, G.M. (ed) (1976), *Modelling in Data Base Management Systems*, North-Holland, Amsterdam

O'Brien, J.A. (1994), *Introduction to Information Systems*, Irwin, Burr Ridge, IL

Olle, T.W., Verrijn-Stuart, A.A. and Bhabuta, L. (eds) (1988), *Computerized Assistance During the Information Systems Life Cycle*, North-Holland, Amsterdam

Orlikowski, W.J. and Baroudi, J.J. (1991), Studying IT in organizations: research approaches and assumptions, *Information Systems Research*, 2 (1), 1–28

Orlikowski, W.J., Walsham, G., Jones, M.R. and DeGross, J.I. (eds) (1995), *Information Technology and Changes in Organizational Work*, Chapman and Hall, London

Ovsenik, J. (1989), On the rise and significance of the concept of organization (of work) in the modern society, in Kaltnekar and Gricar (eds) qv

Parsons, T. (ed) (1968), *American Sociology*, Basic Books, New York

Popper, K.R. (1972), *Objective Knowledge: an evolutionary approach*, Oxford University Press, London

Porter, M. and Millar, V. (1985), How information gives you competitive advantage, *Harvard Business Review* July–August, 152

Poulter, J., Checkland, P. and the NHS Central HISS Team (1996), *Guidelines for the use of Soft Systems Methodology*, NHS Central HISS Team, Winchester

Price, A. (1979), *Battle of Britain: the Hardest Day 18 August 1940*, Book Club Associates, London

Pugh, D.S., Hickson, D.J., Hinings, C.R., MacDonald, K.M., Turner, C. and Lupton, T. (1963), A conceptual scheme for organizational analysis, *Administrative Science Quarterly*, 8 (3), 289–315

Pugh, D.S. and Hickson, D.J. (1976), *Organizational Structure in its Context: The Aston Programme*, Saxon House, Farnborough

Randall, N. (1997), *The Soul of the Internet*, International Thomson Computer Press, London

Rathswohl, E.J. (1991), Applying Don Idhe's phenomenology of instrumentation as a framework for designing research in information science, in Nissen, Klein and Hirschheim, (eds) (1991) qv

Reed, M.I. (1985), *Redirections in Organizational Analysis*, Tavistock, London

Reed, M.I. (1992), *The Sociology of Organizations: themes, perspectives and prospects*, Harvester Wheatsheaf, Hemel Hempstead, London

Reed, M.I. and Hughes, M. (eds) (1922), *Rethinking Organizations*, Sage, London

Rexford-Welch, S.C. (ed) (1955), *The Medical History of the Second World War: the RAF Medical Services, Vol II The Commands*, HMSO, London

Richards, B. and de Glanville, H. (eds) (1996), *Healthcare Computing 1996*, BJHC Ltd, Weybridge

Roberts, J.M. (1980), *The Pelican History of the World*, Penguin Books, London

Robey, D. and Zmud, R. (1992), Research on the organization of end-user computing: theoretical perspectives from organization science, *Information Technology and People*, 6 (1), 1992, 11–27

Robinson, R. and Le Grand, J. (eds) (1994), *Evaluating the NHS Reforms*, Kings Fund Institute, London

Rockart, J.F. (1979), Chief executives define their own data needs, *Harvard Business Review*, March–April, 81–93

Rockart, J.F. (1988), The line takes the leadership – IS management in a wired society, *Sloan Management Review*, Summer, 57–64

Roszak, T. (1986), *The Cult of Information*, Lutterworth Press, London

Schäfer, G. with Hirschheim, R., Harper, M., Hansjee, R., Domke, M. and Bjorn-Anderson, N. (1988), *Functional Analysis of Office Requirements: a multiperspective approach*, John Wiley and Sons, Chichester

Schultheis, R. and Sumner, M. (1995), *Management Information Systems: the manager's view*, Irwin, Chicago

Searle, J.R. (1969), *Speech Acts*, Cambridge University Press, London

Secretary of State for Health and others (1989), Working for Patients (White Paper), HMSO, London

Shannon, C.E. and Weaver, W. (1949), *The Mathematical Theory of Communication*, University of Illinois Press, Urbana, IL

Sheth, J.N., Gardner, D.M., Garrett, D.E. (1988), *Marketing Theory: evolution and evaluation*, John Wiley and Sons, New York

Shields, R. (ed) (1996), *Cultures of Internet: virtual spaces, real histories, living bodies*, Sage, London

Schofield, J. (1997), New skin for the old skeleton; and: The battle for Java's purity, *The Guardian*, 3 and 10 April

Schön, D.A. (1983), *The Reflective Practitioner*, Temple Smith, London

Silverman, D. (1970), *The Theory of Organizations*, Heinemann, London

Simon, H.A. (1960), *The New Science of Management Decision*, Harper and Row, New York

Smith, A. and Medley, D.B. (1987), *Information Resource Management*, South Western Publishing Co, Cincinnati

Smyth, D.S. and Checkland, P. (1976), Using a systems approach: the structure of root definitions, *Journal of Applied Systems Analysis*, 5 (1), 75–83

Somogyi, E. and Galliers, R.D. (1987), From data processing to strategic information systems – a historical perspective, in Somogyi and Galliers (eds) (1987) qv

Somogyi, E. and Galliers, R.D. (eds) (1987), *Towards Strategic Information Systems*, Abacus, Tunbridge Wells

Stamper, R. (1973), *Information in Business and Administration Systems*, Batsford, London

Stamper, R. (1987), Semantics, in Boland and Hirschheim (eds) (1987) qv

Stamper, R. (1991), The semiotic framework for information systems research, in Nissen, Klein and Hirschheim (eds) (1991) qv

Stamper, R., Althaus, K. and Backhouse, J.(1988), MEASUR – Method for eliciting, analysing and specifying user requirements, in Olle et al (eds) qv

Stowell, F. (ed) (1995), *Information Systems Provision: the contribution of soft systems methodology*, McGraw-Hill, London

Stowell, F. and West, D. (1994), *Client-led Design*, McGraw-Hill, London

Strate, L., Jacobson, R. and Gibson, S.B. (1996), *Communication and Cyberspace*, Hampton Press, London

Strauss, A. (1978), *Negotiations: Varieties, Contexts, Processes and Social Order*, Jossey-Bass, San Francisco

Susman, G. and Evered, R.D. (1978), An assessment of the scientific merits of action research, *Administrative Science Quarterly*, 23, 582–603

Susman, G. (1983), Action research, in Morgan (ed) 1983 qv

Teng, J.T.C. and Galletta, D.F. (1990), MIS research directions: a survey of researchers' views, *Data Base*, Fall, 1–10

Thomson, D. (1966), *Europe Since Napoleon* (revised edition), Penguin Books, Harmondsworth

Thuan, E., McBride, P., Broadbent, M., Samson, D. and Wirth, A. (1988), Identifying the task of an information system: towards a general model for information processing in organizations, *Working Paper 10, Graduate School of Management, University of Melbourne*

Toffler, A. (1980), *The Third Wave*, Morrow, New York

Toffler, A. (1990), *Powershift: knowledge, wealth and violence at the edge of the 21st century*, Bantam, New York

Trauth, E.M. and O'Connor, B. (1991), A study of the interaction between information, technology and society, in Nissen, Klein and Hirschheim (1991) qv

Tricker, R.I. (1982), *Effective Information Management*, Beaumont Executive Press, Oxford

Verrijn-Stuart, A. (1986), Themes and trends in information systems, in Langefors et al, (1986) qv

Vickers, G. (1965), *The Art of Judgement*, Chapman and Hall, London. (Reprinted, Harper and Row, London, 1984 and Sage, London, 1995.)

Vickers, G. (1972), Communication and Appreciation, in Adams et al (eds) (1987) qv

Vickers, G. (1974), Letter to Peter Checkland, some of which is reprinted in Checkland, 1985 qv

Vickers, G. (1984), *The Vickers Papers*, edited by Open Systems Group, Harper and Row, London

Walsham, G. (1993), *Interpreting Information Systems in Organizations*, John Wiley and Sons, Chichester

Ward, A. (1989), *A Nation Alone: the Battle of Britain 1940*, Osprey Publishing, London

Warmington, A. (1980), Action research: its method and its implications, *Journal of Applied Systems Analysis*, 7, 23–39

Watson, T. (1986), *Management, Organization and Employment Strategy*, Routledge and Kegan Paul, London

Weaver, P.L. (1993), *Practical SSADM Version 4*, Pitman, London

Webster, F. (1995), *Theories of the Information Society*, Routledge, London.

Weick, K.E. (1995), *Sensemaking in Organizations*, Sage, Thousand Oaks, CA

West, D. (1990), 'Appreciation', 'expertise' and knowledge elicitation: the relevance of Vickers' ideas to the design of expert systems, *Journal of Applied Systems Analysis*, 17, 71–78

West, D. (1992), Knowledge elicitation as an inquiring system: towards a 'subjective' knowledge elicitation methodology, *Journal of Information Systems*, 2 (1), 31–44

Whitley, R. (1984a), *The Intellectual and Social Organization of the Sciences*, Oxford University Press, Oxford

Whitley, R. (1984b), The development of management studies as a fragmented adhocracy, *Social Science Information*, 23, 775–818

Wilson, B. (1984), *Systems: Concepts, Methodologies and Applications* (2nd edition 1990), John Wiley and Sons, Chichester

Winograd, T. and Flores, F. (1986), *Understanding Computers and Cognition*, Addison-Wesley, Reading, MA

Winter, M.C., Brown, D.H. and Checkland, P. (1995), A role for soft systems methodology in information systems development, *European Journal of Information Systems*, 4, 130–142

Wood, D. (1969), *The Narrow Margin: the Battle of Britain and the rise of air power 1930–1940*, Arrow Books, London. (Revised edition; first published 1961 by Hutchinson.)

Woodward, J. (1965), *Industrial Organization: Theory and Practice*, Oxford University Press, London

Wright, R. (1969), *Dowding and the Battle of Britain*, MacDonald, London

Youvits, M.C. (ed) (1982), *Advances in Computers* vol 21, Academic Press, New York

Zannetos, Z.S. (1984), Decision sciences and management expectations: fulfilled, frustrated and yet to come, in Brans (ed) 1984 qv

Zuboff, S. (1988), *In the Age of the Smart Machine*, Basic Books, New York

Zwass, V. (1992), *Management Information Systems*, Wm. C. Brown, Dubuque IA

Author Index

Subject Index